The Cayman
Islands in Transition

The Cayman
Islands in Transition:
The Politics, History, and Sociology of a
Changing Society

J. A. Bodden

Ian Randle Publishers
Kingston · Miami

First published in Jamaica, 2007 by
Ian Randle Publishers
11 Cunningham Avenue
Box 686
Kingston 6
www.ianrandlepublishers.com

**A catalogue record for this title is available at the National Library
of Jamaica**

ISBN 978-976-637- 322-1(pbk)

Cover and book design by Ian Randle Publishers
Printed in United States of America

*The transition taking place in the Cayman Islands is graphically
represented in the picture. While a fisherman clears his net, tourism
dominates the background with a large cruise ship anchored in the
harbour. George Town, the capital of the Cayman Islands welcomes
thousands of cruise ship visitors each year with sometimes six cruise
ships per day.*

Photo by permission of David Wolfe.

For Kalesha, Leigh, James, and Anika
You are the future.

The eyes of the future are looking back at us and they are praying for us to see beyond our own time.

– Terry Tempest Williams

Contents

Preface and Acknowledgements

This book was born out of my interest in the history, sociology, and politics of Caymanian society and my background as a Caymanian politician. It has also been informed by ideas emanating from the many public and private discourses on the evolution of Caymanian society in which I have taken part. My fascination with the political transformation of Caymanian society has provided the intellectual stimulation that enabled me to carry this enquiry through to completion.

Some of what appears in this book had its genesis in an article which was written in 1978. Published in the September and October 1978 issues of the *Nor'wester* magazine, that essay provoked heated public debate. In writing this book I have sought to maintain the course embarked upon in that article while acknowledging the changes that nearly thirty years have brought. The peculiarities that define the Cayman Islands as a frontier society with a totally imported population constitute the leitmotif of the work.

I offer this book as a contribution to the emerging academic discipline of island studies and, equally significantly, as one of the first examinations of Caymanian society by a Caymanian – an addition to the small but growing corpus of literature on the emerging society which is the Cayman Islands.

In the painstaking and meticulous process of completing the book, I have incurred a great debt of gratitude. I first wish to acknowledge my debt to the many friends and colleagues who have participated in discussions with me over the years. Of these, I hold Gilbert McLean, Steve McField, and Theresa Lewis-Pitcairn in especially high esteem, for while we may not always have reached consensus, their ideas were always engaging, mature, and stimulating. Political experience and parliamentary debates were also important sources of motivation for this work, and I hope that the views expressed here will serve to elevate current conversation and inspire constructive debate about the issues facing Caymanian society.

I owe a special debt to Professor the Honourable Rex Nettleford, Vice Chancellor Emeritus of the University of the West Indies, who many moons ago suggested the term 'voluntary colonialism' to describe the Caymanian political decision, at the breakup of the West Indian Federation, to go its own way when Jamaica opted for independence. I also wish to express my gratitude to Dr Carlyle Corbin, Minister of State for External Affairs in the US Virgin Islands, Dr Livingston Smith of the University College of the Cayman Islands, Dr Elsa Cummings, President of the International College of the Cayman Islands, and Dr. Philip Pedley, formerly director of the Cayman Islands National Archive, for volunteering to provide advance comments on this work.

As with any undertaking of this nature, the project could not have come to maturity without the diligence of those who worked behind the scenes. Mrs Erlene Hunte, my personal assistant during my tenure as Minister of Education, Human Resources, and Culture, provided invaluable support. My sincere gratitude and appreciation go to archivists Ms Tamara Selzer and Ms Charisse Morrison of the Cayman Islands National Archive for their courtesy, enthusiasm, and energy in complying with my requests for information and research material. I found the CINA Reading Room warm and accommodating, and the staff was always courteous and welcoming.

I hold a special respect for and owe an immense debt of gratitude to my editor, Claudette Upton. She laboured far beyond the demanding obligations of her unsung profession to give these chapters intelligible form, logical structure, and meaning. The consummate professional and, in my opinion, editor par excellence, she deserves kudos.

My most lavish praise and extensive appreciation, however, are reserved for my wife, Nancy. This long-suffering paragon of patience had the unenviable task of computerising, reorganising, and interpreting numerous versions of the manuscript. During evenings, weekends, and public holidays too numerous to mention, she endured my frustrations and complaints while offering frontline editorial opinion and serving as a guinea pig for my sometimes pedantic expressions and pedestrian prose. Her dedication and commitment were, as usual, my greatest source of inspiration, and this work could not have been completed without her efforts.

Introduction

> Men make their own history, but they do not make it just as they please; they make it under circumstances directly encountered, given and transmitted from the past.

> (Karl Marx, German political philosopher, 1818–1885)

Every historian has an agenda. In the totally imported colonial society of the Cayman Islands, which has for some time now been experiencing a frenzy of change, it is important that any commentator who purports to articulate the societal transformation clearly define his or her agenda. This writer's agenda is a search for understanding and probity in Caymanian history and politics.

It is also an agenda, self-imposed, to understand and respond to the need to interpret the attempts to achieve self-determination which sit at the centre of the society's evolution. The chapters focus on the specific ways that Caymanians and expatriates have grappled and continue to grapple with the concrete issues of settlement, history, colonialism, domination, prejudice, growth, modernity, coexistence, globalisation, and the desire for self-determination.

In a work of this nature, in which a multidisciplinary approach is employed, it is not necessary for events to be placed in strict chronological sequence. Rather, the work is so constructed as to allow the reader an understanding of how these events significantly affected and affect political behaviour, societal expectations, and historical interpretation. Further, it casts the whole phenomenon of British colonialism in Caymanian society into perspective and shows how colonialism and cultural imperialism as practised by some expatriates (especially those ubiquitous white Anglo-Saxon Protestants) trigger a reaction among Caymanians which is contributing to divisiveness in the society.[1]

History, politics, and societal expectations constitute a challenging triad in the current evolution of the Cayman Islands. The resolution of the society's response to the challenges of change and development will require bold and innovative decisions, which may prove hazardous for those who articulate and execute them. These tensions are exacerbated by the colonial political structure and the fragility of the foundations on which a cohesive multiculturalism must be formed. A complicating factor is the relationship between administering power and colony – a relationship which, if the recent past is any indication, has been clouded by duplicity, obfuscation, and confusion. There does not seem to be any desire on the part of political directorates (past or present) to evolve politically from the current state of voluntary colonialism.

Other themes recur throughout the chapters, and emphasis is placed on certain societal constructs – such as the characterisation of the Cayman Islands as a 'frontier society'[2] where colour and class distinctions contributed to the Islands' emergence as a 'pigmentocracy'[3] from the early settlement years.

The work opens with the chapter 'From Columbus to the Present: Caymanian History within the Larger West Indian Complex'. This chapter places Caymanian history within that of the West Indies, although it makes the important distinction that Caymanian society was a 'society with slaves, rather than a slave society'. Slave societies were those societies where the free whites were significantly outnumbered by their black slaves. This was not the case in the Cayman Islands, where there were at least as many white, coloured, and free black people as enslaved blacks. There were other differences as well, among these the fact that the white populace was only marginally economically superior to the black people. The *buckras*[4] (white people) were so economically strapped that in the years of servitude the black people had to provide the soap when doing their masters' laundry. This practice is unique in the annals of Caribbean slavery and highlights the poverty-stricken state of Caymanian whites compared with that of their contemporaries in the rest of the Caribbean.

From this point, the reader is ushered through the period of colonialism (1838–1938). A catalogue of important events follows, including the breakup of the West Indian Federation and the adoption of voluntary colonialism as a governance mechanism.[5] The chapter ends with a discussion of how political events and banking changed Caymanian society from the 1970s onward.

Chapter 2 is entitled 'Settlement, Society, and Population: The Evolution of the Modern Cayman Islands'. Several important points come to the forefront in this chapter, among them the reiteration of the Cayman Islands as a totally imported colonial society. As a corollary, the distinction is made between 'established Caymanians' and 'expatriate Caymanians'. I have intentionally avoided the inaccurate term 'indigenous Caymanians' as there is no record of any aboriginal inhabitants (Amerindians) on these islands.

'Creole' as a concept is introduced and discussed in this chapter, and the concept of frontier society is further elaborated. The chapter describes the Caymanian 'diaspora' and makes the point that there were two periods in the colony's history when emigration was necessitated by economic constraints. Offering a detailed elaboration of colour in Caymanian society (pigmentocracy), the chapter ends with a substantiation of the central thesis that the future success of the Cayman Islands lies in the ability to sustain the synergistic and symbiotic relationship between established Caymanians and their expatriate (status-holding) counterparts.

'Engendering Democracy: An Analysis of the Relationship between Administering Power and Colony', the third chapter, traces the colonial relationship between the United Kingdom as administering power and the Cayman Islands as colony, and charges that, far from being democratic, the relationship is based on power.

The power relationship between administering country and colony manifested itself on the occasion of an Order-in-Council abolishing capital punishment in the Cayman Islands, and, more recently, of a second Order-in-Council legalising homosexual acts performed in private by consenting adults. These Orders-in-Council came into effect as a result of the Cayman Islands Legislative Assembly's refusal to amend the Islands' laws as requested by the British government. The requested legislative changes were deemed culturally dissonant by Caymanian society. The United Kingdom Parliament exercised its prerogative and imposed Orders-in-Council to bring the legislation into line with that of the European Union. It is with this in mind that reference is made to the Melian Dialogue during the Peloponnesian War. This reference exemplifies the principle that right is superseded by might, and that the weak cannot dictate terms to the strong.

A further substantiation of the power-based relationship between administering country and colony is to be found in the conduct of officials of the Crown in the Cayman Islands. The earliest record of official malfeasance in the modern Cayman Islands dates back to 1962, when the colonial head of state, Jack Rose, contravened established constitutional procedures and ignored political protocol, as described by Hannerz (1974, 90–91).

Having orchestrated the rejection of Ormond Panton (leader of the majority party) as an Executive Council (ExCo) member in 1962, Rose added insult to injury by allowing the nominated (appointed) members of ExCo to participate in the selection of the two elected members. Ormond Panton was completely excluded from anything to do with ExCo on this occasion. The contemptuous attitude of the colonial authorities is shown in the following excerpt from the Monthly Intelligence Report for December 1962–January 1963:

> A recent attempt to set fire to old Government House, now used solely as the central office was unsuccessful. During the night a fire was built, using dried grass, paper and paraffin, in a staff lavatory. The main timber wall of the building was charred, but the fire did not spread as the door had been closed and the draught excluded. The old wooden building, once alight, would have been gutted, and the loss of almost all Government records and papers would have been a very serious loss to the community. Public opinion places the responsibility for this arson attempt with disgruntled politicians. The prime suspect is O.L. Panton, who is notoriously capable of wild action and speech at times.[6]

No evidence is included to support the libellous statement made. Also conspicuous by its absence is any reference to a police investigation or to an attempt to obtain forensic evidence to bolster the allegation.

As preposterous as that allegation appears, it is the handwritten note on page 5 of the document which bears out the treachery and distrust found in these colonial officials. In that note a Mr Donohue suggests:

> ... that the defeat of Dr. McTaggart (the Administrator's bitterest opponent in ExCo for further constitutional advance) led to his resignation and that of his party colleagues & therefore the loss of represented leadership of their party in the govt.
>
> The violence reported reflected the character of politics in the territory, self-seeking – & unscrupulous ... I do not put it past Dr. McTaggart to make a second attempt to burn govt offices about his ears.[7]

So intent were these colonial officials on besmirching the character of the local elected representatives that they could not get their maliciousness coordinated. This is obvious since one official suspected O.L. Panton, while the other suggested it was Dr Roy McTaggart. It was a matter of conjecture for some time how Dr McTaggart, a stalwart citizen, legislator, and civic-minded person, did not receive an award for his outstanding leadership. If what obtained in that report bore any influence, small wonder that his services went unacknowledged by the colonial establishment.

The incidents described also serve to highlight another aspect of the peculiar relationship between the colonial head of state and his officials at the ExCo (cabinet) level: his relationship with the official members is different from that with elected members and ministers. This distinction seems designed to ensure that ultimate power resides at all times with the colonial authority, irrespective of ability.

There seems to have been a pattern of contempt on the part of the colonial administrators for local politicians and political aspirants who demonstrated populist tendencies. Whether it was a result of the establishment's contempt for Commissioner Andrew Gerrard's attempts in the early 1950s to make Caymanian society more egalitarian is not at all clear. In any case, Gerrard's successor, Allan Donald, was not of the same disposition as Gerrard, and there is no evidence to suggest that he had any intention of continuing Gerrard's work of transforming the civil service (and, by inference, Caymanian society) into one based on merit rather than colour.

On the contrary, Commissioner Donald may have set the tone for Jack Rose's later malice by soaking up scandal from the inner circles of Caymanian society. It is fascinating to learn how much interest was paid to gossip by some of the colonial authorities. One would think that in the interest of proper administration, credence would not have been given to certain lurid rumours. As the following excerpt from Commissioner Donald's correspondence to His Excellency, Sir Kenneth Blackburne, KCMG, OBE, Governor of Jamaica, shows, gossip and innuendo did play their part in colonial administration in the Cayman Islands:

> You have, I believe, already heard mention of the notorious "Dr." Rose (Dispenser of Jamaican origin, who, I believe, narrowly escaped conviction for abortion in Jamaica some years ago, and has since been in the Cayman Islands, where, also some years ago, a friendly jury got him off a manslaughter charge, also arising from abortion). He has a shocking reputation here – allegations of illegal operations, gambling, and other knavery, but nobody has ever been able to get a charge to stick. He is a leading light in the Vanguard Progressive Party, and narrowly missed election in the

last elections for George Town. He is the ogre at whom all the talk of stiff residential and property qualifications is primarily directed, and after him all our noticeable population of "slick" Jamaicans (who, of course, are much more noticeable than their useful and industrious compatriots) are tarred with the same brush. I cannot blame Caymanians for their feelings: Rose is supremely competent as a demagogue and speaker, charming and respectful to meet, utterly unscrupulous and disreputable, and with no stake in these Islands whatsoever, even after some seven years here. His wife and family are in Jamaica. Rose came for what he could get out of it and he was doing pretty well. With a steady increase in education and worldly wisdom, and latterly even more so with the advent of Dr. MacGregor, it is believed that he has lost a great deal of his "medical practice", which is now probably largely limited to illicit work, at least among those who can afford fat fees. He is said to be very anti-white. He wields great influence among the black, many of the well-educated as well as the least literate, and is credited with having an almost magic way with women. This is the man and this is the type that the better-class Caymanian dread seeing in the Assembly, or even voting. This is the reason for [Ducan] Merren's keenness to impose these restrictions. It is also certainly a contributory cause of his [Ducan Merren's] opposition to female suffrage, and his avowed reason for it.[8]

Commissioner Donald, it would seem, set the standard for the official attitude that followed. His vilification of 'Dr' Rose and other Jamaicans of colour who, along with their Caymanian colleagues, were prominent in agitating for modern political rights, including universal adult suffrage, is enlightening. Commissioner Donald apparently expected a protracted obsequiousness from the black people in Caymanian society and could not endure, or was not prepared to accept, the political shift which was about to take place. Donald's actions, then, must be taken as his response to attempts to change the social realities of Caymanian society, which he perceived as a challenge to the colonial power structure and to his prestige and power as Commissioner.

The reference to '[Ducan] Merren's keenness to impose these restrictions' had to do with proposals to legislate draconian residency requirements for non-Caymanians (who at that time were exclusively Jamaicans) in an attempt to prevent their participation in elections.

There was at the same time a serious attempt to stifle female enfranchisement. In this attempt, the chauvinist elements, including Commissioner Donald, had the support of the colonial authorities, who claimed that since British women could not sit in the House of Lords, Caymanian women could not be allowed to sit in the Assembly of the Cayman Islands.

This position was taken in spite of the United Nations Convention on the Political Rights of Women, to which the United Kingdom was a signatory. Agitation continued for the enfranchisement of women, and 1958 was a particularly active year in terms of petitions and even demonstration. However, it was not until 16 October 1958 that a select committee of justices and vestrymen granted universal adult suffrage.

The most recent incident to arouse disquiet in Caymanian society involved former Attorney General David Ballantyne and Financial Reporting Unit Head Brian Gibbs. Their collusion with the British spy agency MI6 caused a jury to acquit four alleged money launderers in the so-called Euro Bank case. That operation, which was a clear subversion of the justice system as well as a trespass on the human rights of the accused, was carried on with the tacit approval of the British government fraternity.

Other instances substantiate this suggestion of a power relationship; however, the most convincing case has to do with the fact that all laws of the Cayman Islands must be assented to by the representative of the Crown before they come into effect in the Cayman Islands. The administering power can withhold assent on any legislation passed by the Legislative Assembly of the Cayman Islands, with the result that such legislation cannot come into effect.

In further discussion of the relationship between administering power and colony, the suggestion is made that the relationship is a symbiotic one. It is posited that the Cayman Islands benefits by the perceived stability brought by its status as a colony of the United Kingdom. The argument is made in some circles that it is this close association which attracts investors and financiers, who prefer to do business in a jurisdiction where their investments are safe from the possibilities of expropriation and nationalisation.

Of course there are obvious benefits for the administering power. Not the least of these is the fact that the Cayman Islands as a colony places no strain on the purse strings of UK taxpayers. The colony has never throughout its history been grant-aided, nor, for that matter, has it been a regular recipient of development aid or European Union funds. Even in the aftermath of hurricane Ivan, when there was great need and high expectation, the United Kingdom did not offer more than token assistance.

Regardless, the Cayman Islands continue to provide economic opportunities for literally hundreds of UK citizens who come to the Islands on work permits. Most of these people are employed in the white-collar professions in the private sector, and a significant number of them maintain attitudes of cultural and racial superiority and a sense of empire more appropriate to the era of Curzon and Kipling. Their numbers are evoking a rising disquiet among younger college-educated Caymanians, who see them as competitors for prestigious positions in the business houses of the private sector.

Connell (2001, 118) draws attention to this challenging situation when he observes:

> Immigration has substantially affected the demographic composition of several of the territories leading to a high proportion of foreign-born whites (somewhat earlier in Bermuda than in the Cayman Islands) to what was otherwise a population primarily of African descent. Both immigration and substantial but earlier emigration, continuing into the postwar years, have posed problems for the definition and distinctiveness of island identities.

To this can be added the observation that immigration seriously challenges the advancement prospects of young Caymanians. Additionally, it causes inflation of residential property prices to the point where young Caymanians can ill afford to own their own homes. All of this leads to the observation that as their society developed, the modern Cayman Islanders have placed economic prosperity ahead of constitutional and political advancement (Smith and Wallace 1991).

In commenting upon the almost unique disposition of the Cayman Islands, Fergus (2004, 1) writes:

> The Cayman Islands may now be ready to provide leadership for other BOTs in the region but for its first 327 years it was contentedly inferior in constitutional status. And whereas the Eastern Caribbean colonies and Jamaica, its surrogate mother country, were plantation colonies, the Cayman Islands were a contrast in economic activity. It is their new fortune, together with a political culture of conservation, that makes the Cayman Islands such a fascinating subject of study within the current context of constitutional modernization in the remaining British Caribbean territories.

Commenting on the entrenched conservative attitude toward constitutional advancement, Fergus continues:

> Meanwhile the Cayman Islands have not only been conservative but fiercely and fightingly so. Attitudes to the introduction of the position of Chief Minister symbolize the constitutional conservatism of the Cayman Islands. Caymanian phobia of constitutional advancement was still alive at the turn of the twenty-first century. In contrast, party politics had emerged in Montserrat since 1951 and the Chief Ministerial position in 1960. In the case of the TCI, it was the black power movement which catalyzed the launch of party politics in 1976, and with it, the ministerial system. Quarter of a century on, Cayman was still antagonistic to this modest advance. (p. 4)

Connell (2001, 120) is also instructive in broadening our understanding of these attitudes regarding constitutional change:

> [T]he National Team won 12 out of the 15 seats in the 1992 general elections. One of the issues in the election was the desire of the National Team to oppose constitutional change and especially the creation of a new post of Chief Minister; one of the successful team members observed that the establishment of a Chief Minister would be "a major step, which leaves only one step before declaring independence ... Every move forward relating to the Chief Minister is a move towards independence ..." Discussion of constitutional change had been initiated in Britain in 1990, where the lack of any constitutional provision of a political head of state was viewed as anachronistic and leading to undue decision-making by the Governor, in a political context argued by the Constitutional Commissioners to be less advanced " – and we believe, less effective – than those enjoyed by other Caribbean dependent territories for the last 20 to 30 years". This view was nevertheless rejected in the Cayman Islands, and very few changes of any kind followed the review.

These excerpts tellingly encapsulate the Caymanian attitude to constitutional advancement. Indeed, the Constitutional Commissioners themselves cited the Caymanians' apparent lack of interest in constitutional advancement. In so doing, the Commissioners, in common with other commentators on this subject, cited the Caymanian concern with the Islands' economic prosperity (Smith and Wallace 1991).

Constitutional modernisation notwithstanding, the Cayman Islands are moving forward as an economically prosperous and progressive community. Many residents equate the financial status of the white expatriate element with economic prosperity throughout the community and confuse such prosperity with political maturity. As a result, these people refer to the Caymanian Islands as 'this country' or 'this nation' and in other terms which connote self-determination, political independence, or nationhood.

Such a description is, strictly speaking, incorrect. The Cayman Islands, not having severed colonial ties with the administering power, are still very much a colony. It is less contentious and certainly more correct to refer to the Islands as 'the society' or 'the jurisdiction'. Both terms connote a significant geographical and political entity while avoiding a challenge on political grounds regarding nationhood.

The society which is now the Cayman Islands really came into its maturity at the conclusion of the Vision 2008 exercise. It was the networking, teamwork, consultation, and cooperation involved in this 'visioning exercise' which led established Caymanians, expatriates, guests and well-wishers to realise that the Cayman Islands could become more than a frontier society – or at least evolve into a frontier society with a difference.

Vision 2008, in tandem with the Quincentennial celebrations, left Caymanians of all walks of life and from all ethnic and national backgrounds with a sense of pride and community. It is unfortunate that an exercise which held out such prospects for the blending of all elements of the society and which was carried out with such commitment has not been followed through. Disappointingly, political leaders did not grasp the significance of the synergy that resulted from Vision 2008 and the Quincentennial celebrations and use it to embark upon a meaningful societal dialogue and a renewed search for self-determination – in short, to create a new community.

The metaphorical mother/child relationship has continued long past the time when the 'child' would have reached the age of consent, yet there is not even an attempt to wean the 'child', let alone to encourage it. Self-determination for the Cayman Islands has stalled, and it seems accurate to remark that few, if any, of those in influential political circles have any real understanding of the concept.

It is of critical importance for the Cayman Islands to pursue the quest for self-determination, after first arriving at a national consensus as to what it should entail. Political directorates must be forced to come to grips with the importance of such an exercise. The most effective way of arriving at a consensus would be through a referendum, although one can hardly expect encouragement from the United Kingdom since referendum is not a Westminster instrument of decision-making. It is apparent that the interest, enthusiasm, and energy which once surrounded the proposal for a referendum have dissipated. Cynics would explain this as no more than a false alarm – one of those 'issues of political convenience' which opposition elements have so successfully employed over time to gain majority favour.

With international agencies threatening to end the Islands' tenure as a major financial centre, and with no overt support from the administering power in preserving its financial integrity, the Cayman Islands must agitate for a new paradigm. In its agitation, however, it must hold firmly to its option as a major financial centre. Such is the position taken by the author in the fourth chapter, 'Banks, Hedge Funds, and Trusts: The Rise and Fall of the Cayman Islands as an International Financial Centre'. The reference to 'the fall' is certain to evoke challenges from both pundits and players, but nothing lasts forever, and it is unrealistic to expect that the economic success the Islands have been experiencing in recent years will go on ad infinitum.

In many respects the Cayman Islands are unique among international financial centres. While the jurisdiction now stands among the most meticulously regulated, that was not always the case. Two factors were in play, the first of which relates to the construct of a frontier society. The phrase conjures up a notion of reticence, no questions asked, complicity, confidentiality, and even anonymity, if necessary. In such a frontier society, 'straw men' abounded and collusion was second nature. The second factor is that geographical fortune placed the Cayman Islands a convenient distance from the front doors of the United States, the major capitalist economy, and Canada, another influential member of the G8. Add in the legal expertise available in the Cayman Islands from the late 1960s to about the 1980s, when the pressure of regulation set in, and one has all the ingredients for an auspicious beginning.

In fairness to the Cayman Islands, however, it must be said that the Cayman Islands were not doing anything that was not being done by other jurisdictions, including the United States, United Kingdom, and Switzerland. Rather, the Cayman Islands were doing it better, more meticulously, and in a more attractive location.

The jurisdiction is still doing it better today, as it has better regulation, more efficient services, better communications, and a higher level of professionalism than most of the competition. As an international financial centre, the jurisdiction has consistently held its position as the fifth largest and complied with the most demanding systems, and most recently was praised as a well-regulated jurisdiction by the International Monetary Fund.

Small wonder, then, that there are those who would take issue with the author's reference to the fall of the jurisdiction as an international financial centre. If the Cayman Islands are to 'fall', when will this be? The answer – the only answer –is that nobody really knows. It seems much more constructive to elaborate on factors which could cause the Cayman Islands to 'fall'.

At the Cayman Business Outlook 2006, the news media in the Cayman Islands carried reports of the threat to the Cayman Islands economy posed by outsourcing to India and China. The pundits feared that the Cayman Islands would lose valuable business to these countries, which are known to provide services much more cheaply.

The argument is submitted that as a result of its small size and non-reliance on factory workers, the Cayman Islands are not as susceptible to losses caused from competitive outsourcing as are some larger, more populous jurisdictions. Also, the Cayman Islands offer the full range of financial services from company registration through trust establishment, hedge fund management, and insurance to banking, plus the ancillary services. The high quality of the services offered, coupled with the Cayman Islands' meticulous regulation, makes it unlikely that the services can be duplicated in jurisdictions with no history of offering them. That effectively rules out India and China as competitors to the Cayman Islands as a financial services centre.

However, there is no room for complacency. To maintain its competitive advantage, the Cayman Islands must embark upon enlightened policies and articulate best practices which ensure that educated Caymanians have every opportunity to advance in their chosen fields, here in the Cayman Islands.

And therein lies the challenge. At the time of writing, there is a good deal of confusion and controversy surrounding an immigration policy. The law was changed in 2005 to disallow work-permit holders from staying in the Islands for more than seven years. The limit was recommended by a committee established with the concurrence of both government and opposition during the 2001–2005 tenure of the United Democratic Party. As a result, the cabinet approved the recommendation, and it became both law and policy. The rationale was that it is necessary to maintain a level playing field for qualified young Caymanians.

Once in effect, however, the policy was the subject of vociferous objections from several sectors of the business community, which argue that it will cause the loss of senior expatriate personnel. Two questions arise: What kind of businesses are these which did not realise until their employees' work permits were expiring that this proposal would be unworkable? and What efforts have been made to recruit and train Caymanians for these positions?

There is no reason to be optimistic that established Caymanians, in more than token numbers, will gain access to and experience in critical areas of international finance, since the hiring practices of the major law firms and business houses in the Cayman Islands have not changed in 25 years. In money-management matters, it is expatriates who make the selections and expatriates who are selected. Should the practices persist, change in the Cayman Islands will come as it does in every other society where such obvious exclusionary practices spawn resentment and eventually hatred.

No entity, it seems, public or private, is taking into consideration the growing disquiet among young Caymanian university graduates. Prejudice and cultural imperialism exists to such an extent that established Caymanians are often considered only for entry-level positions. This is where the pundits at Cayman Business Outlook 2006 got it wrong. Outsourcing will not affect the Cayman Islands as detrimentally as will discrimination, prejudice, and unfair employment practices which limit the opportunities open to established Caymanians.

The best strategy that the Cayman Islands can adopt to ensure its future success lies with education, training, and fair employment practices. Why have not the various financial service providers and major law firms in the Cayman Islands come together to establish, for example, a financial services institute? Such an institute could form part of the University College of the Cayman Islands or the International College of the Cayman Islands. Given the number of service providers and the available expertise, both funding and faculty could be readily found within the Cayman Islands.

It would also be prudent to begin training interested Caymanians in foreign languages, including those of the G8 countries and of emerging powers such as China.[9]

There is to date no indication of such proactive measures, and the Cayman Islands will not maintain its prestige if it lulls itself into a false sense of security. Nor will it continue to hold international investors' confidence if unrest ensues, or if large numbers of Caymanian college graduates begin voting with their feet as a result of failure to obtain meaningful employment in Cayman.

Charting the jurisdiction's rise as a reputable financial centre, the chapter chronicles several financial scandals and shows how, with characteristic elasticity, the Cayman Islands not only rebounded but utilised past experiences to bolster confidence and credibility through strengthening their regulatory regimes. The Cayman Islands then emerged as a premier centre for the hedge fund market, captive insurance, and trust and estate management. In examining these new products, the author suggests that hedge funds are open to exploitation by unscrupulous people.[10]

The concluding chapter, entitled 'From Frontier Society to International Financial Centre: A Nuanced View', is best described as a *tour d'horizon*. Charting the Islands' development from 'the islands time forgot' to the twenty-first century, the chapter elaborates on the importance of land in Caymanian society. Detailing the growth of the real estate market, a phenomenon whose beginnings are traced to the Seven Mile Beach development, the chapter makes the point that, while land was the source of wealth, it held no monetary value in 'old Cayman'.

It is suggested that a critical mistake was made in later years in that, rather than selling leaseholds – as was done for the West Bay land purchased by Benson Greenall – landowners began to sell absolute titles. There was no legislation controlling land ownership and speculation by foreigners (absentee landowners). The result was that within three decades land became such a valuable commodity that whole areas were priced beyond the reach of even wealthy Caymanians.

In contrast to many other Caribbean territories which have laws prohibiting non-residents from buying land for purely speculative purposes, the Cayman Islands have never considered any form of alien land-registration law. Such legislation would have protected Caymanians against foreign speculators and developers whose only interest was playing the market for personal or corporate profit. The first sign of the importance of land in the modern Cayman Islands appeared in 1969, in the form of concerns raised in objection to the planned Land Development (Interim Control) Bill, 1969.

The law was passed on the political directorate's second attempt to have the Assembly accept the bill. It is interesting to note that the only objections came from three George Town members (Hannerz 1974, 129). Controversy soon surrounded the new legislation, especially the regulations. Among these were a prohibition against the removal of sand from the island's beaches for construction purposes. During this time it was a common practice to remove sand from the beach, and the political directorate, quite rightly, recognised that the practice was a danger to the island as a developing tourist destination.

Other regulations dealt with zoning, the height and density of buildings, land for public purposes (public open spaces) in subdivisions, water and sewerage requirements, and a certificate of fitness for occupancy for each newly completed dwelling.

It is characteristic of the frontier mentality to resist certain forms of organisation and structure, and it did not take long for objections to galvanise into one gigantic island-wide protest march. April 20, 1970, is recorded as the largest organised political demonstration in the history of the modern Cayman Islands.[11] Opposition aside, however, every point of objection at that time has been incorporated into subsequent legislation and accepted as important to the society's development.

Following upon these momentous events, the chapter turns to banks and banking, introduces the concept of the 'revolution of rising expectations', and examines the nexus between modernity, money, and materialism. The author then focuses on politics, populism, and political parties and offers an explanation of the breakup of the political directorate which ultimately resulted from the general elections of 2000.

From tracing the resuscitation of party politics in the Cayman Islands, the chapter deals with what the author considers emerging problems in Caymanian society and the challenges of maintaining a viable tourism industry, before concluding with a synopsis of the position of the Cayman Islands as a financial centre. In keeping with current society-wide sentiments, the chapter ends by posing the rhetorical but seminal question: For whom are we developing the Cayman Islands?

This book demonstrates belief in the multicultural, multinational, plural society which the Cayman Islands should become. It is essential to promote respect, understanding, tolerance, and a mutuality of interests, and to use knowledge to confront the pervasive evils of prejudice and ignorance. If we are to move forward, we must be determined to speak the truth boldly. In so doing, there is a need to explore the intellectual sources and existential resources which feed our courage to understand one another, to engage in a national social dialogue, and to fight for the democratic ideal. Three related and fundamental questions motivate my writing: Who is Caymanian? For whom are we developing the Cayman Islands? What of our future?

My perennial wrestling with these challenging issues is rooted in past experience. It is my sincere hope that this book, like the 1978 article (Bodden 1978) which presaged it, will evoke energetic debate and, ideally, promote understanding of how Caymanian society is constructed and what should be done to maintain its vibrancy.

My ideas of development have been formulated from the writings of P.T. Bauer (1976, 1981, 1984, 1991), Amartya Sen (1999), and the indomitable René Dumont (1966). Added to the mix is my identity as an established Caymanian (Caribbean) man with roots in the African (black) diaspora. It is the combination of my study of these masters and my own personal history which gives me the confidence to place my interpretations on the table for discussion and dissection.

I have read and re-read Dumont's magisterial work, *False Start in Africa,* so many times that it has become a kind of testament for me. His criticism of development implemented unwisely is a graphic reminder that bad practices cannot lead to good results. It is with this in mind that I state that for some time now, the Cayman Islands have been witnessing a 'false dawn'.

Since I published my original article in 1978, the situation has been grossly compounded. I hear no voice expressing reservations about the building of new mega-communities designed for a whole new populace. No one has yet publicly remarked that such communities are going to usher in a new society for which the Cayman Islands are unprepared.

There is no preparation of significant numbers of young Caymanians to take advantage of the knowledge economy. Established Caymanians, it seems, are too willing to spend time denigrating expatriates when what is needed is an embrace of modernity. Expatriates with selfish motives spend their time decrying the 'lack of education and training among Caymanian school leavers' while making no practical effort to alleviate the situation. Instead of lighting a candle, they, quite predictably, curse the darkness. There are few attempts at examining what modernisation should mean to the Caymanian society.

To be modern in Caymanian society is to use one's critical intelligence to stand up for democracy, prosperity, and pluralism. To be modern means avoiding the destructive 'us against them' alignment. Modernity demands that we promote dialogue, seek understanding, and demand respect.

There are too many instances in Caymanian society where situational ethics and political expediency prevail over fairness and the democratic ideal. It is my studied opinion that we are not eager enough to be open, broadminded, and receptive. The political norms in any society are influenced to some degree by the ethical standards expected of private individuals. The oldest insights into such ethics turn on the principle of reciprocity. 'Love your neighbour as yourself', from Leviticus, is one of the earliest we have. Rabbi Hillel, of the generation just before Jesus, clarified the moral logic of reciprocity when he admonished, 'Do not do to others what you would not have them do to you.'

Jesus expressed the same idea in somewhat different terms, in what we call the Golden Rule: 'therefore all things whatsoever you would that men should do to you, do you even so to them: for this is the law and prophets' (Matthew 7:12). This general precept is seen as a great truth upon which much of Western ethical and even political thinking stands. And yet, for all their willingness to express their religiosity, many Caymanians, as well as expatriates, resort to situational ethics rather than the dictates of their conscience.

Finally, to the challenge as to who is Caymanian. To be Caymanian in the modern sense is to be part of a democratic operation that is grappling with the challenges of living in a small society and coming to grips with its complexity. Although the Cayman Islands form a totally imported colonial society which is romanticised into a paradise, a land of opportunity, it is in reality a fragile experiment, perched precariously astride two conflicting streams – one established, one expatriate.

To be Caymanian is to give ethical significance to the future by viewing the present as capable of transcending the past and thus arriving at a new sense of society, community, and individual. From the peculiarities and xenophobia of the frontier society in its earliest stages to the arrival of economic migrants in the twentieth century and beyond, to be Caymanian means to be able to give credence to the possibility that future prospects can trump present troubles.

To be Caymanian is to raise perennially the daunting democratic question: When will the so-called privileged elite among the expatriate elements refrain from condescension and hypocrisy and treat established Caymanians as equals? To be Caymanian is to say that, as a person with clearly established ancestral rights and privileges in the society, I can accept expatriates as equals, even with their prejudices and cultural imperialism, as long as they are willing to accept Caymanian society as their own.

To be Caymanian is to have come from Africa, Jamaica, Canada, Australia, the United Kingdom, the United States, Costa Rica, Honduras, Cuba, Afghanistan, the Philippines, and all the myriad other places from which those desirous of adopting our community hail. That so many others wish to belong to this society makes it incumbent on us to respond with empathy and understanding – thus attaining the true democratic ideal.

Can the society which is the twenty-first century Cayman Islands meet such challenges? Or are we limiting ourselves to maintaining our rank among the major international financial centres and becoming just another 'sun, sand, and sea' tourist destination? Are we, in fact, in danger of becoming a community of philistines whose only objective is to amass personal wealth? I am reminded of Commissioner Gerrard's Budget Speech to the Assembly of Justices and Vestry on March 16, 1955, an excerpt of which follows:

> [T]he prevalent spirit in the Dependency today is the spirit of self-satisfaction and complacency. There is an illusion that, having become part of the modern world, the Cayman Islands can accept all the benefits of the Dependency's new status, and accept none of the liabilities. There is an illusion that the Dependency can be part of the modern world, and yet stand aside from what is happening in the rest of the world – an illusion that in the Cayman Islands everything can remain unchanged while the community continues to become more and more prosperous ... it is impossible.[12]

Edmund Burke, that quintessential statesman and political philosopher, expressed it this way 175 years earlier: 'If our patrimony is cast aside, if we insist on lingering smug and apathetic, we shall come to know servitude of mind and body.'[13]

It is now time to turn to challenges for which appropriate responses must be crafted – by the government, because it is the government's responsibility to create a level playing field and to set the standards; by established Caymanians, because we bear a moral responsibility to acknowledge that the society cannot grow without accommodating others. And established Caymanians must come to grips with the diaspora, when our forebears left their home in significant numbers in search of economic prosperity. We must remind ourselves that Caymanian society is a totally imported society.

Expatriates bear an equal share of moral obligation. They must be less hypocritical, less prejudiced, and more willing to integrate. They must realise that to be segregated is to be dangerous, to run the risk of becoming disaggregated, dysfunctional, marginalised, and isolated.

The ideas and analyses presented in this book are one interpretation of political, historical, and sociological events. They are but one vision of the society which is the Cayman Islands. The interpretation of events, the commentary and assessments are marks which define the history, politics, and sociology of what it means to be a modern Caymanian:

> [This] then is the sort of man the historian should be: fearless, incorruptible, free, a friend of free expression and the truth, intent, as the comic poet says, on calling a fig a fig and a trough a trough, giving nothing to hatred or to friendship, sparing no one, showing neither pity nor shame nor obsequiousness, an impartial judge, well disposed to all men up to the point of not giving one side more than its due, in his books a stranger and a man without a country, independent, subject to no sovereign, not reckoning what this or that man will think, but stating the facts.[14]

Chapter 1

From Columbus to the Present:
Caymanian History within the Larger West Indian Complex

To study Caymanian history is to become aware of the intractable problems faced by a total colonial society. This exploratory chapter seeks to provide an introduction to Caymanian history within the larger West Indian context. It is intended for anyone who appreciates the challenges involved in conducting historical enquiry into a society whose emergence assumed academic importance only in the latter part of the twentieth century, and where there is a dearth of modern historial research. Throughout the writing, cognisance has been taken of Hobsbawn's (1997, 79–86) explanation that social history is made up not only of structures and mechanisms of persistence and change with general possibilities factored in; what actually happened needs to be given equal importance.

In that context, then, Caymanian history requires an elaboration which gives us a vivid idea of the complexities of the society being explored. Such an achievement is particularly pertinent in an exercise of this nature, in which an analysis is employed to chart the evolution of the Cayman Islands in the context of the larger Caribbean or West Indian complex.

For the most part, the terms 'Caribbean' and 'West Indian' refer to the British Caribbean islands. Where comparisons are made with non-British territories, the relevant nationality is identified. The comparative perspective is used to place the sighting and settlement of the Cayman Islands, and slavery and emancipation in Caymanian society, into the wider context of those same events and circumstances in other Caribbean territories. The comparative approach is continued as the reader is ushered into the twenty-first century.

Discovery and colonisation

The Cayman Islands, the first recorded sighting of which was made by Christopher Columbus in May 1503, initially held little or no importance for colonisation purposes by the European powers. The three islands did not figure prominently – if at all – within the settlement complex of the "Europeanisation" of the Caribbean.

One can extrapolate from Hirst (1910, 6–15) that the Cayman Islands entered British consciousness as a British intrusion on the Spanish American Empire under orders from Oliver Cromwell. Such an auspicious beginning notwithstanding, the presence of the British Empire in the Cayman Islands was never grand until the twentieth century. The territory was, compared with most other Caribbean territories, a frontier society, small in size and with a topography which made plantation agriculture uneconomical and unfeasible.

Additionally, there was no evidence of a permanent indigenous population, so from the very outset, the Cayman Islands have been a totally imported colonial society. In other words, like many other West Indian colonies, Cayman was colonised by outsiders who came voluntarily or involuntarily. Complementing this concept of an imported colonial society is the heavy emphasis on racial particularism or 'pigmentocracy'. While initial settlement patterns in the Cayman Islands dictated against such an emphasis, later settlement and societal stratification suggest that by the nineteenth century such distinctions existed (Kieran 1992, 46, 49).

Subsequent to the events of the late eighteenth century, the Cayman Islands – although attached to Jamaica as a dependency for colonial administration purposes – were left almost entirely to fend for themselves. This benign neglect had far-reaching implications, one of which was that many Caymanians came to view themselves as being apart and distinct from the rest of the Caribbean. This attitude was manifest after the breakup of the West Indies Federation and Jamaica's movement into independence in 1962.

It was as a result of these two related events that the Cayman Islands distanced themselves from Jamaica. The granting of crown colony status, with its unique brand of internal self-government, ushered in a type of colonialism that was new to the West Indies.

This 'voluntary colonialism' (which was crafted especially for Caymanians) allowed the Cayman Islands to emerge as a premier financial centre by the end of the twentieth century. While many other Caribbean territories grappled with the challenges of political independence and self-determination, the Cayman Islands took advantage of its symbiotic relationship with the United Kingdom and developed its own economy.

The following *tour d'horizon* examines the events that allowed the Cayman Islands to develop as they have, as cogently expressed by one commentator:

> The people of the Cayman Islands have been fortunate in that they have not experienced the serious and retarding problems which have affected some former British West Indian islands. The metropolitan country has long provided West Indians with a convenient scapegoat for intractable social, economic and political ills. (Wallace 1977, 229)

A fortuitous combination of circumstances enabled Caymanians to avoid those ills, at least until the late 1990s. More recent events demonstrate, however, that the immunity is not permanent – an island society with a history of colonialism cannot escape forever the challenges inherent in that circumstance.

Settlement, imperialism, slavery, and its aftermath

From the outset, the Cayman Islands were a total colonial frontier society. By this I mean that most, if not all, of the early settlers were people who were on the fringes of society, and all came from outside the Cayman Islands. In all probability, the majority of 'new Caymanians' at that time would have been deserters from the British garrison in Jamaica, social outcasts, fugitives from the law, runaway slaves, speculators, and exploiters.

The frontier mentality – which, to a great extent, was necessitated by the risks involved in living in such a peripheral society – was in many respects peculiar to Cayman. During these early years, settlements on the north and west sides of Grand Cayman were subject to raids by Spanish forces from Cuba.

Logic dictates that the islands of Cayman Brac and Little Cayman would have been settled first, since they are closer than Grand Cayman to Jamaica and Cuba. The strategic insignificance and small size of the 'lesser islands', however, apparently did not inspire thoughts of permanent settlement in those who may have landed there.

In a sense, the frontier society that developed in the Cayman Islands, taken in tandem with their small size and topographic unsuitability to large-scale agriculture, spared them the turbulence of alternating control by other European powers. It also allowed the residents to operate relatively free of interference from the British authorities in Jamaica.

Such an unfettered development occasionally led to complaints of lawlessness and excessive independence from visiting colonial authorities (Kieran 1992), whose governing system of benign neglect – or complete disregard – was unlike other systems which existed in the larger West Indian complex.

The early Caymanians' disregard for order may have resulted from the transient nature of the society, which suggests that those who came had interests other than culture, learning, civility, and decorum. Lowenthal (1972, 36) puts the situation of the West Indies into perspective when he states that because 'men of substance and taste found the Caribbean unfit to live in, the territories failed to acquire a true elite'.

Given that the larger islands of the Caribbean experienced an absence of 'men of substance and taste', it would seem unlikely that Caymanian society was any different. In fact, as Hall (1964, 18) informs us: 'In British West Indian colonial society a man became a member of the elite only when he qualified as a potential absentee.... Colonial elite was a contradiction in terms [to men] ... whose means permitted them to be elite rather than colonial.'

This knowledge broadens our understanding of the position of British expatriates in Caymanian society. In the first place, this group's claim to superiority had as its basis that most colonial marker of nobility – white skin. There is no historical evidence to suggest that this self-assumed elite brought any other distinguishing characteristics which would have aided the general prosperity of Caymanian society during the early settlement period.

What made the relationships different in Cayman, vis-à-vis the wider Caribbean, was that the physical and environmental characteristics of the Cayman Islands dictated that symbiosis, rather than adversarial relationships, was the norm.

Several facts about the settlement of the wider Caribbean should serve to inform us about this symbiosis and other conditions in the Cayman Islands at this time. First, female mortality among arrivals in the Caribbean was high (Knight 1990, 71)). In the absence of specific figures, one must assume that the same applied to settlement in the Cayman Islands. It is remarkable, then, that there does not seem to have been any serious conflict in Caymanian society brought on by a shortage of females during these early years. The explanation for this absence of upheaval lies in the fact that the Cayman Islands at that time was an 'exploitation colony'.

According to Knight (1990, 74–81), there were two types of colonies, 'settlement colonies' and 'exploitation colonies'. Settlement colonies were those colonies where Englishmen could settle down to a sedentary lifestyle, whereas in exploitation colonies, people tended to make their fortunes and then leave.

Consider living in a society where there was no regular traffic to the metropolitan country or, for that matter, to the other Caribbean islands. Life in the Cayman Islands at that time offered hardships and deprivations beyond those found on the islands that were plantation societies.

The settlers in the Cayman Islands were a different type of expatriate, not necessarily cosmopolitan in nature. In all probability a great many of these colonists were people who preferred not to live in an organised society where they had to obey prescribed laws and regulations.

Such a situation prevailed well into the nineteenth century, when the lawlessness of the Caymanian population became the subject of colonial despatches (C/O 137/198 F235). Hirst (1910, 34) offers some insight into how the Cayman Islands became an unruly society when he describes the occupation of 'wrecking' as 'first cousin to "piracy"'. Wrecking was a practice whereby Caymanians enticed passing ships to investigate an object that was meant to look like another vessel. The wreckers sometimes used a mule or donkey equipped with a lantern to walk along the seashore, or lit a huge bonfire along the seashore. Passing ships, inquisitive as to the identity and cargo of other ships, would try to come within communicating distance. Having no knowledge of the area, these unwitting sailors would often founder on the reef surrounding the shoreline. Once stuck on the reef, the ship would be virtually helpless, and the islanders would take to their canoes and, under pretext of offering assistance, would plunder and salvage the stricken ship. Caymanians gained a certain notoriety from this practice, and discerning captains exercised a justifiable wariness when sailing in Caymanian waters.

In his description of the population, Hirst (ibid.) commented:

> Considering the class of people forming the population little can be said or even suggested regarding their social life. At the close of this period of our history, religion was not considered a "sine qua non" of local society, consequently we have not to record the erection and endowment of churches, schools, chapels and other edifying institutions. ... Neither does there appear to have been any system of Government.

This situation in the Cayman Islands at that time stood in stark contrast to that in Jamaica, Barbados, and the British possessions in the Windward and Leeward Islands. Did the policy of benign neglect of the Cayman Islands fail to produce a commercially acceptable commodity? Owing to an insignificant slave market and minimal production of sugar, cotton, tobacco, or any other commodity desirable to Europeans, the Cayman Islands were allowed to continue to exist as a frontier society until well into the nineteenth century.

The seventeenth and eighteenth centuries were years of flux in the Caribbean. During these years the islands were transformed from settlement colonies to exploitation colonies. In each instance, slavery was the fundamental institution which drove the economy and fuelled the rivalry between the various European maritime powers vying for supremacy in the Caribbean.

After the successful British challenge of the Spanish monopoly in 1655, the Caribbean became a lucrative frontier for the aspiring powers of England, France, and Holland. This era ushered in three significant occurrences in the history of the Caribbean.

The first was the debunking of the notion that the Spanish were supreme and invincible in the maintenance of their empire in the Americas. While the Dutch West India Company controlled Dutch commerce in the Americas, England controlled its Caribbean commerce through the Navigation Laws. These laws stipulated that any trade in colonial products must be shipped in English ships with English captains and 75 per cent English crews (Knight 1990, 59). The Spanish had no such system, and their attempts to exclude other European powers from trading with the Spanish American colonies were subverted by the colonists themselves. Spain, however, still held an advantage in that the lucrative viceroyalties of New Spain (Mexico), Peru, and all of Central America were sources of gold and silver.

Since the other European powers were excluded from this wealth, they resorted to alternative practices. Trade in slaves captured along the West African coast and predatory raids on Spanish treasure ships as well as on the Spanish New World empire became primary preoccupations of the British, French, and Dutch during this time. As the plundering of Spanish treasure reached its peak in the late seventeenth and early eighteenth centuries, the slave trade also became more popular, owing in no small part to the rise of plantation societies.

Emanating out of the increase in the slave trade and the development of plantation societies was the establishment of what Brathwaite (1971,

161–68) describes as 'creole society'. Lowenthal (1972, 32–33) and Knight (1990, 124–25) suggest that the term *creole* originally described African slaves born in the New World. In due course, however, it was used to describe anyone, black or white, born in the New World.

The creolisation of Caribbean society was synonymous with the rise of the plantation societies and gradually brought into play the notions of caste, class, and status designations. As the plantocracies grew, it became necessary to maintain certain distinctions between the various societal elements. As a result, most Caribbean Islands became pigmentocracies. This meant that there was a heavy emphasis on racial characteristics (Knight 1990, 123; Lowenthal 1972, 32–51). The term *pigmentocracy*, popularised by the historians Tannebaum (1947), Elkins (1968), and Freyre (1976), means that the entire social order was characterised on the basis of skin colour.

Brathwaite (1971, 167) provides an elaborate description of the pigmentocratic mentality in the hierarchy of the offspring of black and white unions in the Americas. It is logical to assume that the Cayman Islands, with close geographical proximity and colonial ties to Jamaica, was influenced by this emphasis on racial particularism. Whether such an emphasis was superficial or entrenched is a fertile area for more detailed research. Existing social stratification along colour lines in Caymanian society suggests, however, that emphasis on racial particularism may be more pronounced than many would care to admit.

To the extent that the Cayman Islands were influenced by the notion of pigmentocracy, such an influence would have had its genesis around the late eighteenth to early nineteenth century, when Caymanian society sustained sufficient numbers to make such distinctions meaningful. According to Kieran (1992, 2), before that time Caymanian society comprised mainly two types of colonists:

> The position was relatively distinguishable in the Cayman Islands because of the absence of an indigenous population and major plantations requiring vast numbers of slaves. The original population of settlers were reputed to have been deserters from Cromwell's Army of 1655, following the capture of Jamaica from the Spaniards, and escaped slaves.

The exigencies of life on a small frontier outpost with no guarantees of survival precluded any rigid social stratification during the formative years. Additionally, Caymanian society was, in contrast to other Caribbean societies, a lawless society during the early settlement years.

The significance of this lies in the fact that group survival had far more to do with ability, loyalty, and the will to survive than with the arcana of colour stratification.

Lying in the navigational path of the Spanish treasure fleets returning to Europe from South America, and with an abundance of turtle and fish in the surrounding sea and coastal inlets to serve as careenages, the Cayman Islands were natural haunts for pirates and other seafarers during the eighteenth century. This situation brought its own administrative challenges and substantiates the contention that the Islands, to the extent that they became pigmentocracies, did not achieve this status until the nineteenth century.

Edward Long, writing in 1774, indicated that the residents of the Cayman Islands chose their own governor and made their own laws. Kieran's (1992, 3) reference to a 'Chief' or 'Governor' being chosen by the inhabitants highlights the unique governance practised in the Cayman Islands at that time, compared with other British West Indian possessions, especially Jamaica.

The description of the Cayman Islands as a frontier society with a distinct local culture and in which the metropolitan country displayed little or no interest seems at odds with the rest of the Caribbean at that time. Since the Cayman Islands were not producers of any of the commodities desired by the metropolitan country, it is reasonable to conclude that they did not warrant the expenditure of any money by the metropolitan authorities.

For their part, Caymanian settlers resented their administrative association with Jamaica and seized every opportunity to undermine and frustrate the authorities. This adversarial relationship reached its peak during the period leading up to emancipation, when Caymanian slaveholders refused to cooperate with the Slave Registration Act 1817.

Although the Cayman Islands were not, strictly speaking, a slave society, their position became more untenable and unacceptable as events unfolded in the nineteenth century. As Parliament passed the Abolition Act 1807, the Slave Registration Act 1817, and, finally, the Emancipation Act of 1834, the Cayman Islands moved at their own pace (Higman 1984, 7). Clearly, Caymanian slaveowners, like those elsewhere, did not appreciate being deprived of their chattel.

Cayman Islands slaveowners mounted an organised resistance to efforts by the authorities in Jamaica to create the conditions for apprenticeship and eventual emancipation. This resistance once again set the Cayman Islands apart within the Caribbean.

Kieran describes the situation in the Cayman Islands in a way that sets out the complexities of the society that existed at this time. His depiction also sheds some light on the contentious relationship between the Caymanian authorities and those of the metropolitan country and Jamaica:

> The difficulties which led to the anomaly as to the status of the slaves in the Caymanas arose because of the provisions contained in the Slave Registration Act 1817. The importation of slaves into the British slave owning colonies was made unlawful and more particularly the registration of slaves was to be a prerequisite to the payment of compensation ... The overall objective of registration was not concerned with the welfare of the slaves but to protect the assets of the Plantation Owners. There was no registration in the Caymanas in furtherance of the provisions of the Slavery Abolition Act so there appeared to be ample grounds for the slaves to be considered free from 1st August 1834. (Kieran 1992, 25)

The argument that the Cayman Islands were never a true slave society is illustrated by the following statistics. Figures are provided for the Islands' population in April 1826 as follows (CO 137/198 f318):

Free males	357
Free females	332
Subtotal	689
Slave males	467
Slave females	422
Subtotal	889
Grand total	1,578

Higman (1984, 41) provides figures for the slave population of the Caribbean at the time of emancipation which support the contention that the Cayman Islands, comparatively speaking, were never a slave society.

Colony	Area (mi²)	Slave pop.	Year of colonization
Barbados	166	83,150	1627
Antigua	108	28,130	1632
Montserrat	39	6,400	1632
Virgin Islands	59	5,135	1672
Bahamas	5,548	9,995	1648
Trinidad	1,864	20,655	1797
Jamaica	4,411	311,070	1655
Anguilla	35	2,260	1650
Cayman Islands	100	985	1734

The census of 1802 provides a breakdown of the population in each settlement in the Cayman Islands, including racial identification. These numbers make it clear that Cayman, while not a slave society *per se*, was a society in which there were more people of colour than white people.

District	White families	Slaves	Coloured families
East End	1	0	2
Frank Sound	1	1	2
Bodden Town	24	233	8
Little Pedro	2	4	9
Spotts	3	20	—*
Prospect	2	20	—*
South West Sound	7	21	—*
George Town (Hog Styes)	17	95	5
West Bay	8	25	3
Boatswain Bay	8	25	3
North Side	1	3	2

*— = unknown

Even with what the preceding figures tell us of the entrenchment of white families throughout Grand Cayman, there is no way of ascertaining whether they were whites born in the Caribbean. Given the settlement pattern in the Cayman Islands, it is likely that these were creole whites from Jamaica. Birthplace would logically have significantly influenced attitudes, since whites born in the Caribbean would, by virtue of their upbringing, have had more social contact with black and mixed-ancestry people. The fact remains, however that, for the most part, the Cayman Islands were influenced by the class and colour prejudice prevalent in Jamaica and Caymanian society would be expected to reflect some of these prejudices.

In the period immediately following emancipation in Cayman, there was probably some conflict along colour lines between former slaveholders and their former slaves. It is also likely that this period ushered into the Cayman Islands the beginnings of acute colour consciousness, since emancipation removed the obvious class distinctions of slaveholder and slave.

Throughout the wider Caribbean, following emancipation the black lower class was made up of semi-skilled labourers, both rural and urban, peasants, and other types of workers. George Lamming, the Barbadian novelist and commentator, has implied that to be black in the West Indies is to be poor (Lamming 1987, 1992). To be black in the West Indies also meant to be disenfranchised, to be cut off from the existing channels of mobility, and to be at a psychological disadvantage.

The concept of the 'white man's burden', which provided a psychological as well as an ideological underpinning for the colonial system, became imbedded in pseudoscientific concepts of racial superiority. Emancipation and its aftermath made it essential for the Europeans and creole whites to firmly entrench the concept of black inferiority. Thus the concept of a pigmentocracy became standard, and a heavy emphasis on racial particularism characterised the entire Caribbean social order.

The legacy of colonialism, 1838–1938

Emancipation and its aftermath brought the entrenchment of the British imperial system to the Caribbean. The metropolitan country drew its strength from three areas: the religious community, the working class, and the imperialists and free-traders, especially those supporting unrestricted trade and expansion of the empire.

By the time of emancipation Britain was changing from a primarily trading nation to an increasingly sophisticated economy based on finance, manufacturing, and trade. The change meant that trade with the West Indies took on a different dimension (Knight 1990, 168). It also meant that the imperialist perspective on the West Indies took on a different significance.

Events in Jamaica before and immediately after the Morant Bay Rebellion of 1865 brought a change in colonial administration. The mishandling of the rebellion by Governor Eyre provoked a vociferous post mortem of representative government and British emancipation policy (Holt 1992, 307). 'Responsible government' with its characteristic representation by the planter class and its manipulation by prejudiced colonial governors gave way to crown colony government, a set of political arrangements by which increased authority devolved upon the colonial electorate rather than the Crown.

It was during this period that British policymakers had begun to make distinctions in the administration of the colonies. The white colonies such as Canada, Australia, and New Zealand were to be groomed for independence, while the black colonies were singled out for 'benevolent guardianship' (Holt 1992, 235), which was practised under the euphemism of 'representative government'.

For the Cayman Islands, the period immediately following 1838 had, in addition to these other challenges, local residents' resistance to the stationing of troops of the West India Regiment, which by this time had become a West Indian symbol associated with the demise of slavery in the Caribbean. According to Kieran (1992, 45), 'The Governor was continually being advised of the difficulties ... in the Caymanas, especially with the presence of the West India Regiment detachment, which had arrived in 1834.' The presence of the soldiers, as events were to show, did not deter the unrest engendered by the exploitation of free blacks in Jamaica.

While the Cayman Islands were spared the political fallout that Jamaica experienced following the Morant Bay Rebellion, they were further removed from the colonial mainstream under 'benevolent guardianship'. It appears that the only connection the Cayman Islands had to the authorities in Jamaica during this time was through the West India Regiment detachment.

The relationship of Caymanian civil society to the West India Regiment detachment was characterised by animosity and resistance. Apparently, the years of existence without overt colonial administrative control had reinforced the Caymanians' negative attitude toward authority. The rift between the populace and the West India Regiment was primarily based on the fact that the enlisted men were black. The white establishment was still upset with the change in Cayman's blacks' status from slavery to freedom. To now have their settlement garrisoned by black soldiers seemed an intolerable insult for which the Caymanian settlers were unprepared. Their resentful attitude was characteristic of the frontier society.

For the black and coloured population of Grand Cayman, there were other concerns. There is no evidence to suggest that former slaves in the Cayman Islands experienced any of the economic bondage, political subservience, and social limbo that defined the ex-slave experience in Jamaica. Regardless, slavery in the Cayman Islands still brought deprivation, disenfranchisement, and other social and political evils, as argued below. What is unclear about the condition of blacks and coloureds in the Cayman Islands at that time is exactly what share of the social goods and benefits accrued to them. In the absence of data specific to the Caymanian situation, we are left to infer, based on the Jamaican experience, that the newly freed blacks not only were marginalised in terms of economic and political power but also received only rudimentary health, welfare, and educational benefits.

Lowenthal (1972, 67) illustrates the problem faced by the black and coloured population in the West Indies who were trying to acquire some form of schooling at this time:

> Education was also inequitably dispensed. West Indian whites, like Europeans, thought schooling suitable only for the elite; in the West Indies that elite went "home" to be educated and the territories were left with scarcely the rudiments of a school system. Emancipationists had spoken of the need to train former slaves for life in a free society but little was done. Small educational grants came from the metropolitan governments and from churches, smaller sums from local legislatures ...

Schooling conceived in this spirit was felt undesirable for the masses, in whom it would only confirm distaste for the life of hard physical labour. Primary schooling spread slowly and touched most folk superficially.

Immediately following emancipation, elements of the black population on Grand Cayman, mainly in the districts of Bodden Town and George Town, began to agitate for the establishment of formal schools for the ex-slaves.

There was at this time in the Caribbean a recognition that it was necessary to provide some form of education for the freed black people. In Jamaica, apart from some religious denominations, the effort was spearheaded by the Mico Charity in London. This charity, supported by funds from the Mico Trust, operated Mico Charity schools and later founded the Mico Teachers College to train teachers and missionaries for a return to Africa and the Caribbean.

Two Mico Charity schools were started on Grand Cayman in 1838, one in Bodden Town and the other in George Town. Within six months the enrollment at the Bodden Town school expanded from 23 to 97 and included children from all backgrounds. Andrew Malcolm, the teacher who led this educational effort by opening the first school in Bodden Town on November 29, 1838, had to overcome numerous challenges. There were physical conditions that interfered with operations, such as an infestation of mosquitoes; there was opposition and subversion by former slaveholders, who complained that Malcolm identified too closely with the needs and circumstances of the former slaves.

There is not much information on Malcolm's efforts except what exists in the Bodleian Library at Oxford University. It is known that Malcolm's efforts had such a profound impact upon the parents of the children attending his school that they petitioned the Mico Charity in London on two occasions.

The first petition, sent in July 1840, expressed fears about Malcolm's imminent departure from Grand Cayman. After Malcolm left, parents sent another petition to London requesting that the Mico Charity authorities encourage Malcolm to return to Grand Cayman. The records show that most of the signatories were illiterate, since their printed names are accompanied by a mark of 'X'.

Education of the children of former slaves got off to a similarly slow start elsewhere in the Caribbean, largely owing to resistance on the part of the planter class. Much credit must be given to the religious denominations and the Mico Charity schools, which persevered in spite of such resistance.

By the end of the 1800s significant changes were taking place within Caymanian society. All three islands were permanently settled, and there was an obvious cultural affinity with the sea. The advent of steam navigation and refrigerated cargo meant that ships plying the North Atlantic route from South America no longer had to re-victual in the northwestern Caribbean. As a result, the Cayman Islands went through a period of isolation. Caymanians, in true frontier spirit, used this isolation to further hone their navigational and boat-building skills. Turtle fishing in the waters surrounding the Cayman Islands became an even more necessary and popular vocation, and soon Caymanian sailors were a familiar sight from Pickle Bank to the Miskito Cays.

From frontier society to representative government

The earliest organised system of government in the Cayman Islands had its genesis in 1750, in the appointment of one William Cartwright as stipendiary magistrate. A bombastic, officious character, he served until 1775, and his years of service were characterised by his overbearing and tyrannical nature.

He reportedly was especially harsh and cruel to slaves, often sentencing them to severe lashings and on occasion to public execution north of the Hog Styes. There appears to be no historical record of Cartwright's appointment, although it is widely assumed that he was from George Town and that his official title was only Stipendiary Magistrate and not Governor, which he later assumed (McLaughlin 1982, 11–12).

Cartwright was succeeded in office by the Bodden Towner William Bodden Sr. He held a commission as chief magistrate by the Right Honourable Earl of Balcarnes, Lieutenant Governor of Jamaica. This commission, dated January 13, 1798, also included his two brothers, James Bodden and Joseph Bodden.

During this period a closer relationship developed with the authorities in Jamaica, and, although the relationship was far from ideal and certainly not to the liking of the Caymanian oligarchy, it brought some form of accountability. Significantly, in 1802 Governor Nugent of Jamaica sent Edward Corbet on an official visit to the Cayman Islands. Corbet made a number of important suggestions in his report. Among them was the suggestion that someone from George Town should be appointed, as a matter of convenience, to be associated with the Boddens but serve the George Town inhabitants.

Governor Bodden served from 1776 until 1823. He was a forceful man, and his term of service brought considerable improvement to Grand Cayman. One significant change was the renaming of the place called Hog Styes, now George Town. It was then that the district began to gain prominence because of its preferred harbour. It was at this time also that two forts, one at George Town and the other at Prospect, were constructed for the defence of the island.

For administration purposes, magistrates in the Cayman Islands had the same power as those in Jamaica, except that when new measures were to be adopted, they had to be submitted by the magistrates for the public's approval. The practice was true frontier democracy and was fraught with problems, as indicated in Corbet's report of 1802.

The report tells of an incident culminating in the deportation to the United States of an 'ill-disposed individual' by the 'united voice and compulsion of the inhabitants'.

This type of government continued until 1898, when the powers of the custos, or chief magistrate, were vested in a commissioner, who combined administrative duties with those of a judge of the Grand Court of the Cayman Islands (McLaughlin 1982, 12). The commissioner was selected by the secretary of state for the colonies and appointed by the Governor of Jamaica. With the coming into effect of this arrangement, the Cayman Islands were transformed from a frontier society in which Caymanian authorities operated almost independently of colonial administrative controls to a frontier society which was being drawn into the realm of accountability and responsibility. Undoubtedly, however, the most significant event of the time in terms of economic impact was the transfer of the capital in 1898 from Bodden Town to George Town, which had been the residence of the commissioner.

Several factors made this transfer logical and predictable. In the first place, the threat of Spanish raids from Cuba was eliminated by this time, and a merchant class had become noticeable around George Town. The harbour at George Town was operational almost year round, and the depth of the water enabled large vessels to more easily be accommodated in this port. Bodden Town as a seaport was handicapped by the year-round southeast trade winds, shallow water, and extensive coral reefs.

The first election of representatives to the Cayman Islands Assembly took place in December 1831 (C/O 137/193 S CC 480). A bicameral system with eight magistrates and ten elected vestrymen first met at Cayman's only 'great house', Pedro St James. With its second meeting on January 2, 1832, the Legislative Assembly of Justices and Vestry of the Cayman Islands became fully functional. At this meeting it was agreed that it had become necessary to increase the number of elected representatives. Accordingly, the Act to Regulate the Legislative Assembly of the Cayman Islands was passed on January 2, 1832.

The first elected representatives were from Bodden Town, Prospect, South West Sound, George Town, and West Bay. Elected by registered male property holders between the ages of 18 and 60 years, these men formed the beginnings of representative government in the Cayman Islands.

The corresponding period in Jamaica saw the further evolution of the conflict between the oligarchy and the former slaves and free blacks. Developments during the first decade of freedom were to greatly complicate the practice of representative government. Colonial systems of justice became increasingly biased in favour of planters' interests and against those of the freed slaves.

The passing of responsibility for government to the Colonial Office in London did not alleviate the problem. Colonial Office officials continued to be preoccupied with the inadequacies of the West Indian assemblies. A grand opportunity was missed when the colonial authorities failed to heed the warning signs exhibited in Jamaica in 1839 (Augier et al., 1960, 221).

The upshot of this failure was the Morant Bay Rebellion of 1865 and the ensuing royal commission, which brought additional changes to the existing system of representative government. The Cayman Islands were not directly involved in these activities, and despite their association with Jamaica, they were affected only peripherally. Caymanian society at this time was not totally dependent on Jamaica, as the resourcefulness of the Caymanian residents enabled them to be self-sufficient in foodstuffs and many building materials.

Constitutionally, the end of the 1800s brought a change in the position of custos to that of commissioner, with an assigned salary. Concomitant with this development was the condition that commissioners were to be appointed from outside the Islands. There followed a number of commissioners who continued to oversee improvements. Roads were built, new schools were constructed, a Police Force Law was passed, and a special residence for the commissioner was built. From 1906 until 1912 the post of commissioner was held by George Stephenson Shirt Hirst. He was a medical doctor by training and later became a respected chronicler of Caymanian history (McLaughlin 1982, 13)

The period 1914–1932 witnessed an expansion of Caymanian society to the point where international affairs began to have an influence upon local matters. World War I brought deprivation, and a few Caymanians were lost at sea, the result of the North Atlantic submarine war. Several successive commissioners did nothing spectacular until 1934.

In 1932 the Cayman Islands were struck by the most devastating hurricane in the history of the colony, with considerable loss of life and destruction of property. Conditions following the hurricane were aggravated by the stock market crash and the ensuing Great Depression in the United States.

Challenging times call for visionary leadership, and in 1934 the colony was fortunate to welcome Commissioner Allan W. Cardinall, who laid the foundations of the modern Cayman Islands. Few of Cayman's colonial leaders demonstrated prescience and vision comparable to Cardinall's. Arriving during perhaps the most depressed era in the Islands' history, Cardinall embarked on an amazingly robust development programme (McLaughlin 1982, 15–16).

By the time his tour of duty ended, Commissioner (later Sir Allan) Cardinall left the Cayman Islands with a modern infrastructure of roads, a hospital, schools, a hotel aid law, and an efficient and professional civil service. Such a social and political transformation by a colonial administrator was surpassed only by the performance of Andrew Morris Gerrard between 1953 and 1956.

If the Caymanian oligarchy expected the status quo with regard to black people in public life to continue, they were soon upset by the outspoken, able, and unflinching Gerrard. An atypical colonial officer, he soon came to realise the contradictions and duplicity among some elements of Caymanian high society. Realising that he had come to a community in the West Indies where the social pretensions to aristocracy were based merely on skin colour, and where his official position allowed him to remain aloof and detached from the disingenuous, he opened up the social life of Government House to the coloured element, to the dismay of the white oligarchy.

It was at this point that the British political legacy, represented by Gerrard, distanced itself from the social legacy perpetuated by a majority of the Caymanian oligarchy. Nothing could have better illuminated the changes which were about to take place in Caymanian society than the tone set by Gerrard in his routine dealings with the people.

A new social dialogue was about to take place, and it soon became clear that this unreserved and unapologetic but able commissioner held no brief for discrimination based on skin colour or pretensions of racial purity. In August 1953, under his visionary leadership, Owen Roberts airfield was completed. Shortly thereafter, a 28-bed hospital with a maternity ward, X-ray block, and nurses' quarters was built in George Town (McLaughlin 1982, 23).

Pragmatic in his approach to development, Gerrard went to great pains to introduce tourism into the Caymanian economy. Largely as a result of early tourism advertisements in the *Saturday Evening Post* magazine, enquiries flooded his office. It was also during his tenure as commissioner that Benson Greenall built the first hotel, the Galleon Beach, on lands leased from the government. Barclays Bank, drawn largely by the increasing amounts of remittances from Caymanian sailors sailing on ships flying flags of convenience, superseded the Government Savings Bank as the Islands' premier bank. As a special dispensation from the secretary of state for the colonies, Gerrard's tour of duty was extended so he could witness the completion of the airport on Cayman Brac (McLaughlin 1982, 23).

It should come as no surprise, then, that during Gerrard's term as commissioner he continued the modernisation set in motion by Sir Allan Cardinall. His farewell address to the members of the Assembly of Vestrymen and Justices was characterised by his understanding and appreciation of Cayman and Caymanians. In addition to the infrastructural successes mentioned above, by his demeanour he succeeded in changing the Caymanian social hierarchy from a colour- and race-based one to a class-based one. It was this accomplishment, perhaps more than any other, that paved the way for Caymanians of colour to enter the civil service in greater than token numbers (Lewis 1968, 332).

Sailors, seamen, and the emergence of national society

It was during Gerrard's tenure in office that the postwar shipping industry attracted hundreds of Caymanians to ply their skills as merchant seamen. No survey of Caymanian history would be complete without an acknowledgement of the contribution of Caymanian sailors and seamen to the economic, social, and cultural development of the Islands. The use of the phrase *sailors and seamen* is deliberate and peculiar to this work, since the term *sailor* is used here to describe the men engaged primarily in the turtling trade and earlier trading ventures using ships with sails. 'Seamen', on the other hand, connotes those involved in maritime activities on steam- or diesel-driven vessels more representative of the modern era. With the failure of the Cayman Islands government's turtle-canning factory and contention with Nicaragua over turtle-fishing rights, turtling as a viable industry fell into a steep decline.

Gordon Lewis, writing almost 40 years ago, offers a vivid description of the challenge which faced the Caymanian community as it emerged, mid-century, from its frontier-society cocoon:

> It is this cultural traditionalism which today constitutes the basic problem of Caymanian society. For with the post-1945 decline of the turtle industry a serious challenge of cultural adaptation has arisen. The decline was due, in large part, to intractable factors: the decline of maritime traffic and its food needs, the competition from other delicacies in the metropolitan markets, the growing difficulties with the Nicaraguan Government concerning Caymanian fishing rights in the Nicaraguan territorial waters. The island economy thus faces the need for fundamental adjustment to new conditions. (Lewis 1968, 331)

That adjustment arrived in the form of a demand by US shipping companies, flying flags of convenience, for skilled, non-unionised seamen to crew their ships. The aftermath of World War II brought a tremendous industrial growth spurt. Iron ore, steel, and petroleum products to fuel the automobile and allied industries were in great demand. Bulk carriers, sometimes fabricated from World War II Liberty ships, became popular, and Caymanian seamen – English speakers with considerable maritime experience, who were willing to work with no union and for low wages – became the crews of choice.

In addition to their normal commercial activities on turtling and trading vessels, a significant number of Caymanians volunteered for service in the Trinidad Royal Naval Volunteer Reserve during World War II. This organisation was an adjunct of the Royal Navy, and its main responsibility was to protect the oil reserves on the island of Trinidad as well as carrying out anti-submarine and maritime patrols in the Caribbean and the North Atlantic. Such experiences enhanced the employability of Caymanian seamen, allowing many to achieve the highest ranks as engineers and captains on multimillion-dollar supertankers and bulk carriers. Lewis (1968) describes the development of this enterprise:

> [T]he Caymanian sailor has an intimate affection for the sea that no human force, including that of his close knit family life, can change. This helps account for the gradual change that has taken place in the employment picture, with an increasing transfer of both crews and officers to Dutch tankers, American merchantmen and Jamaican steamers. Their remittances, especially from American sources (the export income of the economy is almost entirely in dollars) are basic to island prosperity. (p. 331–32)

At its zenith this vocation employed about 1,000 Caymanian seamen, out of a population of 10,000 islanders. It was the remittances from these seamen that brought the Cayman Islands to the attention of Barclays Bank in the early 1950s. By the 1960s it was apparent that, with remittances from Caymanian merchant seamen as the catalyst and the efforts of Administrator John Cumber to attract international business, Cayman was gaining importance as an economic jurisdiction.

It is significant that the cultural traditionalism so fundamental to Caymanian society came under stress as a result of an influx of foreign nationals who came to work in banks and financial businesses from the early 1970s. At various times during their tenure, both Sir Allan Cardinall and Andrew Morris Gerrard warned against opening up the Cayman Islands to outsiders (McLaughlin 1982, 18). The influx of foreigners brought challenges that had been, up to that time, largely unknown in the Cayman Islands.

As events unfolded, however, Cayman held a certain attraction for outsiders, and the shrinking of empire and the independence movement in the other Caribbean territories placed the Cayman Islands both literally and figuratively as the 'last frontier'. It is not surprising that the British officials and expatriates who came to the Cayman Islands during this time were, for the most part, markedly different from their predecessors. A significant number of them had been displaced when other Caribbean islands – Jamaica, Trinidad, Barbados, and the Bahamas – became independent, while others came from African countries under the circumstances of an expired welcome.

Many of these new arrivals in both officialdom and civil society saw themselves as intellectually and culturally superior to the established Caymanian populace. Often they referred to Caymanians pejoratively as 'the natives'. Lewis (1968, 109) shed some light on exactly how widespread this attitude was when he wrote, 'It is evident enough, reading the literature, that the majority of the English educated class, as well as its expatriate bureaucrats in the colonies, believed, as an article of faith, in the cultural, sometimes the racial inferiority of the West Indian person.'

In many instances, the expatriate prejudice against established Caymanians of colour is *sub rosa* and not likely to be displayed openly. Association in the workplace and on social occasions only rarely reveals any reservations based on colour. The hypocrisy, however, is revealed in the expatriates' private enclaves, often in subdivisions or condominium developments totally isolated from established Caymanians. It is here, in these residences, that the expatriates' true contempt for Caymanians can be expressed.

Established Caymanians are aware of this hypocrisy and, indeed, have their own prejudices against many of these outsiders, whom they contemptuously lump together as 'expats'. Though there is a mutuality of prejudice, it rarely reaches the point of aggressive or threatening behaviour. The social fabric is held together by the realisation that what exists is a synergistic and symbiotic relationship, which must be maintained if both groups are to continue to prosper. The Cayman Islands have never been a jurisdiction where blatant hostilities against outsiders were expressed. It is largely the acceptance of this symbiotic relationship by established Caymanians that has allowed Cayman to devise the concept of 'voluntary colonialism', which is one of the most interesting aspects of Caymanian society and one reason that there is great promise for its further evolution into an equitable multicultural community.

Federation, failure, and voluntary colonialism

With the end of World War II came a desire for autonomy on the part of various colonies of the British empire. Beginning on the Indian subcontinent and spreading into Africa by the 1960s, victory in war brought a yearning for liberation from the imperial mantle.

The West Indies presented a unique challenge, and, with encouragement from the metropolitan country, a federal venture was crafted. History should have been kind to such an undertaking since Jamaica, Trinidad, and Barbados, as the larger territories, had similar colonial experiences. But personality clashes, arguments over cost, and political patronage led to an irreparable breach, and by 1961 federation was no more.

What should have been a predictable outcome brought a quandary for the Cayman Islands. Previously attached to Jamaica for administration purposes, the Cayman Islands' legislators now faced the difficult choice between independence as a part of Jamaica and some other, hitherto undefined alternative.

The 1950s were years of significant political change that placed the Cayman Islands on the threshold of political modernity. From 1863, when they were formally annexed to Jamaica, until July 1959, the Cayman Islands had no written constitution (McLaughlin 1982, 24).

The 1863 Act of Parliament set up an assembly composed of justices of the peace and vestrymen. It was an unusual system, which allowed the Jamaican Assembly the authority to make laws for the peace, order, and good government of the Cayman Islands and to amend or repeal any laws passed by the Cayman Islands Assembly of Justices and Vestrymen.

The situation gave Caymanians cause for concern, although in practice there was little or no interference from the Jamaican authorities. Colonial Office correspondence for this period reveals that some Caymanians feared being dominated by a larger and more populous Jamaica. Additionally, Caymanian politicians wished to maintain 'a considerable degree of autonomy under the Governor, rather than the government of Jamaica' (WI/64/19/01). With a new Jamaican constitution in preparation, the suggestion was made that it was undesirable to clutter it up with 'complicated references to the Dependencies'.

The proposal was for the United Kingdom to pass a special Act of Parliament dealing with the dependencies of the Turks and Caicos Islands and the Cayman Islands as entities separate from Jamaica. Sir Hugh Foot, Governor of Jamaica at the time, suggested a new United Kingdom Act which permitted the Turks and Caicos Islands and the Cayman Islands to have their own constitutions enacted by Order-in-Council. In an address to the Assembly in November 1956 he told Caymanians:

> You have local autonomy within your grasp. Go forward and take it confidently. You will then find that being masters in your own house, there is every reason to maintain your profitable and honourable association with Jamaica, and to create a similar relationship with the other British territories of the West Indies who believe in the same things that you do. (WIS 59/289/02)

From 1956 onward there was great political agitation in the Cayman Islands, compared with previous years. Several important issues came to the forefront of political discussion. Women were barred from both voting and running as candidates, and informed Caymanians made reference to the United Nations Convention on the Political Rights of Women.

Campaigners for women's suffrage in the Cayman Islands were told by the secretary of state for the colonies that 'the United Kingdom Government itself is not able to accept the Convention at the present time if only because of the non-admittance of women to the House of Lords' (CO IRD 152/01, Feb 18, 1957). The campaigners were undeterred, and on May 29, 1957, a petition with island-wide support was presented to the Assembly of Justices and Vestrymen.

The following year a group of prominent George Town men wrote to the commissioner, nominating Mrs Ena Watler as a candidate for George Town in the upcoming elections. The nominators received a reply in June 1958, informing them of the commissioner's inability to accept the nomination but offering hope that the situation would change within a year or so.

Almost simultaneous with the agitation for female enfranchisement was the organisation of the first political party in the Cayman Islands. In a letter dated August 8, 1958, and addressed to the commissioner, five Caymanians told him of the formation of the Cayman Vanguard Progressive Party and its executive.

Such political activity by interest groups was apparently motivated by political events in the wider Caribbean. Federation fervour was raging throughout the larger British colonies, and, although Caymanians realised their relative unimportance, they believed that their interests could be assured only if they made their position known. It was for this reason that a historic mission to King's House in Jamaica was undertaken on January 14, 1957.

The so-called Big Four – T.W. Farrington, justice; O.L. Panton, vestryman; Ernest Panton, justice; and E.D. Merren, vestryman – articulated the Cayman Islands' position. According to the *Cayman Times* newspaper of January 21, 1957 (p. 2), the purpose of the visit was:

> To represent the great importance which Caymanians give to their main aim, which is to achieve the maximum autonomy in the management of their own affairs.
>
> To urge that the special position of the Cayman Islands should be recognised and accepted, particularly in matters of taxation, trade and migration.
>
> To request that when the new Constitution of Jamaica is introduced, the composition, rights and powers of the representative institutions of the Cayman Islands should be set down by constitutional arrangement.
>
> To request that when the new West Indian Federation Constitution is formulated provision should be made under which the need of the Cayman Islands may receive special consideration.

The politics of these years brought out the prejudices that existed in Caymanian society. There was a serious distrust of women's ability to make rational political choices. In correspondence between the Cayman Islands commissioner, Allan H. Donald, and Sir Kenneth Blackburne, Governor of Jamaica, reference was made to 'the behaviour of certain groups of women stated to be supporters of the Cayman Vanguard Progressive Party affecting seriously the chances of the Vestry passing the Sex Disqualification (Removal) Bill'.

Prejudice against the Cayman Vanguard Progressive Party (CVPP) was widespread, with certain party members of Jamaican nationality singled out for official opprobrium. Establishment behaviour serves as a reminder that the Cayman Islanders did not see themselves as belonging in any political alliance with Jamaica.

The prejudice and opposition of the merchant establishment ensured the early death of the CVPP. That political parties could galvanise public opinion was not lost on some Caymanians, however, and when political parties next manifested themselves it was with significantly more durability and permanence – although not, as yet, with the penetrating influence that political parties had elsewhere in the Caribbean.

The significance of the CVPP in Caymanian history lies more in symbolism than in lasting achievement. After all, the party as an active organisation lasted less than two years. Events would show, however, that agitation for change originated not with the merchant establishment but from the middle class, which included a mixture of so-called white and coloured elements.

By the time the old Assembly of Justices and Vestrymen voted itself out of existence in 1959, several new developments were obvious. Significantly, a number of the justices and vestrymen took the opportunity to close out their political terms. Concomitant with their departure was the emergence of younger, more articulate, and more visionary representatives.

When the new constitution came into effect on July 4, 1959, one of these legislators had succeeded in generating enough support among his colleagues to organise a functioning political party. The National Democratic Party, headed by Ormond Panton, was well poised to take advantage of the recently declared universal suffrage and the advances in Cayman's constitution.

Several significant changes occurred as a result of the new constitution. For example, the title of the colonial head was changed from 'commissioner' to 'administrator'. The Assembly of Justices and

Vestrymen was changed to a Legislative Assembly with an executive council. Twelve elected members, along with three nominated members and three official members, were the complement of the Legislative Assembly, and women were allowed to stand as candidates for the first time in the Islands' history. It is also significant that the Cayman Islands agreed to form part of the West Indies Federation in 1961 (McLaughlin 1982, 25).

The West Indies Federation, shaky from its beginning, collapsed outright in 1961. Its collapse placed the Cayman Islands in a political quandary. For the first time in history there appeared to be a 'crisis of existence' facing the Cayman Islands (Hannerz 1974, 65–68; Lewis 1968, 333–34). Two questions were critical to the Caymanian legislators. Should the Cayman Islands retain close political ties with Jamaica? Or would it be more politically astute to remain attached to the United Kingdom in a yet-to-be-defined relationship?

The importance of the predicament was underscored by an address given by the then Governor of Jamaica and the Cayman Islands, Sir Kenneth Blackburne. After a preamble which included commentary on the proceedings up to that time, the governor outlined what he saw as the advantages and disadvantages of association with the United Kingdom and Jamaica respectively (Legislative Assembly, Jan 18–19, 1962: 1–18).

After the governor's elaboration, it became clear that Jack Rose, the administrator, had not been accurate in his famous 'black ball, white ball' speech from the porch of the Old Court House building in George Town on December 14, 1961: there was another way besides alliance with Jamaica in which internal self-government could be achieved.

To his credit, the second elected member for George Town, Dr Roy McTaggart, led the proposal that the future of the Cayman Islands lay in seeking some arrangement with the United Kingdom whereby the Islands would retain their constitutional links with the metropolitan country while running their internal affairs virtually unmolested. It is this arrangement that this writer describes as voluntary colonialism. This symbiotic relationship with the United Kingdom has served the Cayman Islands well until now. Voluntary colonialism has allowed the Cayman Islands to derive considerable economic benefit over the past four decades.

Arising out of the decision to seek internal self-government were two events that were of paramount importance in the development of Caymanian politics. The first was that the Legislative Assembly, in anticipation of the granting of internal self-government, voted on February 9, 1962, to introduce a 'membership' system of government as a prelude to the ministerial system, which, it was understood, would accompany internal self-government. Since the executive council had not been elected or appointed under the membership system, it was considered appropriate for its members to resign their seats so that a new executive council could be elected under the membership system.

During this reorganisation it was discovered that the Legislative Assembly (which had been elected three years before the demise of the West Indies Federation) had no mandate from the people to proceed on these important yet controversial matters. As events unfolded, the Cayman Islands went through a constitutional transition that legitimised the Cayman Islands as a direct dependency of the United Kingdom (Lawrence 1975, 17).

It was at this juncture that the National Democratic Party (NDP), under the leadership of Ormond Panton, established itself as an organisation representing what turned out to be the popular opinion. The merchant establishment, consisting largely of the older representatives, countered by forming a rival organisation, which they called the Christian Democratic Party (CDP) (Hannerz 1974, 73).

The election of November 22, 1962, made history in the Cayman Islands. Not only did the NDP win seven seats, but the first woman was elected to the Legislative Assembly. Victory at the polls, however, proved the only source of inspiration for the triumphant NDP leader. In an obvious gesture of bias and contempt, Administrator Jack Rose nominated three members to the Legislative Assembly without consulting the leader of the majority party. These appointments were so unacceptable to NDP leader Ormond Panton that he proposed the mass resignation of his members (Bodden 1978, 13). Such a move would undoubtedly have attracted the attention of the Colonial Office, had it been unanimous. As it turned out, however, the leader took no steps to ensure collective behaviour, and the party members, in a classic display of Caymanian individualism, did not actually tender their resignations to Mr Rose.

Only the leader and another prominent party member from George Town were honourable enough to follow through and resign. The gesture had the negligible effect of calling a by-election to fill the two vacant seats. Ormond Panton was again a candidate for one of the two vacant seats, and again he was successful. By this time, however, it was difficult to rationalise the indiscipline of some party members. This, coupled with the intransigence of the administrator and his nominated members, further eroded the effectiveness of the NDP to the point at which it was impotent to deal with the growing opposition to full internal self-government.

The demise of the NDP meant that the CDP also became politically irrelevant. With the extinguishment of party politics went any hopes for constitutional reform. Fortunately, it was discovered in 1965 that, through incompetence, the 1962 constitution had not been ratified. As a result, a new Order-in-Council was made on October 29, 1965, and passed in the Cayman Islands Legislative Assembly on November 4, 1965 (Lawrence 1975, 18).

Elsewhere in the Caribbean, Jamaica withdrew from the federation and gained independence from the United Kingdom in August 1962. This achievement by Jamaica inspired several other former federated states to follow suit, and later Trinidad, Barbados, and some smaller islands in the eastern Caribbean sought self-determination.

While these territories enjoyed political buoyancy in their newfound status, the Cayman Islands continued to labour under voluntary colonialism with a questionable constitutional instrument. It was not until 1970 that the Legislative Assembly was able to agree to request that a constitutional expert be sent to the Cayman Islands.

Arriving in January 1971, the constitutional commissioner had wide discussions throughout the Cayman Islands. One immediate outcome was that in October 1971, the title 'administrator' was changed to 'governor'. In 1972, the following changes were accepted (McLaughlin 1982, 29):

- Nominated (appointed) members were discontinued.
- The three official members would be the Chief Secretary (Deputy Governor), the Attorney General, and the Financial Secretary.
- Four elected members were to form the elected executives on the Executive Council and were to be elected by the members of the Legislative Assembly.
- Executive Council members were assigned portfolios on various subjects by the Governor.
- The voting age was reduced to 18 years.
- Provision was made for a Speaker to be appointed by the governor when the Legislative Assembly passed a resolution mandating such.

- The life of the Legislative Assembly was increased to four years from three.

The changes gave the Cayman Islands a constitutional instrument which, if not thoroughly modern, brought the jurisdiction to the threshold of political modernity.

Politicians, bankers, and change

The 1970s were years of significant change in Caymanian society. While the Islands did not experience any of the turmoil which shook up some other Caribbean territories during these years, there was one major political demonstration in the Cayman Islands.

Since the later part of the 1960s land development had gained prominence throughout the Islands as a source of wealth. Many Caymanians sold their land to mainly wealthy North Americans, and such sales fuelled an economic boon. Controversy followed, however, as the political directorate decided that it was time to change the old regional Planning Law 1935 and modernise the system.

The replacement for the old system of land registration and safeguarding of Crown property and interest appeared onerous and demanding, and seemed to deprive people of long-established rights. The new proposals had the unintended consequence of agitating some influential members of society who, in addition to being landowners, held real estate interests. After protracted island-wide discussion and much agitation, a demonstration was planned for the coming days.

The demonstration took place on Monday, April 20, 1970. While there are no official figures as to the number of people who participated, the demonstration seems to have been large enough to impress the government. In preparation for the demonstration, islanders from all over Grand Cayman congregated at the Princess Royal Park. From this venue, they proceeded to government headquarters. Two things were immediately significant: several prominent individuals had organised the demonstration, and nothing like it had been seen in the Cayman Islands before (Hannerz 1974, 130–50).

Given the absence of endemic political and ideological problems, no one expected the Cayman Islands to be rocked by the level of political agitation experienced in other Caribbean territories at this time. Activists such as Walter Rodney and Maurice Bishop were espousing a leftist radicalism that was to leave its mark on modern Caribbean history.

While the repercussions did not affect the Cayman Islands, political change was destined to affect Caymanian society through more traditional means.

Such change came in 1972 when, upon first being elected to the Legislative Assembly, the members from Bodden Town – namely James (Jim) M. Bodden and G. Haig Bodden – brought a different style to Caymanian politics. Dubbed the 'Voices of Opposition' by *Northwester* magazine (September 1974, pp. 6–13), these two members brought a direct and relentless approach to politics, and political debate in the Cayman Islands took on a new character.

By the time of the general election in 1976, these members had built a noticeable political machine with representation from throughout the island. It should have been obvious to Benson Ebanks and Warren Conolly, the two leading members of Executive Council, that these were more politically demanding times. They refrained from challenging the opposition to their political directorate during the formative period of their administration. This reticence allowed the opposition, which cohered around Jim Bodden and Haig Bodden, to strengthen and swell. Later this opposition manifested as the Unity Team, by which time it had attracted island-wide support. This was the first time the Islands had witnessed the frenzied atmosphere of mass politics since Ormond Panton and his National Democratic Party in the 1960s.

Despite more than one insinuation that their political careers rested on the outcome of the 1976 general election, and despite assistance from a small but determined cadre of supporters, the incumbent Executive Council members did not throw the whole weight of their efforts behind the campaign, apparently relying instead on the hope that the voting populace would remember their past record.

While the incumbent political directorate had made significant infrastructural strides – including the construction of a government administration building, new docking facilities in George Town, and a new Legislative Assembly building (*Northwester*, June 1974, pp. 17–30) – they lost a great political opportunity by not publicly informing the Caymanian people of these accomplishments. Because of their aloofness and negligence, the opposition was successful in charging that the political leadership was arrogant and uncaring. Not to challenge these accusations was the most politically unwise action of all. Indeed, their lack of reaction seemed more indicative of a political corpse than of the vibrant, modernising force they purported to be.

In the event, the movement known as the Unity Team swept all but one seat. Dominating both the Legislative Assembly and the wider society, this organisation consolidated its support and dominated again in the 1980 general election.

The Unity Team's leadership style and mass organisation techniques brought such success that on one occasion one of the Bodden Town representatives boasted that, if they were to dress a broomstick and ask for their constituents' votes, the broomstick would gain a seat in the Legislative Assembly (*Nor'wester,* November 1976, 7).

It was during the tenure of the Unity Team that the Islands experienced a tremendous economic growth spurt. Land sales boomed, and the banking business took on serious international proportions. In true frontier spirit, events were rapidly pushing the Cayman Islands into becoming a major centre of international finance.

Encouraged by the bullish real estate market, many Caymanians sold their inherited land, some of which had been in their families for generations, for what appeared to be attractive prices. What followed was nothing short of a 'revolution of rising expectations', in which Caymanians entered into a consumption-based social milieu followed by an elevation in the standard of living. These changes were followed by a sobering reality.

There appeared for the first time significant numbers of expatriates whose primary function was to service the growing financial industry. It became obvious that elements of the established society were uncomfortable with these newcomers (Hannerz 1974, 114–15).

The newcomers, who represented a new affluent and cosmopolitan class, came to the territory for a variety of reasons. Most were attracted by new business opportunities and tax advantages. Yet it was the expansion of the governmental apparatus that drew most of the criticism, and, perhaps rather unfairly, the government was made to carry a large share of the burden of dissonance between Caymanians and expatriates.

It is important to note that when Caymanians speak of expatriates, they invariably are referring to Caucasians from the 'first world'. People from the Caribbean are usually referred to by nationality – for example, Jamaican, Trinidadian, Guyanese. The term *expatriate* is reserved for citizens of Europe, Canada, the United Kingdom, and the United States.

There exists a certain dissonance between some Caymanians and elements of the British expatriate community. Not infrequently, Caymanians will refer to British people as 'limeys' – a pejorative reference to the long-ago practice of British sailors bottling lime juice for long voyages to protect against scurvy. Some members of the British expatriate community, for their part, refer to Caymanians as 'the natives' in the colonial tradition from which they have come.

Dissonance notwithstanding, there is a symbiosis that has allowed these elements to coexist in a way that is peculiar to Caymanian society. It is this symbiosis which, by 1974, had enabled the Cayman Islands to benefit from the openly pro-Bahamian policies of Lynden Pindling when he took office as prime minister of the newly independent Bahamas and espoused a nationalist philosophy.

The Cayman Islands experienced a setback in 1974, however. Some years earlier, a French Canadian with a flair for unorthodox banking practices had formed a banking establishment called Interbank. Government officials should have paid closer attention to the bank's practices, though to this day there are some who believe that the bank's failure had less to do with its founder's inabilities than with a conspiracy among jealous rivals from the more orthodox banking sector.

Whatever the cause, this first major bank failure in the Islands sent the economy into shock. It took years to recover – although in many respects the lessons were soon forgotten. Caymanian society was profoundly changed, in that some of the wide-open financial speculation indicative of frontier-type societies was gone. The crash of Interbank eliminated the single unorthodox banking house, which had stood in stark contrast to the more sedate and conservative branches of the multinational banks. Regulation and oversight were, however, still rudimentary, as was obvious when the Bank of Credit and Commerce International (BCCI) crashed in the 1990s. The Cayman Islands government had not grasped the lessons of the Interbank failure. The international community, as a result of the corruption which had brought down BCCI, demanded that regulation and accountability be established in Cayman's banking industry. The improvements in the practice of banking conveyed some sense of regulatory responsibility and were implemented just in time to attract more international business.

With the economy in transition, the popularity of the Unity Team and its leader was called into question. The general election of 1984 saw the emergence of a credible enough alternative that many were predicting the end of the Unity Team era, as the leaders appeared to be suffering from political malaise. In the event, the once-dominant Unity Team political directorate was reduced to its original state – two representatives from Bodden Town. The following years brought an end to Unity Team politics, although there were large elements of society that insisted on regarding its leader as a benevolent godfather.

Caymanian politics during these years took the Islands away from regionalism and wider Caribbean issues such as the Caribbean Common Market (CARICOM) and regional free trade. The Dignity Team, which had been in opposition to the Unity Team, formed a loose coalition and was successful in forming the political directorate after the 1988 general election.

The concept of a political 'team', as opposed to a political party, is a phenomenon peculiar to the Cayman Islands. The rationale is that, as an informal organisation, a political team cannot easily alter the constitutional status of the territory. Since great emphasis is placed on the Cayman Islands' maintaining their voluntary colonialism status, voters find it easier to support a political team than an outright political party, which could – quite conceivably, some think – agitate for self-determination.

The team-versus-party debate has fuelled sentiments in Cayman for many years. Successive political directorates have managed to convey the impression that constitutional advancement will invariably lead to independence. As a result, political developments are shrouded in a kind of hypocrisy, and the political directorate can be held hostage by a sterile and hidebound bureaucracy.

Over the years certain political players have used as a favourite tactic the accusation that their opposition are 'radicals' who will destroy the economy and draft the Cayman Islands into independence. References have been made to other societies, in the Caribbean and elsewhere, in an attempt to persuade the voting populace that those in opposition not only are incapable of leadership but also are of questionable ideology. The people positing these sentiments consider themselves as representative of the middle class. In keeping with the Caymanian colour/class dichotomy, they are invariably representative of the merchant class.

For many years, then, a disquiet arose when newcomers, not of the old established Caymanian merchant classes, won political seats. Sometimes the disquiet was contained by marriages of political convenience, such as existed after the breakup of the Unity Team when one original member of the Unity Team Executive Council was instrumental in forming a rather loose coalition with defectors from the Dignity Team. This agglomeration, known island-wide as 'the back-benchers', was successful in its attempt to unseat the political directorate in the 1996 general elections. With this defeat, the Dignity Team had no obvious remnants left, thus paving the way for a completely new political team to emerge.

As is not unusual in marriages of convenience, however, the organisation that emerged changed its membership and called itself the National Team. Led by the former prominent Unity Team member along with three of his old colleagues, this political directorate controlled government and legislative affairs until the general election of 2000, when the antipathy it had aroused among the electorate and its inability as an organisation to respond to Caymanians' desire for transformation and modernity resulted in the routing of its leadership. The National Team leader and two of his ministerial colleagues lost their seats in the Legislative Assembly. Two members who had successfully contested the elections, in true Cayman style, found a welcome elsewhere in the political landscape that is island politics.

Ex post facto analysis suggests that the National Team self-destructed during the years 1996–2000. In the campaign leading up to the election, the focus was on economic mismanagement, corruption, and an inability or unwillingness to settle a festering immigration problem. With the National Team's demise, all traces of the old political establishment were removed, and former team politicians and their supporters were left to occupy the political periphery.

November 2000 ushered in a new political era in the Cayman Islands, an era marked by a younger, more educated set of political leaders. After the jockeying and lobbying which characterised the old system had settled, a new political directorate, promising a fresh approach, took the reins of government.

At the outset, prospects appeared good for a new style of open and transparent government. The government consisted of a diverse but able coalition which could have delivered much, given the members' conviction that personal ambitions should be put aside. In the end, however, an inability to craft a definitive style on the part of the Leader of government business turned what should have been a robust political directorate into an unholy alliance.

In November 2001, the coalition imploded through its own political bankruptcy, brought on by the leader's failure to effect an acceptable national agenda in which the political directorate laid out its solutions to the challenges facing the economy, immigration, employment, education, and the social contract.

Arising out of this implosion was the first political party in the Cayman Islands in recent times. Led by a veteran legislator from West Bay, the political directorate formed themselves into a registered political party, the United Democratic Party (UDP), and administered the affairs of state along strict party lines.

Displaced members of the previous political directorate, along with two other members of the Legislative Assembly, merged into an opposition group called the People's Progressive Movement (PPM). The birth of this organisation signified that the Cayman Islands were once again operating in the realm of formal party politics. This development, coupled with the debates surrounding it, brought the Cayman Islands to a point previously experienced only briefly during the early 1960s. At the time of the 2005 general election there were two formal political parties competing for votes. When the election results were tabulated, the PPM emerged as the majority party, gaining all nine of the seats it contested.

The victory stunned most of the UDP and its supporters. Defeat, however, should not have come as a total surprise, since it was the UDP's own blunders, betrayals, and general lack of dynamic preparation that allowed the PPM to wrest the political momentum from the incumbent party.

Certainly the campaign mounted by the PPM in 2005 appeared to be well funded. There is reason to believe that at least one major corporation supported the PPM, since the UDP had, in protracted negotiations, sought to limit its franchise and introduce competition in the area in which it held a monopoly. In all likelihood there were other companies and corporations which were uneasy with the UDP's stated intention to introduce reformed labour legislation with guaranteed basic employment rights, minimum-wage provisions, and practical overtime regulations. Such legislation would have brought the jurisdiction into line with the International Labour Organisation's best practices and also would have complied with the requirements of the United Nations Committee on Economic, Social, and Cultural Rights.

Another factor in 2005 was the issue of the more than 3,000 residents who had been granted Caymanian status (citizenship) by the UDP political directorate. The negative response to this gesture was so powerful that not even the ambitious and far-reaching recovery programme that the UDP had put in place after hurricane Ivan appeased the majority of the electorate.

An intransigent and unwilling business community was led by the Chamber of Commerce, which saw itself as an arbiter of Caymanian affairs more powerful than the political directorate. The usual excuses and scaremongering tactics were employed in an attempt to discourage support for modern labour legislation. In the end, factions within the UDP parliamentary group colluded with special-interest groups in the private sector in an effort to derail the legislation. Conspicuous by their absence when the vote was taken were several key members of the UDP's legislative group. In the absence of any credible explanation for these absences at such an important time, one can only comment that such contempt and disunity made a mockery of the principle of collective responsibility in Caymanian party politics.

Under the Westminster system, if the party is not in support of a bill proposed by a minister, the minister is informed well beforehand of the party's position and thereby given the opportunity to withdraw it, sparing himself the embarrassment of having his party colleagues not support the proposed legislation. In other Caribbean jurisdictions, a betrayal such as the one over the employment legislation would have resulted in the minister's resignation, and perhaps in a vote of confidence in the leader.

It is exactly this kind of behaviour that leads many Caymanians to be sceptical and suspicious of party politics. Nonetheless, the party system has taken on an air of permanence and will probably define the political landscape for some time to come.

The Cayman Islands fall behind the rest of the British and formerly British Caribbean in political sophistication, although it is often argued that Cayman's unique political methods have facilitated the opportunity to thrive economically. That position must now be qualified by the observation that during the past five years there has been an uncharacteristic public interest in constitutional modernisation.

Exactly what form this modernisation will take has not been clearly articulated. A number of civic organisations, led by the Chamber of Commerce, have been calling for greater 'self-determination'. In other Caribbean territories, a Chamber of Commerce would not be permitted to interfere in what is clearly the domain of the electorate and its representatives. The Chamber of Commerce in the Cayman Islands has a history of hijacking political issues by using the opinions of its membership to intimidate political directorates into adopting economic policies that are in line with the Chamber members' desires. The Cayman Islands would be wise to consider the Barbados model. There, the political directorate maintains strict responsibility for policy decisions and good governance while the private sector sticks to what it does best – that is, managing profitable corporations and enhancing employment by encouraging and managing the association of capital and labour.

The Cayman Islands Chamber of Commerce has set itself up as a powerful special-interest political lobby. Just how its idea of constitutional modernisation, clouded as it is with special interests, fits with that which has to represent the interests of the entire Caymanian population, remains to be seen. It is difficult to see the Chamber's intrusion into this area of public affairs as anything other than an attempt to maintain the dominance of the merchant establishment in Caymanian society. The Chamber's opposition to the establishment of trade unions calls into question its commitment to democracy and human rights, since the right of employees to form trade unions is universally accepted.

Caymanian society will regress even further if politics become dominated by the moneyed establishment. This was the situation that existed in the Bahamas until Sir Lynden Pindling wrested power from the so-called Bay Street Boys. Bermuda has only recently shown new dynamism since the predominantly black Progressive Labour Party has come to power, and with it some form of political representation for the working class. For the Chamber of Commerce to be allowed to define self-determination in the Caymanian context will mean the death of parliamentary democracy as we know it and economic bondage for the working class. As of this writing, there has been no publicly aired elaboration of what self-determination would entail. There is, however, reason to believe that many people in the political establishment would like to see devolution of some of the powers of the governor.

It is doubtful that the United Kingdom as the administering power would be prepared to consider such a request. With constitutional modernisation talks set to resume, it will be interesting to learn just how self-determination evolves. A few years ago it became obvious that the symbiotic relationship with the United Kingdom, previously hailed as a model, was fraying at the edges.

The chill in the warm relationship was a result of findings by the chief justice of the Cayman Islands in a case officially listed as Indictment 6 of 2001: *The Queen v. Donald Stewart, Brian Cunha, Ivan Burgess, and Judith Donegan*. During the trial it was revealed that the attorney general and the head of the Financial Reporting Unit (FRU), while in the employ of the Cayman Islands Government, were also associated with MI6, the United Kingdom's espionage agency. It was further revealed in the grand court that an ongoing intelligence operation against certain companies in the Cayman Islands had been organised with the approval of high-level UK operatives, the attorney general, and the head of the FRU. The revelations seemed more like the script of a James Bond film than like the reality of daily life in the usually sedate Cayman Islands – except for the fact that the jurisdiction's chief law officer was himself an organiser of the plan to subvert the law and compromise justice.

The revelations set off a firestorm of political and social protest. Public and private sectors joined to express concern to the governor that Cayman's successful financial industry risked being undermined by this conspiracy. Compounding the difficulty was the fact that under the constitution, the governor would have been apprised of the operation by both the attorney general and the head of the FRU – a built-in mechanism by which the administering power ensures that its representative is kept informed about all sensitive matters within the jurisdiction. In this instance, the governor, as the administering power's representative, bore as much culpability as the attorney general and the head of the FRU. No embarrassment, however, reached the office of the governor – though many must have realised that the governor, in the normal course of events, would have been informed all along.

Relations between the government of the Cayman Islands (including the two remaining official members of the cabinet) and the UK authorities became strained. There was also a public uproar regarding what was perceived as a subversion of Caymanian legal and judicial authority by a UK agency. Absurdly, at one stage the governor, who was the United Kingdom's appointee and who must have been fully aware of the espionage, was the mediator between the UK authorities and the Caymanian political directorate.

After protracted discussions and threats from the UK Secretary of State for Foreign and Commonwealth Affairs, an accommodation was worked out. The head of the FRU was allowed to flee the Cayman Islands to avoid being arrested. The embattled attorney general, meanwhile, shunned by his cabinet colleagues and by officialdom, was allowed to vacate office with a significant cash settlement and no official public opprobrium. The conditions were demanded by the UK authorities, which to this day remain adamant that no offence was committed and refuse to discuss their actions at the time.

As for the indictment in the Grand Court of the Cayman Islands, the defendants were exonerated by the court. This was not so much a result of any convincing proof of their innocence as of the corruption of justice and attempted subversion of the system.

As a result of these actions, many in Caymanian society have come to realise that the relationship between the United Kingdom and the Cayman Islands is not as ideal as had been assumed. The fallout from this incident, hereafter referred to as the Euro Bank debacle, has left many questions unanswered. It is posited here that the damage may have been irreparable, in that it has spawned a previously unknown suspicion of the UK authorities on the part of Caymanians.

These suspicions have opened a rift between Caymanian society and the UK authorities. Many Caymanians have come to realise that the United Kingdom, as the administering power, views the Cayman Islands' position as a leading offshore financial centre as inimical to the United Kingdom's own interest in international finance. This is also manifested in the United Kingdom's disposition with respect to the Cayman Islands in matters of international financial regulation and protocol: the Cayman Islands are left to fend for their own interests while the United Kingdom pursues its agenda, which is to ensure that the City of London continues as the world's premier international financial centre.

History shows that such rifts are but symptoms of a deeper, more profound problem. Although the progress of the Cayman Islands up to now has been inextricably bound up with the territory's symbiotic relationship with the United Kingdom, it is clear that the relationship as it exists is no longer in the Islands' interests – and the Islands cannot expect to continue to trust that relationship when the United Kingdom regards its interests as being threatened.

The Cayman Islands, with their intricate cultural heritage, their consititutional existence steeped in voluntary colonialism, and their arcane and powerful social mechanisms, have done well over the past several decades. The people of the Cayman Islands have been fortunate that they are just now experiencing the serious and retarding problems of a changed relationship with the United Kingdom.

New challenges have arisen, and the reappearance of party politics can be considered as an institutional response to the frustrations of confronting new political challenges in a traditionally personal style.

These are indeed interesting times for the Cayman Islands, and it is no exaggeration to remark that the Cayman Islands may have reached its Rubicon. If the twentieth century saw the full manifestation of voluntary colonialism, the twenty-first holds out the promise of a completely new form of metropolis/colony relationship.

We turn to that future when we examine the nature of the relationship in 'Engendering Democracy: An Analysis of the Relationship between Administering Power and Colony'. In the interim, let us examine the settlement patterns and the nature of Caymanian society as it evolved into the entity it is at present.

Chapter 2

Settlement, Society, and Population:
The Evolution of the Modern Cayman Islands

Any understanding of the complexities of Caymanian society must be predicated upon the notion that there are no indigenous Caymanians. All Caymanians are imported people, from many different jurisdictions. To a large extent, the differentiation is between 'established Caymanians' – that is, those who can trace their ancestry from the earliest settlement in the Islands and have clearly established lines of ancestral privilege – and expatriates, who, even when they possess Caymanian status, have not been in the Islands as long as the established Caymanians. The distinction is strictly academic and holds no legal merit, nor does it purport to determine which is the more important of the two elements. My thesis is that, origins notwithstanding, the success and future of the Cayman Islands lie in the ability to maintain the synergistic and symbiotic relationship between established Caymanians and their expatriate (status-holding) counterparts. I hope it will provoke readers to think, question, and examine for themselves the societal constructs which make up modern Caymanian society.

To begin with some historical background, I propose that Cayman Islands society is, to a large extent, a creole society. 'Creole' as a concept first gained prominence in Caribbean academic circles in the 1970s. Naturally, the concept is related to colonialism and its ancillary practices. It is a provocative argument, and the reader is invited to judge its relevance and appropriateness to the Caymanian context.

As a colony of the United Kingdom, the Cayman Islands existed on the periphery of what was once the British Empire. Over the years following World War II, what had been the world's greatest empire shrank to little more than a second-rate world power with a scattering of Overseas Territories and Crown dependencies. Among these remaining possessions, the Cayman Islands are of prime importance, both as a successful colony which from its settlement has never been grant-aided and which from the 1980s has been a world-class financial centre. The shrinking of the British Empire has sharply reduced the number of colonial holdings where British colonial administrators can be posted to gain valuable administrative experience. Since decolonisation at the end of World War II, there has also been a change in the type of official sent to the remaining Overseas Territories.

While it was widely thought during the colonial period that a variety of experiences strengthened one's administrative and managerial abilities, that appears to have changed. In the case of the Cayman Islands, Alan Scott, appointed in 1992, was the last experienced colonial governor. His successors have all been relatively low-level British diplomats from postings in Boston, Zambia, and other non-front-line jurisdictions. Sent to the Cayman Islands to pass the time in a pre-retirement posting, rich in social activities, these governors have nothing more exciting and challenging to confront than the apprehensions and preparations that accompany the seasonal tropical storms and hurricanes.

In this writer's estimation, none has displayed the prescience, vision, and administrative abilities of Allan Cardinall in the 1930s or Andrew Morris Gerrard in the mid-1950s. The conclusion to be drawn is that as the colonial agenda has changed so has the calibre of diplomats recruited to serve as governors. There are those who suggest that the governors of the twenty-first century should be more like chief executive officers and less like the 'goodwill ambassadors' – or political hacks – who display little, if any, ability to move the society forward and whose interest seems limited to anticipating their end of tour. Certainly there is merit to this suggestion, especially in light of the fact that a maturation process has taken place among Caymanian politicians and the Caymanian civil service has proven that it is quite capable. It will be interesting to see what evolves if the elected ministers are given administrative responsibility for their ministries, as will likely happen should the current exercise leading to self-determination reach maturity.

Under the current Cayman Islands constitution, ministers have no authority to hire or dismiss staff members, nor do they have authority to assign or re-assign personnel. This authority falls under the office of the governor, who usually delegates it to the chief secretary.

The financial management initiatives which came into effect under the Public Management and Finance Law have brought some changes in ministerial authority. As a result, ministers now have the authority to scrutinise departmental reports regarding the ministry's level of success in realising outputs as expressed in budget documents. In cases where outputs have not been achieved, the minister now has the discretion and authority to withhold payments, including salaries, until the picture improves.

The bureaucracy is, however, still reflective of colonial precedents and practices. For example, the chief officer (formerly called the permanent secretary) in a ministry seems to hold more authority than the minister, since the chief officer signs off on the minister's application to the governor for official or personal leave, and the reverse is not the case. Indeed, there have been cases where discord existed between a minister and the ministry's chief officer, and the chief officer took leave without officially informing the minister.

I believe that the settlement patterns of the Cayman Islands carried with them certain predispositions. In the first place, class and colour categories existed from the early years of settlement. Social differentiation in the Cayman Islands mirrored that of nearby Jamaica and resulted from the social and political links between the two settlements. This linkage took form with the formal annexation of the Cayman Islands to Jamaica in 1863 (Lewis 1968, 332; Craton 2003, 150).

Indeed, Craton (2003, 36) writes that the first land grants in the Cayman Islands were issued in 1735 to people residing in Jamaica. It seems logical to conclude that, given its association with Jamaica, the population of the Cayman Islands would naturally have been drawn from Jamaica. Popular folklore suggests that the earliest settlers were an aggregation of shipwrecked sailors, runaway slaves, deserters from the garrison in Jamaica, free men with land grant deeds, and freebooters or buccaneers.

It is this writer's contention that the apparent absence of an indigenous population makes it both accurate and appropriate to describe those generations descending from the early settlers as 'established Caymanians', in contrast to those people who have come to the Cayman Islands as economic migrants since the 1960s boom. It is to these migrants – which, for purposes of this work, are confined mainly to the Caucasian elements – that the term 'expatriate' is applied.

Such an apparently strict differentiation is based on the established norm in Caymanian society whereby West Indians and other regional residents are identified by their respective nationality – as, for example, Jamaicans, Trinidadians, or Guyanese – rather than as expatriates. When 'expatriate' is used, it usually refers to nationalities other than those of the neighbouring jurisdictions; indeed, it refers almost exclusively to residents from metropolitan countries such as the United Kingdom, Europe, United States, and Canada.

The frontier society

In earlier chapters reference is made to the Cayman Islands as a frontier society. Frontier societies invariably attract many different types of people. The composition of Caymanian society today enables us to envisage what the social construct was in earlier times. Such a construct bore both similarities to and differences from other contemporary Caribbean societies.

An important difference lay in the disposition of the early settlers towards outside authority. Brian Kieran captures this well in his book *The Lawless Caymanas* (1992). The period leading up to and immediately following emancipation of the slaves was an especially challenging one and illustrates why the label of frontier society is appropriate. According to Kieran (1992, 29), 'The general libertine attitude of the populace towards authority was a cause for concern.'

An early manifestation of this attitude took the form of racial tension which occurred as a result of the interaction between black soldiers of the West India Regiment and white Caymanian residents. Both Kieran (1992) and Craton (2003) describe these incidents in ways which lead to the conclusion that Caymanian society, like most other West Indian societies at the time, was stratified along colour lines.

Racial stratification continues to exist, although there are those who would prefer to believe that there are no such reservations in Caymanian society. To the extent that such differences exist, they have never been an obvious deterrent to the maintenance of the symbiotic relationship between whites and blacks since the period immediately following emancipation.

However, it is patently fallacious to assume that representative government, when it began in the Cayman Islands, included any consideration of the black population. Indeed, while electoral politics was different from what had existed before, the system was far from representative, in that black people were still disenfranchised. This is in keeping with the concept of a frontier society, where only those with the power of money or some other acceptable commodity (including, of course, force) could claim fair representation.

Democracy, as we have come to call the concept of universal adult suffrage, came to the Cayman Islands only in the mid-twentieth century.

Previously, those participating in elections, both as candidates and as electors, had to be property owners or persons in good standing on the poll tax records – which, of course, excluded women.

The majority of the population, being descendants of black people, had little or no encouragement to involve themselves in politics during the years before the establishment of universal adult suffrage. Realistically, the major objective of the newly freed slaves was their survival and entrenchment in a society in which it was necessary to own land for food production and also as a status symbol. This was of particular importance in the frontier society of the Cayman Islands, as land equated to permanence and wealth – in fact, to the whole notion of prosperity and stability.

In any frontier society, land is a powerful economic commodity. In the Cayman Islands, land ownership not only signified wealth and social status but commanded honour and respect. While it is true that land was a common commodity among established Caymanians long before the economic boom beginning in the late 1960s, distinctions were made between those who owned only small parcels and those who held sizable tracts. A more detailed discussion of the importance of land in Caymanian society is found in chapter 5, 'A Nuanced View', but suffice it to say here that land ownership was so common among the relatively few black people in the Cayman Islands that there were no chattel houses, as there were in other Caribbean jurisdictions where black people were in the majority and deprived of the ability to own land.

The years following the abolition of slavery witnessed fundamental changes in the political, economic, and social structure of Caymanian society. The most startling political change was the population shift that allowed George Town, which had for some time been the commercial capital, to supersede Bodden Town as the political capital. Economically, the Islands experienced a decline in agricultural production since most former slaves withdrew their services from their former owners (Craton 2003, 106–8). This meant a decline in the standard of living of many of the white families, since their wealth was derived primarily from the proceeds of slave labour.

While slavery in the Cayman Islands was of a different nature from that practised in Jamaica and other British West Indian plantation societies, no slavery was ideal. The fact that the Cayman Islands were, strictly speaking, not a slave society, should not be interpreted to mean that there were no tensions between masters and slaves. During slavery there seems to have been little or no reason to practise rigid stratification based on colour. In the aftermath of emancipation, however, with free black people outnumbering whites and coloureds, it would have been most unusual if the plantocracy had not relied upon common practice in Jamaica and elsewhere to maintain superiority over the free blacks.

The Cayman Islands at this time represented a fully fledged pigmentocracy, in addition to being a frontier society. Class and colour as determinants of social status in the society took on powerful significance. It was at this time also that the significance of the expatriate phenomenon first manifested itself in the Cayman Islands. The earliest known expatriate to become prominent in Caymanian society was Nathaniel Glover. Glover was a slave-owning American who had settled in Bodden Town around the 1830s (Kieran 1992, 27; Craton 2003, 79–80). He made such an impression upon certain elements of the Caymanian establishment that he managed to gain appointment as a magistrate. This appointment was later revoked by the Colonial Office on the grounds that Glover was an American citizen (Craton 2003, 97).

It was this very symbiosis, originating with Glover, between established Caymanians and expatriates, which was to prove most problematic to the integrity and most challenging to the cultural distinctiveness of the established Caymanian. As is not atypical in frontier societies, there was racial tension between whites, coloureds, and blacks. In many respects, Glover's situation mirrors the ambivalence toward expatriates in Cayman society today. There certainly exists a mutual contempt between some Caymanians and some expatriates.

It is a moot point whether those expatriates who have arrived since the boom of the 1970s would have braved the challenges of the earlier frontier society. The conditions of deprivation in this outpost produced a physically tough, spiritually sensitive individual who, whether male or female, was capable of living under extremely demanding conditions. The early settlers did not have as a primary motivation economic prosperity, and the slavery period brought nothing but enduring challenges – among them survival in a society in which black people were disenfranchised and economically disadvantaged.

Emancipation brought new economic realities, as described by historian Michael Craton:

> In the post-slavery economy, conditions were determined by economic realities, and by the will of former slaves as much as by the wishes of their former owners. Restoring anything like a

plantation economy in the Cayman Islands was clearly impossible. All parties alike relied on a subsistence economy and the extension of the turtling industry – along with shipbuilding and what might come in from the chancier business of combing wrecks. (Craton 2003, 111)

As it turned out, turtling, as much as subsistence farming, became the principal occupation of a majority of Caymanian men before World War II. In the peculiar society which was the Cayman Islands, turtling provided the opportunity for master and slave to work closely together, since it was common practice for slave owners to take slaves on turtling expeditions.

Indeed, turtling became such an entrenched way of life in Cayman that the Islands gained a reputation as a valuable port of call for sailing ships wishing to re-victual and take on fresh water on their journey from Central and South American to northern Europe. This practice lasted until the advent of steam navigation and refrigerated cargo stowage made it unnecessary to call in at the Cayman Islands.

Lewis (1968, 331) further points out as mentioned earlier:

[In] ... the post-1945 decline of the turtling industry a serious challenge of cultural adaptation has arisen. The decline was due, in large part, to intractable factors: the decline of maritime traffic and its food needs, the competition of other delicacies in the metropolitan markets, the growing difficulties with the Nicaraguan Government concerning Caymanian fishing rights in Nicaraguan territorial waters.

The years following emancipation also ushered in a 'diaspora' which saw Caymanians migrating to the Bay Islands of Honduras, the Swan Islands, Providencia (Old Providence) and San Andres in the Colombian Caribbean Archipelago, and the Corn Islands of Nicaragua. In the late nineteenth and early twentieth centuries a second wave of migrations occurred as men went to work in Colón, building the Panama Canal; in Costa Rica, for the United Fruit Company; in Nicaragua, in the gold mines; in Cuba's Isle of Pines (now Isla de Juventud), where American investors were selling cheap land; and in Havana, as household help, labourers, and factory hands. Simultaneously, other Caymanians were moving to Jamaica and to the United States of America.

The Caymanian diaspora

Craton (2003) informs us that the period immediately following emancipation was marked by three characteristics: emigration, isolation, and poverty. A major peculiarity of Caymanian society was that its slave-owning class was not noticeably much better off economically than the slaves. This was markedly different from the slave societies of the rest of the British Caribbean and certainly from the slave states of the southern United States. In these jurisdictions the most obvious indicator of social and economic status was the size of the planters' mansions. The Cayman Islands, in contrast, had only two slave-era residences which could pass as plantation houses: Pedro St James, located at Great Pedro, and the Petra Plantation (now Grand Old House) at Southwest Sound. Nonetheless, emancipation brought the Caymanian slaveholders an aggravation of their economic woes, since they lost their legal hold over their workers, and many slaves took the opportunity to move away from their former masters and seek a livelihood of their own.

At about the same time, the once viable sea island cotton industry began its decline as a result of competition from the cotton plantations of the southern United States. The removal of cheap slave labour, along with the large-scale production of cotton by the southern slave states, destroyed the sea island cotton industry in the Cayman Islands and in other British Caribbean islands as well.

With no exports, the Cayman Islands lost importance as a port of call, hence shipping lessened significantly. Contractions in the local economy brought additional pressures as able-bodied Caymanian men in increasing numbers looked to turtle fishing for a livelihood.

The diaspora, while it had some negative social consequences for the people of Grand Cayman, had positive economic effects, since the emigrants sent money home to their families on Grand Cayman, enabling the eventual development of an economic entrepreneurship there. This expansion of the economic scope was also the catalyst for permanent settlement on Cayman Brac and Little Cayman. By the early 1900s, the population of what were then called the Lesser Islands had reached approximately 1,000 (Craton 2003, 130).

Surprisingly, it was the Bay Islands of Honduras which became the primary focus of Caymanian emigration. Consisting of Utila, Roatan, and Guanaja (Bonacca), the islets all appeared to have special attraction to Caymanians, who were familiar with them from fishing in Central

American waters. Britain's expansion in the Caribbean in the eighteenth and nineteenth centuries took in the Bay Islands, which encouraged Caymanians to take quiet possession of them.

By the mid–nineteenth century the Bay Islands population was over 1,500. Of these, 600 had been born in the Cayman Islands, and another 300 to Caymanian parents living in the Bay Islands (Craton 2003, 134).

When the Bay Islands were granted crown colony status in June 1852, it was regarded as a triumph for the Caymanian inhabitants. Largely as a result of pressure from the United States, however, England demitted ownership and revoked the Bay Islands' crown colony status in 1859, much to the disappointment of the residents of Caymanian descent. Many who had settled in the Bay Islands saw this as an ideal time to leave.

The Caymanian diaspora thereafter continued in other areas, including the Caribbean coast and offshore islands of Nicaragua. Such settlements were bolstered by Great Britain's policy of 'gunboat diplomacy', and communities like Puerto Cabezas, Prinzapolka, Pearl Lagoon, and Bluefields developed with significant numbers of Caymanians, whose descendants and relatives still live in the Cayman Islands.

Within the next half-century Caymanians emigrated to and formed family settlements in the Corn Islands and San Andres and Providencia (Old Providence), joining the English-speaking blacks who were either left over from the days of slavery or part of the diaspora and the new colonisation movement.

Hemispheric rivalry between Great Britain and the emerging regional power, the United States, brought the first wave of Caymanian migration to an end. Not long afterwards, during the time of the American Civil War, Grand Cayman again came into prominence when it was used as a regular port of call for vessels of both the Union and Confederate navies. Interestingly, there is evidence to suggest that one or both of these navies may have recruited Caymanian seamen. The following excerpt from a report of acting Rear-Admiral Charles Wilkes, Commander of the US Navy's West Indian Squadron, bears this out. Dated January 2, 1863, it was written on board the US flag-steamer *Wachusett* at Havana:[1]

> In my last note I informed you of my intended departure with this steamer, the *Wachusett*, and *Sonoma* in search of the *Alabama* [a

Confederate Navy warship]. I had some knowledge of the intention of Semmes [a Confederate officer] while in the *Sumter* and concluded he would resort to the same places to recruit in the *Alabama*. One was the Grand Cayman Island, and for it we sailed with all speed. ... On the fourth day we reached the Grand Cayman and found the *Agrippina* bark [another Confederate vessel] had left only three days before. This is the vessel which supplied the *Alabama* with 200 tons of coal at Martinique. She had been waiting for the *Alabama* nine days and left very suddenly and at night in consequence of a signal having been made in the offing, supposed to have been by the *Alabama*.

While the diaspora had many beneficial effects, cementing social and family ties between Caymanian descendants in the various settlements and exposing Caymanians to the wider world, its positive economic effects were felt by the Caymanian merchants and shipowners involved in the turtle trade headquartered on Grand Cayman. Many families whose descendants are prominent in Caymanian business and financial circles to this day came to prominence during the diaspora.

This period of history reminds us that Caymanians themselves were immigrants and that established Caymanians first settled the Islands during the early years of the eighteenth century. It was the period from 1850 to 1910 which saw the most significant early ingress of people from Jamaica and other parts of the world (Hirst 1910, 253). Much later, during the economic boom of the late 1960s and beyond, came the economic migrants from the Caribbean region, Europe, and North America.

These migrants, coming for the most part on work permits which allowed them to be employed in the Islands, were attracted to the frontier society because of the economic opportunities available. They did not make Caymanian society prosperous; rather, they enhanced its prosperity by offering expertise and services that established Caymanians could not provide.

Those most responsible for the opening up of the Cayman Islands and the economic prosperity which resulted were the merchant seamen, the children of the diaspora, and those Caymanians who remained at home and who – by their characteristic frontier frugality, conservative political disposition, and economic good sense – ensured that the Islands became attractive to outsiders. It is to these people, now largely unheralded, that most credit must be given for laying the foundation upon which modern economic prosperity was able to develop.

Ethnicity, race, and class in Caymanian society

Few regions today can match Cayman's cultural diversity. The blend of people who migrated into the Caribbean both before and after slavery represented a mix of dialects, languages, beliefs, and mores. The settlement pattern during the era of the plantocracy brought European traders, African slaves, and, later, indentured labourers from India and other Asian countries. Such diversity, though, was limited mainly to the larger agriculture-based islands of Jamaica, Trinidad, Guyana, and, to a lesser extent, Barbados.

In the Cayman Islands, while settlement patterns showed no such pronounced influxes of foreigners, since the late 1960s English, Canadian, Irish, and US citizens have joined Jamaicans, other West Indians, and Central Americans (from Honduras, Nicaragua, and Costa Rica) in becoming settlers in Caymanian society. The latest nationalities to complement this ethnic mosaic are Filipino workers and people of East Indian descent, brought under the rubric of avoiding domination by nationals from any particular geographic area. Past political directorates, concerned that the society might be dominated by migrants from one jurisdiction, established quotas to avoid such an occurrence. This is still a concern, and political directorates since 1988 have sought to avoid the problems that are anticipated if too many migrants come from the same country.

Such a decision could be challenged as a *sub rosa* excuse for avoiding the domination of the society by an element reminiscent of the slave society, since it appears that the primary concern is Jamaican nationals. The question must then be posed: is Caymanian society a racist society? No; rather, it is a society in which certain elements, including established Caymanians, cultivate some ethnic, racial, and cultural prejudice.

Many resident expatriates from the United Kingdom and North America also appear to have clear racial preferences toward whites. There has always been a certain sensitivity about fraternisation between British expatriates and West Indians – including Caymanians – on all but the most token level.

That this is so in a frontier society such as the Cayman Islands should not be surprising, since in British colonial settlements the expatriate community always tended to exhibit the most insidious characteristics of imperialist Britain. It is fallacious to say that in the age of empire serious racism did not exist. Racist beliefs were founded upon the misguided notion that the inhabitants of these colonies – 'the natives', as they were pejoratively called – were not only different but were also inferior to the colonisers. This notion was the basis of colonialism as defined by Osterhammel and Frisch (1997, 16–17):

> Colonialism is a relationship of domination between an indigenous (or forcibly imported) majority and a minority of foreign invaders. The fundamental decisions affecting the lives of the colonized people are made and implemented by the colonial rulers in pursuit of interests that are often defined in a distant metropolis.

Rejecting cultural compromises with the colonised population, the colonisers are convinced of their own superiority and of their ordained mandate to rule.

Racism is an inevitable legacy of empire and colonialism. This is the case even today in the Cayman Islands, where certain British expatriates regard established Caymanians, both white and black, as racially and culturally inferior. The same legacy is entrenched in relations *between* established Caymanians. In an elaborate typology, Brathwaite describes this phenomenon in terms of a pigmentocracy:

> The offspring of white-black unions in the Americas were placed on an elaborate ladder of skin colouring:
> Sambo: child of mulatto and negro
> Mulatto: child of white man and negress
> Quadroon: child of mulatto woman and white man
> Mustee: child of a quadroon (or pure Amer-Indian) by white man
> Mustiphini: child of mustee and white man
> Quintroon: child of mustiphini and white man
> Octoroon: child of quintroon and white man.
> (Brathwaite 1971, 167–68)

This legacy of empire was tempered only faintly by the work of the British Anti-Slavery Society, the Quakers, and some other religious denominations like the Scottish Presbyterians, which set their faces against the idea of racial superiority and cultural imperialism and the suppression of African custom, beliefs, and mores. It was the attitude of superiority to anything African, coupled with the establishment of cultural imperialism, that caused the suppression of the religious practices and beliefs of the Africans. European imperialism at the time of settlement was predicated upon the four pillars of commerce, Christianity, conquest, and colonisation, in that order. Irrespective of the territory – whether Peru, with its Inca gold, or Dominica, with its agricultural potential – the pattern of domination was similar for all the conquering European powers.

Study of the emancipation and post-slavery period suggests that the Caribbean was a less homogeneous area during that time than it had been during slavery, when the common practices were more obvious and more compelling. In the Cayman Islands, the newly freed people expected that emancipation would allow them to use the African knowledge and skills handed down through the generations. Under such circumstances, they did not wish to continue working for their former masters. For their part, the former masters realised that the new order was inevitable but hoped that the old order would continue in some form.

For the newly freed slaves, emancipation meant gaining control over their time, labour, and the products of that labour. The former slaveholders somewhat desperately resorted to political power to restrict the ability of the ex-slaves to own productive lands. What resulted was an economic downturn and a stratification of the society that manifested itself in the development of a pigmentocracy.

Culturally, it was the beginning of a rather adversarial relationship. The emancipated Africans reconstructed some aspects of their ancestral traditions. The ruling elite, while recognising that slaves' religious rituals and tribal practices were useful for diffusing tensions inherent in the master-slave relationship, also realised that such practices were always potentially threatening, since they enabled the oppressed classes to congregate in groups and reaffirm their own cultural identities.

Fear of resistance and rebellion preoccupied the planters and former slaveholders. Largely owing to their ignorance of African customs and mores, they outlawed any ritual which they did not understand. One practice that came under suspicion and warranted certain punishment was obeah. It is a fact of some historical significance that even though there were no rebellions in the Cayman Islands, obeah was and remains a banned practice and a criminal offence.

The first recorded prosecution of a case involving the practice of obeah in the Cayman Islands took place on August 16, 1826. The case was listed as *The King* vs. *A Negro Man Slave named Hannibal*. Hannibal was described as 'a man slave, the property of the estate of

Sterling Rivers (deceased)'. According to Hirst (1910, 207), there were three charges against Hannibal. First, he was charged with practising obeah; second, with abusing and threatening his deceased master's wife; and finally, with assaulting and using violence against said wife. The trial was held in the Slave Court at George Town, where a jury of freemen and slaveowners found Hannibal guilty as charged. He was sentenced to deportation from the island of Grand Cayman.

That a person could be charged with practising obeah in the Cayman Islands in November 2006 speaks volumes about the resilience of the belief, and one must wonder what are the enduring qualities of these African beliefs and customs. Throughout the history of the West Indian slave societies, obeah had a place in an alternative system of justice as well as serving as a vehicle to gain sexual power or to exact revenge.

According to Diana Paton, in an article entitled 'Popular and Official Justice in Post-Emancipation Jamaica', obeah was 'an empowering phenomenon, a discourse and practice concerning rights, crime and punishment and various forms of domination and resistance'.

In the often oppressive and frequently violent world of plantation slavery, the practice of obeah enabled the otherwise powerless to seek revenge on enemies, including the white planters whose status and power were far superior to the slaves', and provided a respite from the environment of the plantation. Obeah bears some similarities to candomble, voudun (voodoo), and Santería, including the fact that many practitioners are women.

European and creole whites did not understand African religious ceremonies and customs, so they imputed a criminal character to these rituals and practices. Not surprisingly, this was the prevailing attitude throughout the British Caribbean.

In the Cayman Islands, there seems to have been a jettisoning of anything associated with or reminiscent of the slaveholding era. It is as if the black people were deliberately encouraged to abandon the traditional beliefs, customs, and mores originating in the African diaspora. Vocabulary and linguistic peculiarities have been abandoned in favour of the colonial language and expressions. In a blatant denial of history, even established Caymanians with obvious black ancestry are reluctant to factor in African influences.

Similarly, certain celebrations – for example, Emancipation Day, on August 1, recognised around the British and formerly British Caribbean as one of the most important historical and cultural holidays – has been excised from the Caymanian cultural calendar. And yet, until the late 1950s Emancipation Day was a public holiday in the Cayman Islands.

The celebration was especially vibrant in Bodden Town, the first capital, where it was traditional for a certain prominent black man to hold the annual celebratory dance. This event was a grand affair, attended by most prominent black people from throughout the Islands. The promoter, an upstanding citizen from the Gun Square section of Bodden Town, had a standing contract with the authorities for rental of the Town Hall for this particular event.

It appears that these Emancipation Day celebrations originated in the nineteenth century. But admiration of Queen Victoria and the Caymanian affiliation with Britishness confused the celebrants into believing that it was out of the sheer goodness of the British authorities' hearts that the black people were freed. The people of Bodden Town had a special respect for Queen Victoria, and to this day a memorial cast in her honour stands in that district.

Another event, Jonkanoo, which originated in the African diaspora, also thrived in Bodden Town. Like the celebrations of Emancipation Day, Jonkanoo too has fallen away, although it was regularly celebrated up to the late 1950s and early 1960s.

The disappearance of these two prominent reminders of the African-Caribbean cultural experience in the Cayman Islands was the result of two societal changes. First, their employment on merchant ships meant that the men who were the organisers and patrons of these celebrations were, for the most part, no longer available. Second, these celebrations held no cultural or historical significance for the governments of the day and therefore received no official government support. While other former British Caribbean territories have continued to honour and even expand these traditions – examples are Trinidad's Carnival, Crop-Over in Barbados, and Goombay in the Bahamas – there is apparently little or no interest in Caymanian political circles in reviving them.

Consonant with the characterisation of the Cayman Islands as a frontier society is the importance of early sexual mores. As in other Caribbean societies, visiting and consensual unions were important patterns of domestic life. Legal marriage, while a significant part of the domestic cycle, was frequently delayed until economic stability was established. This was especially so in view of the fact that, as in many frontier societies, most of the men were absent from home for extended periods, working to support their families. More important, many families were matrifocal as a result of a non-formal union.

The Cayman Islands were similar to other frontier societies in that there were moral sanctions against concubinage. While no overt bias against illegitimacy existed, it was only in the past 10 years or so that the Cayman Islands Legislative Assembly repealed the Bastardy Law and enacted legislation granting full recognition and inheritance rights to children born out of wedlock.

As in other Caribbean societies, the black people in the Cayman Islands for the most part were semi-skilled and unskilled labourers, farm or plantation workers, fishermen, and proletarians. The celebrated Barbadian novelist George Lamming has remarked that 'to be black in the West Indies is to be poor'. Unlike other Caribbean societies, in the Cayman Islands to be black was not necessarily to be poor, simply because most Caymanian families – black, white, and coloured – were landowners. Land ownership, therefore, was not in and of itself status-enhancing; it was money, not land, that was required for a Caymanian to be considered wealthy.

To be black in Caymanian society did mean disenfranchisement, social immobility, disqualification from social circles, and, later, exclusion from the front pews of the island's established churches and (until the era of Commissioner Andrew Morris Gerrard) from the civil service.

An ideological underpinning that stems from the colonial system is still manifested, to an extent, in the idea of racial and cultural superiority held by some white people residing in the Islands. By the beginning of the 1970s, however, educational developments were leading to important changes. The introduction of the comprehensive high school allowed more Caymanians of colour to attain a decent education. Education still remains, at least in theory, the *sine qua non* for people of colour to achieve upward mobility and parity.

Educational opportunities were increasing at the same time employment opportunities were becoming available in the civil service and the budding financial industry, and during this period tertiary education began to attract more Caymanians. Credit goes to the International College of the Cayman Islands, which, from 1970, sought to prepare Caymanians for the changing world – though there were cultural imperialists who argued that an American tertiary education was inferior to one gained in UK universities.

The white elite in Caymanian society had always jealously guarded their privileged position. This elite consisted primarily of a self-appointed membership, aptly described by the American sociologist C. Wright Mills (2000, 11) as 'the people of the higher circles':

> The elite, according to this conception, feel themselves to be, and are felt by others to be, the inner circle of the "upper social classes". They form a more or less compact social and psychological entity; they have become self-conscious members of a social class ... They are more or less aware of themselves as a social class and they behave toward one or another differently from the way they do toward members of other classes.

They accept one another, understand one another, marry one another, tend to work and to think if not together, at least alike.

This elite represents the quintessential colonial mentality and, as is obvious in Caymanian society, is limited to Caymanians who think of themselves as pure whites, along with some white expatriates. Their attitudes are premised upon their belief in British cultural superiority. It is a cultural perspective best portrayed by Kipling, Curzon, and the Victorian-era imperialists.

Only in colonialism does ethnocentricity take such a dominating turn. In the Cayman Islands the phenomenon is exacerbated by the uneasy relationship that exists at any particular time between the administering power and the elected members of the cabinet. Then, too, there is the symbiotic relationship between those white expatriates (mainly British) and Caymanians who work in the financial industry and the large law firms which practise almost exclusively corporate law.

This relationship between elements of the expatriate population and the 'natives' is based upon two factors, namely domination and cultural dissimilarity. It is important to note that this 'domination' by the bureaucratic machinery acting for the administering power is not viewed by Caymanians as an illegitimate foreign domination. The past few years, however, have brought challenges to this relationship, and colonialism is no longer always appreciated.

From earliest times until the tenure of Gerrard, the white Caymanian establishment laid exclusive claim to association with Britain. Before Gerrard's time, the visit of Royal Naval vessels was an occasion for the establishment to celebrate their perceived superiority. At these times it was customary to hold social events, usually culminating in two dances held in George Town town hall.

On the first evening, the dance was for the officers of the visiting vessel and the Caymanian white establishment. It was a grand event that provided an opportunity for white Caymanian single women to cast an eye for a possible suitor from among the visiting officers. Indeed, Caymanian women sometimes became engaged to visiting armed forces personnel as a result of socialising at such occasions or meeting in the normal course of events, as was the case with some US military personnel stationed at the American base in George Town during World War II. The occasion also provided an opportunity for whites in Caymanian society to feel important through association with British and American officers in an atmosphere where loyalty to empire was assumed and a white complexion was indicative of high social status.

The second evening of entertainment was reserved for the non-commissioned officers and enlisted men, and black and coloured Caymanians. This was an entirely different sort of evening from that held for the officers. Drunkenness and disorderly behaviour were likely to occur, often as a result of rivalries between the visitors and Caymanian men over the attentions of local women.

Some of the young black men in George Town did not take kindly to the implied discrimination. Normally, on the night of the officers' dance these young men had to be content with gazing through the windows of the town hall. On one occasion, however, it was decided to send a message of displeasure to both the visitors and their prejudiced Caymanian hosts.

The young men who desired an end to the 'two dance' tradition employed a locally grown solution commonly known as cow itch. When it was shaken from a brown paper bag through an open window, pandemonium broke out among the patrons, and several visiting dignitaries fell victim to that most Caymanian of treatments and wound up at the hospital.

It was Gerrard who brought a conclusive end to the practice of having two dances. It is known in some Caymanian circles that shortly after his arrival, when a ceremonial occasion arose, Gerrard made it known that he was having only one dance in the George Town town hall, to which all were invited. Shortly before the formalities were to begin, a white Caymanian of high government rank realized that Gerrard must have made an error. This official informed Gerrard that this was not the way things were done in Caymanian society, implying that there was strict separation between the white people and the people of colour.

With characteristic irreverence and with no attempt to muffle his voice, Gerrard told the official that there was no need to remind him (Gerrard) of the presence of black people at the function, since his previous posting had been in Lagos, Nigeria. With this contemptuous dismissal, Gerrard proceeded, much to the chagrin of the white Caymanians present, to open the dancing with the darkest-skinned woman at the function.

At the conclusion of the dance, amidst expressions of disgust by the so-called white Caymanians, Gerrard let it be known that from then on that was the way social events were to be conducted. Those who objected to associating with the coloured and black people could exercise their option of not attending. Such behaviour by civil servants would be interpreted as a reflection of their personal prejudices and would call into question their fitness to serve the public in a society in which there were significant numbers of coloured and black people.

On the occasion of visits by Royal Navy vessels — for example, on the Queen's Birthday or Remembrance Day — the usual parade was enhanced by a detachment of sailors or marines. The crowds were treated to a display organised to show the importance of the British Empire. Although no situation arose in which loyalties were put to the test, such displays served as subtle reminders of who was in control.

The populace viewed the relationship between the administering power and the Cayman Islands as one in which the all-powerful administering power was the protector of a vulnerable entity. Such an association with the United Kingdom was a source of pride to the 'natives' and indeed, remained so until the election in Britain of the Labour Party government of Tony Blair.

In recent years, the Constitutional Review 2003 and matters related to the European Union Savings Directive have engendered a closer examination of these once-cordial relationships. The British government, in recognition of the irrelevance of empire and the trappings of colonialism, has jettisoned the governor's white military-style uniform and plumed helmet in favour of a business suit, even for ceremonial occasions such as the opening of parliament. There is also a clear dissimilarity between the 'colonisers', in the person of those expatriates who, strictly speaking, are economic migrants, and the colonised, both white and black established Caymanians and other people of colour in the society. One example has to do with the desire among some British expatriates to cling to British values and mores. As well, other white expatriates fraternise with the British elite in a symbolic acknowledgement of their position in the social hierarchy – above the established Caymanians. This is obvious in, but not exclusive to, the private sector, where, for example, the view is held that a legal education obtained in certain UK universities is superior to a similar university degree obtained in the Caribbean region. In a work of this nature such an observation might seem irrelevant and inappropriate, except for the fact that such ethnocentricity is the foundation of some expatriates' prejudice against established Caymanians of any colour.

Such prejudice highlights the mentality of the colonisers, which, in this writer's opinion, is how these expatriates who came as economic migrants see themselves. The Cayman Islands, then – with the exception of the cost of raw materials – fits the following description:

> ... a place where one earns more and spends less. You go to a colony because jobs are guaranteed, wages high, careers more rapid and business more profitable. The young graduate is offered a position, the public servant a higher rank, the businessman substantially lower taxes, the industrialist raw materials and labour at attractive prices. (Memmi 1965, 4)

It is obvious that Caymanian society is composed of many persons of the type to which Memmi referred. Having acquired wealth and status, these people present themselves as an ordained elite, often with the perceived mannerisms of British aristocracy. To many Caymanians they appear to be a powerful elite who, by virtue of their positions as businessmen, bankers, attorneys, accountants, and high-level civil servants, can make or break the career of an established Caymanian.

Younger, more educated and open-minded Caymanians, however, see them as a fickle, exploiting cabal, more to be tolerated than to be respected. Among this cohort of young Caymanians are those who expect to challenge the powerful Caymanian establishment for primacy in the social, economic, and political spheres.

The power of the expatriate elite is not manifested in openness. The powerful expatriates are not likely to be among those writing letters to the editors of local newspapers. Nor are they to be found among the altruists agitating for some political reform. On the contrary, they prefer to remain faceless, cloistering themselves in their glass and steel towers where they labour at increasing their annual incomes.

Returning to their residences in exotic, expensive, and occasionally gated communities, they are unlikely to invite many established Caymanians to dinner. Even where such 'friendly' relationships exist, it is not inappropriate to suggest that their basis is political expediency or some other motive from which the expatriate elite will derive benefit.

These observations about expatriate behaviour are not peculiar to the Cayman Islands. Nor does the writer hold any particular prejudices against the Caymanian expatriate elite. Rather, such behaviour is a fundamental tenet of colonialism. Indeed, the expatriate behaviour and settlement patterns exhibited in the Cayman Islands are no different from those found in colonial Cairo, Kenya, Zimbabwe, South Africa, or Jamaica. The expatriate elite in these colonial jurisdictions adopted this behaviour as a mechanism of survival – in addition, of course, to their belief that they were ordained to bear the burden of the colonised people. They attached a special legitimacy to their residence and in no way perceived themselves as exploiters and pillagers, not even when the natural resources of the colonies were being shipped to the metropolitan country for little or nothing.

Again it is instructive to refer to Memmi (1965, 9):

> It is impossible for him [the coloniser] not to be aware of the constant illegitimacy of his status. It is moreover, in any way, a double illegitimacy. A foreigner, having come to a land by the accidents of history, he has succeeded not merely in creating a place for himself but also in taking away that of the inhabitant, granting himself abounding privileges to the detriment of those rightfully entitled to them.

Although Caymanian society has experienced social harmony between the various sectors, this should not be interpreted to mean that there is no difference between them. Recent developments in the relationship between the administering power and the Overseas Territory suggest a significant difference.

The colonial relationship in which the Cayman Islands are dominated by the United Kingdom is increasingly being called into question. Such a relationship is predicated upon two elements – power and cultural dissimilarity – and so important are these concepts that a brief explanation is necessary.

It should be understood that colonialism, as discussed at this level, is one in which the entire society in the Cayman Islands is robbed of its self-determination and its ability to take full responsibility for its own decision making, in the absence of the administering power's representative. This phenomenon is orchestrated by the United Kingdom through the appointed governor. In practice, this type of colonialism has as its hallmark the subservience of the colonial society to the administering power. Consider the practice of the governor huddling with his official members before their attendance at the weekly cabinet meeting. The huddle excludes the elected cabinet members, who often meet with the governor after the cabinet meeting. What this tells the interpreter is that British colonialism has not changed, that the 'natives' must not be trusted.

Consider that the most recent impasse between the Cayman Islands and the United Kingdom arose over the former's reluctance to implement the European Union Savings Directive. After resisting initial requests to implement a strategy widely perceived to be inimical to its interests, the Cayman Islands gave in to pressure from the UK authorities. Such manipulation is becoming commonplace in the relationship between the two, and it appears that the United Kingdom will not hesitate to exercise its authority through Orders-in-Council.

This leads to the issue of the dissimilarity between colonisers and colonised. In the colonial society which is the Cayman Islands, the notion exists among some older people that the old concept of 'the white man's burden' is still acceptable. Ethnocentricity and arrogance often characterise the relationship between the UK authorities and the Caymanian political directorate. It may be helpful at this stage to analyse the societal behaviour in the context of Caymanian society as creole and colonial.

The term *creole* is hardly ever used in the Cayman Islands, and yet Caymanian society is a solidly creole society. Little or no attention has ever been paid to this cultural concept as it applies to the Cayman Islands. Since one has to assume that the work of the Cayman National Cultural Foundation will eventually lead to such a discovery, it is fitting to open this section with a definition of the term.

In its most general context and as used here, *creole* refers to people and cultures originating from the European and African countries but born in the colony. As a historical and cultural concept, the term gained importance in 1971 when Kamau Brathwaite published his seminal work, *The Establishment of Creole Society in Jamaica, 1770–1820*. In this work, which is also relevant to other Caribbean societies, Brathwaite sought to identify the Jamaican nature of the identity which developed at the point of intersection between the cultures of Africa and those of Europe.

On the concept of creolisation, Bolland (2002, 17–18) commented:

The concept of Creole society, as it has been used in the Caribbean, stresses the active role of Caribbean peoples and the importance of African cultural traditions. In many ways it is the antithesis of the old imperialist viewpoint that denies the "natives" a history of their own and asserts that nothing of any cultural value was ever produced in the Caribbean. By insisting on the fact that the common people – slaves, peasants, freed people and labourers – were active agents in the historical process, the creolisation thesis has made a major contribution to Caribbean historiography. This thesis, which reflects the influence of anthropological approaches, has broadened our conception of the scope of Caribbean social history and reconstituted our ways of looking at the dynamics of social and cultural change. Caribbean societies and cultures can no longer be thought of as the result of a one-way process, of the unilateral imposition of European culture upon passive African recipients. Important as European expansion, slavery, the plantation system and the deracination of Africans unquestionably are, it is now generally recognized that the conjoint participation of different peoples, not least those from Africa, produced from a very early time a distinctive African-American Creole culture.

Caymanian society, then, like other West Indian creole societies, is a society in which little, if any, racial purity exists among descendants of the original settlers. Similarly, too, it is a culturally mixed society in which many overtly African traditions and customs have been superseded by an imperialist psychology.

The idea that many cultural practices which appear to be so vibrant today are the result of a synthesis between sometimes conflicting social and cultural forces is not a new interpretation as far as Caribbean history and society are concerned. Caymanian society is a plural society in which there is a blending of cultural nuances. At present the society seems to be in a state of flux, in which the structural ingredients which emanate from the varied ethnic and cultural composition of the society are at odds with a political process which emerges when established Caymanians put nationalistic pressure on the political directorate – a nationalism which appears reactionary rather than rational. Rather than touting the long-term advantages to be gained from an organised integration, there is too great a willingness to succumb to what appears to be political pressure resulting from the expectations of some established Caymanians. The political directorate has refused to demonstrate maturity and clarity of societal vision by promoting a social dialogue in which the merits of a plural society could be discussed.

The *Cayman Net News,* one of two local daily papers, has taken it upon itself to keep the immigration issue front and centre. On June 21, 2006, its editorial asked 'What is the problem with new Caymanians?' and offered scathing commentary on societal attitudes toward outsiders.

> The xenophobic rhetoric over Caymanian status [citizenship] shows no sign of letting up as demonstrated by the regular correspondence on the pages of this publication, other media and the calls to the talk shows that feature on many of the local radio stations ... This attitude continues to foster the idea that Caymanians should only really be born and that awarding status is something that needs to be controlled and limited as much as possible.

Just a week later, on June 29, the publication issued a call to 'bring back the Caymanian diaspora' as a way of addressing the immigration problem. Calling the Cayman Islands 'an entirely service-based economy which needs talented, specialist and professional people', the writer suggested that descendants of Caymanians who were raised and educated overseas be invited back and offered immediate permanent residency or status, to ensure the continued growth of a qualified work force.

As the earlier editorial indicated, the press and the electronic media provide a popular pulpit for people wishing to bloviate about the sacrosanct position that established Caymanians should hold. The notion of the Cayman Islands as a service economy, largely reliant on an outside pool of expertise, appears to have been lost on both officialdom and the majority of commentators who submit opinions to the media. The rollover policy has created a new category of people in the society. It is suggested here that this new category can best be described as 'disposable people'. This is not the first manifestation of this category of people; they appeared when this policy was initially practised, in the 1980s. At that time, however, those affected were mainly domestics and unskilled construction workers from the Caribbean region, working mainly in households and small to medium-sized businesses which were owned mainly by Caymanians.

The situation continues to fester. A headline in the *Cayman Net News* on July 20, 2006, proclaimed '"Revolution" without rollover'. In the accompanying article, an established Caymanian businessman and former political candidate warned: 'If Government fails to keep the seven-year rollover policy the Cayman Islands may be heading down the path of revolution.'

These are strong sentiments, and yet there has been no attempt by civic organisations or the political directorate to convene a national dialogue which could enhance understanding and the search for a solution. The positions taken in the print media and on radio call-in programmes leave one with the conclusion that human rights and security of tenure are mutually exclusive.

While one prominent human-rights advocate decried the lack of reference to the Vision 2008 exercise, no others have proposed seeking a solution in this venue. It is no exaggeration to remark that if a constructive dialogue is not embarked upon in the near future, Caymanian society will be in danger of a systemic breakdown.

Comparatively speaking, there was no sustained national hue and cry in the 1980s, although the political directorate realised that their policy was counterproductive. It seems obvious that, if such a policy had to be jettisoned at that time because of its retarding effect on the economy and society, the same should be true now. Yet officialdom seems oblivious to the service-based nature of the economy and its absolute dependence on outside expertise in both banking and tourism.

One would expect such *sturm und drang* to be essential ingredients of a frontier society like the Cayman Islands. It will be interesting to observe the acculturation which takes place within the next decade, as the new immigrants realise that a significant number of established Caymanians are hostile toward outsiders. In a developing society, as the Cayman Islands is, there are always attempts to compartmentalise groups. While no constructive purpose is served by such compartmentalisation, it is both socially and culturally important to establish, in an acceptable way, who is Caymanian.

The designation of Caymanian society as both colonial and creole set the stage for this exploration. Attention must also be drawn to the fact that the attempt to define who is Caymanian is a social and cultural exercise; strictly legal constructs and definitions are inappropriate in this context. It appears that such an exercise is necessary; let us examine whether it is worthwhile.

Colonial and creole, established or expatriate – who is Caymanian?

There is no evidence that there were permanent settlers on the Cayman Islands before their colonisation in the eighteenth century

(Craton 2003). It is inaccurate to speak of 'indigenous Caymanians', then, if the term means persons native to these islands.

All Caymanians, as explained in the introductory paragraph of this chapter, are or were imported into the society. This is why this writer has chosen to use the terms 'established Caymanians' and 'expatriates'. However, it is recognised that, culturally and historically, only established Caymanians have ancestral privileges, in the sense that length of tenure favours those residents with knowledge of certain rites, traditions, mores, and values. Those people who were 'established' at the beginning of colonisation have always held a certain superiority over those who came much later as economic migrants. What follows is an attempt to explain the differences and also to briefly explore the symbiosis between the various elements.

Established Caymanians would have to be those whose roots and ancestry are from the settlement period until, for example, the beginning of the twentieth century, with the cutoff point being the 1950s. Such a category would span the ethnic spectrum. In terms of tenure, this could be interpreted to mean that anyone claiming to be an established Caymanian should have ancestral lines extending at least three generations.

For purposes of establishing a clearly defined arrival point, it is accepted that expatriates did not arrive in significant numbers until Lynden Pindling came to political prominence in the Bahamas, defeating the so-called Bay Street Boys, during the 1970s. This event, coupled with the rise of nationalism and the desire for independence in many jurisdictions throughout the then British Empire, led many expatriates who had overstayed their welcome in the former colonies to the Cayman Islands as their 'last frontier'. While these people brought expertise to the Caymanian community, they also represented the change and uncertainty that marked the gradual death of colonialism and the move to more local control and, ultimately, political independence in many former British colonies.

Assimilation into Caymanian society carried none of the challenges and confrontations experienced in many other British territories. Many of the expatriates who came to the Cayman Islands naturally took advantage of the congeniality of their Caymanian hosts. By asserting their own intellectual and cultural superiority, they succeeded in introducing a powerful colonialism and placing an indelible mark on the Caymanian psyche. There are many obvious signs of the expatriates' contempt for established Caymanians and Caymanian society; those seeking examples need to look no further than the hiring practices of the major law firms on Grand Cayman.

We must again ask: Is the Cayman Islands then a racist society? No; rather, it is a society in which the practitioners of colonialism appear to operate in a racist manner. That this is so should not be surprising since this kind of manifestation is a characteristic of any frontier society, particularly one with pigmentocratic inclinations.

From its earliest settlement, Caymanian society exhibited class and colour distinctions. Such distinctions were compounded by the fact that within some prominent white Caymanian families were relatives of black or mixed ancestry. This was the case because the mating pool in the Cayman Islands during the early years was limited. It was not uncommon to encounter 'close-cousin' marriages, but there was also the practice of 'visiting', and consensual sexual relationships between whites and people of colour did produce offspring of various complexions.

Many expatriates in today's Cayman like to be cast in the role of intellectual and economic leaders. The principals of the large law firms are especially fond of arrogating this role to themselves. So arrogant are some of these players that they perceive themselves as indispensable to Caymanian society.

While the prominent positions occupied by these people allow them to be numbered among the most powerful, their intellectual productivity is primarily limited to the production of personal and corporate wealth. They bequeath very little – other than money – to Caymanian cultural and intellectual life. Often these self-appointed paragons of virtue and enlightenment are reserved towards established Caymanians and other Caribbean people, whom they see as 'hewers of wood and drawers of water', inferior by virtue of their lack of a metropolitan education. Exclusion from the elite on the basis of national origin is more than a pinprick on the body politic. It penetrates to the deepest layers of the Caymanian psyche, especially that of established Caymanian and Caribbean intellectuals.

Nonetheless, real advances have been made by the society in shaping a relatively harmonious multiracial and multinational atmosphere.

Such an acknowledgement notwithstanding, the observer of Caymanian society should not be misled into thinking that the tenaciously held opinions among educated established Caymanians, with regard to their vulnerability, are chronically insular. There exists an almost impregnable wall – the so-called glass ceiling so often discussed on radio call-in shows and letters to the editor. Established Caymanians – both black and white – complain of a deprivation of power, influence and authority. A frequent complaint is that they are often passed over for promotions and required to train the expatriate who has been recruited for a position superior to theirs. While there are exceptions, it is the exception that proves the rule.

The picture of a non-white majority being expected to function as a cultural minority in an apparently Eurocentric matrix was shattered by a number of occurrences. Most significant among these events was one which took place on January 27, 2003, in Heroes Square in George Town. The year 2003 held special significance for the Cayman Islands, since in 1503 the islands were sighted by that first tourist, Christopher Columbus. History was made again on that day in 2003, when approximately 5,000 people sat, stood, and otherwise packed themselves in the square to hear a series of inspirational speeches and a roll call of persons, most deceased but some alive, who had left an indelible mark on Caymanian society. It was, by this writer's lights, the birth of a national spirit that allowed Caymanian society to emerge from its cocoon of complacence and lethargy to claim a legacy which, if nourished properly, will lead eventually to self-determination.

Caymanians in political and bureaucratic circles refer to the Cayman Islands as a nation. Strictly speaking, this is inaccurate, since the Islands are an Overseas Territory of the United Kingdom. 'Nation' implies not only self-determination, but political independence. The Cayman Islands can, however, be accurately referred to as a society. It is this concept that had its genesis on the first Heroes Day, January 27, 2003. It is no understatement to say that Caymanian society has not been the same since. The emotion and pride that marked that day will be part of the Caymanian psyche for years.

Quincentennial celebrations in Cayman served as a clarion call for many things. Among the significant events was the launch of *Founded upon the Seas,* the first comprehensive history of the Cayman Islands. This chronicle aptly fitted the state of mind at the time. It appears that established Caymanians are at last ready to come to grips with who they are as a people, as a society with roots in the Caribbean plantation system, and in some sense as products of the African diaspora. Perhaps more important, an increasing number of Caymanians across the spectrum are becoming curious about the history and significance of the Caymanian in the wider Caribbean.

To adopt a Caribbean context is to acknowledge the colonial/creole makeup of Caymanian society. It is also an acknowledgement of the symbiosis which today exists between established Caymanians and their expatriate brothers and sisters who have made their contribution to what is the modern Cayman Islands.

Rex Nettleford's comments about the Caribbean can be extrapolated to the Cayman Islands: '... in the continuous dialectical process of creolisation which gives meaning to the dynamic of the Caribbean's social and psycho-cultural historical transitions as it does to a contemporary description of Caribbean citizens as "part African, part European, part Asian, and totally Caribbean [Caymanian]"' (Nettleford 1995, xiii).

Chapter 3

Engendering Democracy:
The Relationship between Administering Power and Colony

Introduction

To examine the entrenchment of democracy in the Cayman Islands at the beginning of the twenty-first century, we must discuss the character of that democracy as well as fundamental questions about politics and its place in society, the role of the political directorate in the conduct of public affairs, and, perhaps most important, relations with the administering or colonial power.

Democracy, for purposes of this chapter, is taken to mean a system that has as its basis the right of a jurisdiction to self-determination, which need not necessarily culminate in political independence. Taken to its logical conclusion, democracy in our context would mean that the colony is accorded the responsibility of consulting as a full partner with the administering power on such matters as the choice of governor. Of equal importance is the recognition by the administering power of the colony's ability to manage its affairs to such an extent that consideration can be given to devolving some of the powers of the governor. In a situation in which elected ministers have responsibility without authority, such a change only makes good administrative sense.

Given this definition, some theoretical concepts should enhance the historical account of the evolution of the Caymanian democratic system and the influence of the administering power on that system. The development of such a framework is limited by the fact that in a small colonial society such as the Cayman Islands, there is no corpus of knowledge from which to draw peculiar theoretical frameworks.

Additionally, for purposes of this work, any definition of democracy must take into account the right of the administering power to legislate, through Orders-in-Council, laws which it deems appropriate for the Cayman Islands, even in cases where the Cayman Islands' political directorate may not share the views of the administering country. The obverse is also true, since the administering power can refuse to allow any law which it deems inimical to the interests of Caymanian society, even if such a law emanates from the Legislative Assembly of the Cayman Islands.

Given such circumstances, the relationship can hardly pass as democratic, because the Caymanian authorities do not have absolute freedom in crafting their own laws. What exists can more accurately be described as a benevolent guardianship, of which more will be said later.

Naturally, any discussion of democracy in the context of the relationship between the United Kingdom and the Cayman Islands must be influenced by the evolving geopolitical context. The United Kingdom's membership in international organisations – the European Union, the Organisation for Economic Cooperation and Development (OECD), and the Financial Action Task Force (FATF), among others – will of necessity affect its relations with the Cayman Islands.

Notwithstanding that observation, it must be stated at the outset that the Cayman Islands are at once unique and peculiar among colonial jurisdictions. To begin with, Caymanian people, for the most part, have a strong sense of loyalty to the British Crown. They believe in the monarchy, with its accompanying nuances, and among the older elements of the population a certain pride is associated with 'Britishness'.

The adoption of British ancestry by colonial people of mixed racial heritage is predicated upon the notion of British cultural and sociopolitical sophistication. This attitude, prevalent among Caymanian people born in the period between the world wars, does not find such fertile ground among the post–World War II generations.

Among these younger generations, there is a sense of connection with the United Kingdom but not to the extent that it supersedes connection with the wider Caribbean. The connection with the Caribbean has significance in historical linkages as well as sociocultural phenomena. It is this writer's opinion that democracy, colony, and society mean different things to people born since the late 1940s than they do to their elders.

Many in Caymanian society are beginning to question the traditional affinity to 'Britishness' and to view British colonialism, insofar as it extends to the Cayman Islands, as a concept whose time has gone. Certainly, events of recent years – the 1999 White Paper entitled *Partnership for Progress and Prosperity* notwithstanding – have done nothing to illuminate the relationship as anything but that of an association between an administering power and a colony in which the administering power always has the advantage.

Any discussion of engendering democracy in the Cayman Islands, then, must be prefaced by the caution that democracy, as a political concept in the Cayman Islands, is still, comparatively speaking, tenuous. After all, by the mid–nineteenth century British policymakers had set up what seems like a deliberate discriminatory policy in the treatment of certain colonies. Holt (1992, 235) states:

> By 1850 key British policymakers had begun to make distinctions between the future of white colonies, such as Canada, and the black ones, such as Jamaica. The former were to be groomed for greater independence in their local affairs, while the latter were judged to be better suited for a "benevolent guardianship".

It is doubtful that Britain held any intention of promoting democratic government in any of the Caribbean territories. Democracy and economy were inextricably linked, but only to the extent that the colonising power maintained a monopoly on the colonial products. Democracy as a system of government extended only so far as to allow the merchant establishment, and by inference the colonial authorities, to implement strict control over the colonial economy. The primary interest of the colonising power was not the implementation of democratic principles but the organised practice of political manipulation (Lindsay 1981, 5). This political manipulation by the administering power, which is grounded in the art of duplicity, is nevertheless obvious in the relationship.

The Euro Bank trial and its subsequent debacle have served to call into question the paradoxical relationship between administering power and colony. For all the well-meant asseverations contained in the White Paper, the administering authorities were embarrassed by the exposure of contradictory actions against the Cayman Islands government. To claim that fairness exists in a relationship in which the administering power resorts to clandestine techniques to subvert an established system over which it has ultimate control is disingenuous; such a claim discounts justice and the rule of law, which are fundamental to democracy.

The relationship that currently exists between the United Kingdom, as the metropolitan country, and the Cayman Islands, as colony, is best described as a power relationship. Nazer (1999, xv), offers an explanation:

> Power of a third kind refers to the historic ability of the West to use its exceptional advantages in global electronic communication systems, as well as its military, economic and institutional leverage, to establish their political processes and assumptions as universal, culturally transcendent frameworks.

It is precisely this 'power of a third kind' relationship which binds the Cayman Islands and the United Kingdom. Democracy, to the extent that it characterises this relationship, is in effect only when the interests of the United Kingdom are identical to those of the Cayman Islands.

In the global financial arena, the United Kingdom and the Cayman Islands are competitors. The symbiosis which existed between these two entities up to 1960 does not override their rivalry for financial prominence, and, as recent events are making obvious, the Cayman Islands find themselves disadvantaged.

The 1990s brought the realisation that the Cayman Islands had become a major international financial centre. Concomitant with this realisation was the discontent of several Western countries, in particular France, Germany, and the United States, with the existence of the offshore financial industry. Largely through political organisations like the OECD, the European Union, and the FATF, pressure was brought to bear on offshore financial jurisdictions. Many of these jurisdictions, such as the Bahamas, Bermuda, British Virgin Islands, and the Cayman Islands, were former or current colonies of the United Kingdom. It was logical, therefore, that they would expect a certain understanding on the part of the United Kingdom. By the mid-1990s, however, it had become clear that the United Kingdom, by virtue of its membership in these organisations, desired a different relationship with its current and former colonies, at least as regarded international financial matters.

The obvious catalyst for change did not come until 1998, when the OECD published *Harmful Tax Competition: An Emerging Global Issue*. While completely different in origin, two other publications surfaced around this time that had significance for the future direction of the relationship between the United Kingdom and the Cayman Islands. These publications were the Report by the Comptroller and the Auditor General, *Contingent Liabilities in the Dependent Territories* (May 1997), and the White Paper *Partnership for Progress and Prosperity* (March 1999). These documents, had they been taken seriously by the political directorate in the Cayman Islands, should have served notice of an impending new relationship.

The international scene was now defined by the existence of a single superpower. This meant that capitalism had finally triumphed over communism and that democracy could take on unrivalled significance. It also meant that the world's capital would now have added importance, since there was no longer the a rival financial system. It is from this change in international politics that questions about the democratic intent of the administering country and its relationship with entities like the Cayman Islands come into clearer focus.

The situation in which the Cayman Islands are placed as a result of these changes is reminiscent of that of the Melians during the Peloponnesian War. The Melian Dialogue, as this episode has come to be characterised, sets out precisely the position of the Cayman Islands in their relationship with the United Kingdom. The relationship is frequently dominated by the United Kingdom, which, like the Athenians, adopts the position described thus: 'For ourselves, we shall not bother you with specious pretences …; since you know as well as we do that right, as it goes, is only in question between equals in power, while the strong do what they can and the weak suffer what they must' (Strassler 1996, 352).

The UK position with regard to the termination of the services of the attorney general, as called for in 2003 by the whole Cayman Islands, displayed no sensitivity to the wishes of the colonial people. Indeed, the United Kingdom's intransigence and unwillingness to give credence to the wishes of the Caymanian people was a further reminder of might – as evidenced by the Athenians when they reminded the Melians:

> … we have come here in the interest of our empire, and … we shall say what we are now going to say, for the preservation of your country, as we would desire to exercise that empire over you without trouble, and see you preserved for the good of us both. (Strassler 1996, 352)

The contempt and disdain with which the administering power viewed the Cayman Islands is more representative of the routine than it is an aberration. Those seeking examples of this behaviour are referred to the Minutes of the Fifth Ministerial Group on the Dependent Territories, which was held in May 1994.

At that meeting, which was chaired by the Honourable Mark Lennox-Boyd, MP, Parliamentary Undersecretary of State in the Foreign and Commonwealth Office, a number of issues relative to the relationship of the two entities were discussed. Conspicuous by their absence were any representatives from the political directorates of the Dependent Territories. This is indicative of the unregenerate colonialism and undemocratic administration employed by UK functionaries whose Kiplingesque sense of empire leads them to notions of state superiority.

It was at this meeting that the first suggestions of future differences between Dependent Territories and the administering power emerged. Mention was made of the need to 'achieve some regulation of international business companies in the DTs'. It was further hoped that this could be achieved through cooperation rather than conflict. This is an obvious reference to the almost geometric growth of such companies in the Cayman Islands and the British Virgin Islands.

In a typical ethnocentric approach, it was suggested that local constraints in the Dependent Territories included 'lack of a knowledge of the society' and 'limited talent'. It was also mooted that it was time to 'make greater demands on both civil servants as well as representatives, in clear anticipation of their inabilities to meet expectations'.[1]

This record makes it clear that, in spite of the pronouncements which were to follow, the reality was a colonialism intent on stamping a permanent mark on the psychology of the Dependent Territories. Later, when it became obvious that the growth in companies brought increasing financial promise, the UK authorities joined other major nations in vilifying what they termed 'shell companies'.

Thus began a programme of political manipulation which was bound to influence any emerging democracy. In the Cayman Islands, several events combined to debunk the myth of parity in the relationship. When it became obvious that the Cayman Islands ranked among the world's financial leaders, the United Kingdom, which had previously displayed no interest in Cayman's economic growth, suddenly began to apply pressure. Initially, this pressure took the form of demands for greater regulation and discrimination; when Cayman's success continued, the United Kingdom's interference became more overt.

Economic growth, political stability, and the concept of democratisation

The reference point for democracy in the Cayman Islands hinges on the relationship between the administering power and the Overseas Territory.

The question of whether true democracy exists here, however, has to be raised in light of the United Kingdom's failure to grant the Cayman Islands the right to self-determination and the Interim Order-in-Council sent down by the administering country as a precursor to the draft constitution. In that Interim Order, The Cayman Islands (Constitution) Order 2003, the following section related to the leader of government business is inserted: 'The Governor, acting in his discretion, shall appoint as the Leader of Government Business the Minister who in the opinion of the Governor has the support of the majority of the elected Members of the Legislative Assembly.'[2]

In a system with formal political parties, it cannot be truly democratic for the governor to presume such an action. A much more democratic and acceptable custom would be for the party leader, with the support of his political colleagues, to inform the governor of the choice of his political colleagues.

In constructing the equation in the way it is, the administering country has left the way open for mischievous behaviour, the ability to reject the people's choice – as Administrator Jack Rose did in the case of Ormond Panton, the NDP leader after the 1962 election – if that choice is deemed inimical to the administering power's interests. If this is indeed the case, then colonial relations are still at the stage they were when Milton Obote, Kwame Nkrumah, and Patrice Lumumba were undermined by the administering powers in the heyday of colonialism.

For many years, a symbiotic relationship existed between the United Kingdom, as the administering country brought economic prosperity to the Cayman Islands as a colony or Overseas Territory. This relationship had its grounding in the financial industry, but was not exclusive to this area. To this extent, it became more practical for the Cayman Islands to pursue economic development than to agitate for constitutional advancement leading to independence. In any case, the choice of 'voluntary colonialism' clearly indicated that constitutional advancement held little, if any, interest to most Caymanian voters.

As history would have it, an efficient communications infrastructure and proximity to the United States allowed the jurisdiction to develop as a centre for financial dealings. A stable political regime in which no formal party politics existed, coupled with a tolerance for outsiders, set the scene for acceptance of the expatriate community, which was certainly not the case in some neighbouring jurisdictions. Added to this was the image of the United Kingdom as a benevolent and caring 'mother'.

Such a symbiosis worked in the Cayman Islands' favour from the beginning of the financial industry until the end of the Cold War. Then several factors, including changing global politics, began to impinge upon the Caymanian success story. The emergence of the OECD, the World Bank, and the International Monetary Fund as standard-setters for the world's money, along with the absence of Cold War politics as a distraction, meant that the major capitalist nations, operating as the G7, had more time to focus on the harnessing and control of the world's money.

For jurisdictions such as the Cayman Islands, this meant increasing pressure to comply with the ever-growing regulatory demands upon their financial regimes. Initially, it appeared as if these regulatory requirements would allow the Cayman Islands to retain their status as a leader among the world's financial centres. Gradually, however, it became clear that the Cayman Islands could not expect support from the United Kingdom, which, as it turned out, faced its own challenge of retaining primacy within the Eurobond market.

The Cayman Islands certainly had ample evidence of this change of interests on the part of the United Kingdom. From the beginning of the 1990s, the United Kingdom began to exhibit intransigence toward the Cayman Islands in the realm of financial dealings. There were several authoritative, if informal, reports available to the political directorate regarding this impending change. By 1995, it was unequivocally clear to all but the least discerning that the symbiotic relationship was fraying.

The National Team, the Caymanian political directorate from 1993, instead of exercising vision, initiative, and maturity by being assertive when these changes were initially hinted at, pretended that no change was impending, apparently hoping that the problem would fade away. Politically, of course, it seemed in their best interests to portray that everything was in order.

It is instructive at this point to focus on economic growth, political stability, and the concept of democracy in the Caymanian context. The economic growth to which the Cayman Islands have become accustomed occurred without any definitive plan that would ensure that the Caymanian people would be the ultimate beneficiaries by virtue of their access to training and development. There were no laws or consistently credible public policies which prescribed the full participation of Caymanians within the financial, legal, or ancillary professions.

Economic growth in the modern Cayman Islands was initially predicated upon the remittances of Caymanian merchant seamen. Later, land sales complemented these sums, and by the mid-1970s economic spinoffs from the financial industry had become significant. Concomitant with these developments was the burgeoning tourism industry, especially as it related to stay-over visitors from the United States and, to a lesser extent, Canada. These twin pillars could have served the Cayman Islands excellently, had successive governments made the necessary links between economy, development, and democracy.

As it turned out, there was no connection made between the components and, as a result, the Islands had a crown colony constitution, which, while it guaranteed political stability, did nothing to prepare the country for the challenges of democratic responsibility in a micro-state. Crown colony government was not suited to nurture the development of colonies like the Cayman Islands. In the first place, as has been pointed out, ultimate authority lay with the administering or colonising power through its head of state. Wallace (1977, 17) explains:

> The virtue of crown colony rule was its amenability to British public opinion, usually more enlightened than that of the nineteenth century Caribbean legislatures. Yet it was necessarily paternal. The wielders of political power were responsible to a distant imperial government, not to the communities in which they served. As most major administrative posts were long reserved for Englishmen, the system gave West Indians no experience of political responsibility and indeed bred distrust of their capacities.

> It continued the autocratic rule by which the majority of the population had always been governed. When independence was finally achieved in the 1960s, the only type of government which the British Caribbean knew was authoritarian.

Certain elements were willing to use their positions to help perpetuate this authoritarianism. In the Cayman Islands, the merchant establishment had, by virtue of its favoured economic position, been able to control politics up to the 1960s. Members of the merchant establishment set themselves up as benevolent 'padrones', supporting candidates whom they co-opted (Hannerz 1974, 99–105). In turn, these candidates were little more than 'extension cords' for those with the real power.

Such a system allowed the merchant establishment to control the political situation while at the same time wielding complete economic primacy. The dominant class ideology assumed that the privileged white and expatriate elite were the natural leaders of Caymanian society. This was not unlike the situation which existed in neighbouring Jamaica, described here:

> The privileged white and light-skinned elite were assumed to be inherently superior both racially and culturally and this assumption was reinforced by a white, racist social ideology and the dependence of the society on a European imperial power, Great Britain.
>
> The dominant class ideology assumed that land owners, the wealthy, and the highly educated had a natural claim to national leadership, pre-eminent political influence, and social wisdom ...
>
> The power structure maintained itself on the basis of patron-client links between the wealthy light-skinned elite and the black peasant, artisan and unskilled labouring classes ... Equally important was the limited sense of efficacy and subjective feeling of power on the part of the subordinate lower classes and black majority. (Stone 1985, 15)

Hannerz (1974, 99) suggests that by the early 1960s Caymanian society had experienced a change in which the former patrons were removed from their positions of political dominance. It is, however, this writer's contention that these attempts at change did not have much significance until 1976, when the old patron system was replaced by a more dynamic version of that system.

It is also contended here that neither of these systems, which had as their basis economic self-reliance, were truly democratic in the sense that they afforded equality to all elements of the society. Hoffer (1951, 33) offered an insight into why such a system would eventually prove problematic when he made the distinction between freedom and equality as democratic concepts:

> Where freedom is real, equality is the passion of the masses. Where equality is real, freedom is the passion of a small minority.
>
> Equality without freedom creates a more stable social pattern than freedom without equality.

Several occurrences in the Cayman Islands over the past three decades serve to remind us of the relevance of this comment to Caymanian politics. Among these, the 1970 demonstration against the proposed Land Development (Interim Control) Bill 1969 stands out as the most dramatic example. Caymanians had always equated land with wealth, and when the political directorate tried to limit landowners' ability to use their lands in certain ways, the opposition found a fertile platform from which to launch their campaign.

An immediate result of these events was that, by the mid- to late 1970s, the political players had changed. The change, however, was only superficial, in that it did not inform public political intellect or illuminate political aspirations in the wider society. The situation was not unique to Caymanian society; as Wallace (1977, 230), points out:

> Many West Indian states still espouse a highly personal brand of politics ... Political and insular jealousies have not vanished, nor has absorption with local as opposed to regional problems, despite steady growing interest in the latter. Universal suffrage, in the Commonwealth Caribbean less than a generation old when autonomy was finally achieved, has in no country guaranteed a wise and informed electorate.

Politics in practice

The system of politics practised by Caymanian politicians varied during certain periods, particularly from 1962 until 1966. Before that there was a brief period when it seemed that party politics might afford a broadening of the political landscape. In 1958 the Cayman Vanguard Progressive Party, presided over by a black George Town businessman and supported by other leading personalities both black and coloured, announced its intention to field candidates in the upcoming elections (Hannerz 1974, 68).

A calculated personal attack along racial lines by prominent members of the white merchant establishment hindered the party's ability to attract a significant following. This prejudiced attack was so devastating that there was a large-scale rejection of what should have been an attractive manifesto. The party was roundly defeated, and its leaders suggested that the elections had been conducted fraudulently (Hannerz 1974, 69).

The Caymanian political scene then, while characterised by stability in the sense that violence was absent, was not, by our earlier definition, democratic. It was not until the first written constitution of 1959, which ushered in universal adult suffrage, that Caymanians experienced any semblance of democracy.

There followed a period of intense political activity from the 1960s onward. By late 1959 it had become apparent that the West Indies Federation was heading for failure. Events took a decidedly nationalistic turn when Jamaica was granted independence in 1962. This meant that the Cayman Islands, which for years had been administratively associated with Jamaica, had to make new arrangements for a political existence.

Through a process described by this writer as voluntary colonialism, the Cayman Islands opted for crown colony status with internal self-government. Once again party politics were resuscitated, this time with a formal organisation and island-wide support. The National Democratic Party was formed by Ormond Panton, a George Town businessman and vestryman. The merchant establishment, not to be left behind, formed the Christian Democratic Party under the leadership of T.W. Farrington, a veteran legislator from West Bay.

Island-wide political organisation and populist appeal carried the leader of the NDP and his colleagues to a significant victory in the election that followed. It was this election in 1962 which saw, for the first time in the Cayman Islands, a woman elected to public office. Evelyn Wood, a community worker, nurse, and church leader was returned to represent the Bodden Town constituency as a member of the NDP.

The NDP had won an illusive victory, however, for although Ormond Panton was the leader of the majority party, he was passed over for an executive council seat by Jack Rose, the colonial administrator. Such blatant disrespect triggered a crisis of some significance among the NDP members. It was decided that the NDP members-elect would resign en masse, but in the end only the leader and one other member resigned their seats. The failure of the members-elect to support their leader signified that democracy had been scuttled.

The leader attempted to regain the momentum, but attitudes had changed, and, according to Hannerz (1974, 98), 'on election day the National Democratic Party, and with it the Caymanian party system, ceased to exist as functioning realities'.

That the NDP was so disrespectfully treated by the colonial administrator should call into question the officer's motives. Was he appointed to facilitate the political maturity of the Caymanian people, or did he so favour the merchant establishment that he was prepared to dishonour any other entity? Whatever the answer, one thing seemed certain: the experience had killed the resolve of the NDP leader, and with it any hopes of his meaningful participation in party politics.

For 17 years following the election of 1962 and its aftermath, politics in the Cayman Islands were an unorganised political free-for-all. In 1969 the Legislative Assembly passed a resolution authorising a select committee to consider amendments to the Islands' constitution. This exercise yielded no unanimity, and in June 1970 both majority and minority reports were submitted, ending the exercise. No significant improvements were made until 1971, when a new constitution was proposed. Successive legislative assemblies had been reluctant to delve into constitutional modernisation, though the administering country expressed no such reluctance.

Several deductions can be made from this hiatus. First, Caymanians apparently were still more focused on economic development than on political modernisation. By these years the political enthusiasm experienced during the period 1959–66 had become dormant, if not completely dead. Second, during this period many Caymanian men obtained steady work as merchant seamen on ships flying flags of convenience, and presumably they were occupied with the opportunities this work afforded.

It was these opportunities that allowed Caymanian seamen to travel the world, exposing them to different cultures and to a variety of consumer goods. These skilled seamen were employed crewing supertankers and ore ships carrying cargoes around the globe, from the relative familiarity of Caribbean and Central American ports to foreign ports in the northeastern United States, Europe, the Middle East, and Asia. Most Caymanian men during these years displayed neither an interest in nor a disposition for politics. It was of little interest to them whether the Islands' constitution was modernised, as their primary commitment was to the economic well-being of their families.

The report of the constitutional commissioner, the Right Honourable the Earl of Oxford and Asquith, KCMG, suggests that, outside of the politicians themselves, the constitutional modernisation exercise did not elicit much attention. Even up to the present time, economic developments in the Cayman Islands have always assumed more importance than social and political developments. It is a fact that Caymanians have never perceived a significant relationship between economic prosperity and social and political advancement. That economic prosperity was somehow attributable to being a colony of the United Kingdom, thereby benefiting from the protection offered by the administering power, served to further cloud this issue.

The unwillingness to press for constitutional modernisation – and, by inference, social transformation – accounts to a large extent for the marginalisation of some elements in the society. At a time when other colonies in the Caribbean were agitating for greater self-determination, ostensibly to advance the social contract for the general populace, the Cayman Islands, often with the encouragement of political directorates, held fast to the view that economic prosperity and social and political advancement were mutually exclusive.

Citing the records of the independent former colonies in Africa and the Caribbean, the defenders of the status quo effectively disseminated the view that to seek self-determination or constitutional advancement, however limited, was tantamount to destruction. Even with the energies expended by the constitutional commissioners beginning in 1971, therefore, not much attention was paid to this avenue of advancement. In his report, the Earl of Oxford and Asquith stated:

> In the approach to my task I wished first of all to clarify the views expressed in the Reports of the Select Committee of 1970; ...

> To assist in the formation of these judgements I visited the colony, arriving in Grand Cayman on 22nd January 1971. My consultations, spread over a month, included talks with the administrator and senior officials, meetings on several occasions with elected members of the Legislative Assembly and interviews with members of the public, including lawyers in private practice and members of the Chamber of Commerce. I made myself available for interview at all the main centres of population in the islands and about 100 people took advantage of these opportunities. (*Cayman Islands* 1971, 9)

That such a small number of people displayed interest in constitutional advancement, when the population of the Islands stood around 10,000, can only be explained as stemming from a lack of interest in local political affairs. As subsequent constitutional reviews show, the forums for public consultation set up by later commissioners also attracted few participants (Smith and Wallace 1991, 9; Ebanks et al. 2002). Although Caymanians did participate in the later stages of the exercise, there is evidently no pressing desire to take part in the public consultation process.

Reverting to the events of 1971, the changes which were accepted by the community and all political participants were adopted. As a matter of interest, both the majority and minority reports prepared by members of the Legislative Assembly made provision for a section on fundamental rights and freedoms. In spite of such unanimity, however, when the new constitution was received, those rights and freedoms were not included in the document.

Nonetheless, the constitution represented the beginning of a new era in Caymanian politics, and by the time it was introduced as a formal instrument, there were those who were prepared to take advantage of this political situation. Within four years, two of these people had so stamped their imprint on Caymanian politics that the political incumbency lost its position of advantage. With a community-wide organisation known as the HELP society, these two candidates were well poised to succeed what, by 1976, was an apparently defeated incumbency.

As was not entirely unexpected, the general election of 1976 brought sweeping change. Aided by the fact that the obvious leaders, the two candidates from Bodden Town, were unopposed, the Unity Team won every seat in the Legislative Assembly. For the first time both the political directorate and the Legislative Assembly were composed of people from the same political organisation.

Success in the 1976 general election had its genesis in earlier events. In 1972 the death of one of the Bodden Town representatives necessitated the holding of a district by-election. Interestingly, one person who had been instrumental in the deceased candidate's successful campaign took the opportunity to seek elected office. Jim Bodden, whose popularity had grown island-wide, won the by-election amid controversy. As it turned out, the then governor refused to swear him in as a member of the Legislative Assembly on the grounds that he was an American citizen.

When the 1972 general election came around, Jim Bodden again presented himself for election. This time he teamed up with Haig Bodden, a Bodden Towner who was a former civil servant. The duo had the benefit of an organised campaign machine composed of ordinary citizens as well as elements of the merchant establishment.

Also contesting the election were the incumbent, Anton Bodden, and newcomer Mary Lawrence. For reasons that are difficult to comprehend, Anton Bodden did not mount a spirited defence of his incumbency. Mary Lawrence, on the other hand, ran hard, mainly against Jim Bodden and Haig Bodden. The ensuing campaign was full of political rhetoric and accusations, including charges of political malfeasance on the part of Jim Bodden and Haig Bodden.

The election itself proved controversial, if not illegal, since 50 George Town ballots were found in a Bodden Town ballot box. The discovery should have been enough to warrant nullification of the Bodden Town election results and an investigation into how such a thing could have happened.

A petition was filed by Mary Lawrence and several of her citizen supporters. The sitting grand court judge, an aging expatriate, displayed no interest in pursuing the matter, and, as a result of intimidation by the supporters of those candidates who were named as defendants, the original petition was withdrawn. When the petition was refiled, it bore only Mary Lawrence's signature.

Eventually the petition was forwarded from the grand court in the Cayman Islands to the appeals court in Jamaica. To this day, nothing has transpired with this case – a result that was a good indication of what was to follow as a consequence of the election. The fact that the UK government allowed this incident to go uninvestigated and unresolved must call into question the administering power's desire for democracy, justice, and the rule of law when its own interests are not at stake. The case can be made that the administering authorities are often concerned only with preserving the status quo. In a jurisdiction such as the Cayman Islands, where the state must be seen as the guarantor of the right to justice and the rule of law, it is patently fallacious to invoke democracy in the face of such injustice.

In this particular case, events were allowed to go unresolved because only a few people viewed the occurrence as a serious trespass on the rule of law and civil society. The situation was further clouded by the reticence of the incumbent to express disapproval. In many respects, Caymanian political behaviour over the next decade took its cue from this incident.

As Caymanian politics evolved, the political directorate that was the beneficiary of the 1972 election operated in a way not previously seen. Controversy, rhetoric, and sophistry became the elements associated with political debates. Some people claimed that intimidation and exploitation were additional characteristics of the political machinery. Whether such accusations could have been substantiated is a moot point; what is certain is that Caymanian politics and the notion of democracy had entered a new era.

There is an obvious peculiarity about the way the discovery of the 50 George Town ballots in a Bodden Town ballot box was dealt with. The conclusion to be drawn is that this incident and its cavalier treatment by the authorities was nothing short of a travesty of justice and a flagrant denial of due process. While lack of evidence makes one reluctant to accuse the UK authorities of direct complicity, the behaviour of the administering power in this instance cannot be termed blameless.

Why did the authorities in Whitehall tolerate such aberrant behaviour on the part of the judge? Even more puzzling, why was a petition which was accepted for registration treated so dismissively?

Time has only added fuel to the belief that such a flaunting of due process must have been part of a wider conspiracy – especially when one considers that the petition was ultimately forwarded to a higher court in Jamaica, where it languished. It is also important to note that the petitioner and her spouse were harassed, intimidated, and victimised by elements of the Caymanian political establishment – including, allegedly, members of the police service acting as enforcers for political interests.

It is remarkable that both the administering power and the Caymanian establishment allowed such acts to pass unchallenged. This writer's contention is that democracy, to the extent that it exists in the Cayman Islands, is inextricably linked to what the administering power is prepared to accept. Democracy is seldom that principled practice which serves the individual and the state, when the interests of those entities differ from those of the administering power.

In what seems a remarkable coincidence, shortly after the filing of the second petition and the transfer of the case to the Jamaican high court, the justice concerned retired from the Cayman Islands bench and promptly left the jurisdiction.

These events had additional significance in relation to 1976, for it was the first time in the history of the Cayman Islands that the political directorate had assumed prominence over the official arm of the government. This achievement was due mainly to the secure and relaxed style of the then governor. Such leadership from a colonial official was largely due to his experience and personality, and to the realisation that Caymanian elected leaders seemed, in his opinion, quite capable of handling 'internal self-government'.

The next four years were marked by an unprecedented economic growth spurt, buoyed, of course, by world economic affairs. Tourism expanded, banks and financial houses experienced a boom, legal and ancillary services came into greater prominence, and construction, fuelled largely by the growing popularity of condominium complexes, flourished. Land sales generated additional revenues, and there appeared to be great public satisfaction with the Islands' economic success.

Not everyone, however, subscribed to the notion that these were the best of times. A small but vocal element, largely comprising the defeated former members of the Legislative Assembly and their close supporters, began to float the idea that Caymanians were selling out their country.

Like other jurisdictions which place emphasis on economic well-being, Caymanians 'vote their pockets'. It was not surprising, therefore, that in the 1980 general election the Unity Team was returned to power, albeit this time with a reduced majority.

Emboldened by limited success at the polls, the opposition continued to organise and campaign against the Unity Team. Charges of corruption, nepotism, chicanery, arrogance, and the 'stifling of democracy' were ever present. Several controversial developments allowed the opposition, though not as well organised as the political directorate, to make inroads into Caymanian public opinion.

The Unity Team leadership, while making many controversial decisions, appeared to have complete confidence in their actions. By far the most controversial move had been severing the long-standing relationship with a Costa Rican airline and creating a national airline for the Cayman Islands. A credible island-wide campaign was mounted by those opposed to the decision, but the die had been cast, and the Cayman Islands could now boast its own airline, courtesy of the Unity Team. While many felt that problems lay ahead, the Unity Team's popularity meant that for the present there was little or no chance of the decision being seriously challenged.

Meanwhile, the Unity Team's leadership style, although originally anti-establishment, gradually became more mainstream, and its constituency, which had been island-wide and broadly representative, now felt neglected, betrayed, and abandoned in favour of foreign power brokers and big moneyed interests. Significantly, too, the Unity Team, originally accessible to all, became reclusive and authoritarian.

What had started out as a populist 'patron-client' relationship in 1972 through 1976 transformed itself into a highly personal brand of almost authoritarian politics. The original relationship was between large numbers of individuals on the one hand and a powerful and influential patron on the other, who dispensed favours and protected the clients' interests in return for deference and unstinting political loyalty.

It was a relationship that yielded satisfactory political results while it lasted. So content did the leadership become that its original pronouncements of pursuing self-government became eclipsed within the larger economic agenda. There was no attempt to further enlighten and inform the Caymanian community on the importance of advancing their social and political development.

Gradually an influx of foreign interests superseded the local constituency. What had been a firm commitment to the local community and clientele degenerated into an ad hoc, excuse-filled relationship that was often coloured by arbitrary and pressure-driven decision making.

Wallace (1977, 230) offers some insight into such a change:

> The natural temptation for politicians to feel themselves above criticism is increased when their education and tastes set them apart from the majority of their people. Where a new government is with difficulty distinguished from a new state there is a further temptation to consider opposition disloyal and to appeal to personalities rather than principles.

This indeed was the case as the Unity Team political directorate from 1976 resorted to a highly personal brand of politics, in which no member of society was free from the vitriolic criticism and partisanship which they practised – and which became the political norm for the duration of the Unity Team's tenure.

At the State Opening of the Legislative Assembly on April 11, 1979, one member of the political directorate singled out several individuals – opposition members and private citizens – for official opprobrium. The impression was projected that whatever the Unity Team political directorate said or did was to be accepted as well done, and any opposition was to be discredited and banished as a fringe element.[3]

By 1980, enough controversial incidents had occurred to demonstrate that the Unity Team had jettisoned its original principles. The opposition, no longer fragmented, had gained some credibility, and there were repeated calls for enquiries into the conduct of various political decisions. The increase in political attacks on elements not deemed to be Unity Team supporters was a manifestation of the team's political death rattle.

As the general election of 1984 was to show, the Unity Team had exhausted its political capital. When the results were tabulated, only a few of the original members were returned. Time, and the opposition political machinery, had rendered the Unity Team all but impotent.

After the 1984 election, local politics took on a more sedate and less contentious image. There followed four years of steady if unspectacular growth, during which internal self-government continued to function acceptably.

The period 1984–88 was presided over by a political directorate made up of a coalition of members of the former Dignity Team and others. There was no attempt during these years to elicit any debate on constitutional advancement. Caymanian society, it seemed, had settled into its comfortable and accustomed position of focusing on the economy. The political directorate, in contrast to its predecessor, steered the Islands away from controversy. With the economy being the focus of attention, both business and the tourism sector continued to grow; the Cayman Islands began to distinguish themselves as a jurisdiction of choice.

The general election in 1988 was preceded by a robust campaign, participated in by a significant number of political newcomers in addition to the incumbent political directorate and remnants of the Unity Team. There was the usual campaign rhetoric, familiar to the Caymanian political landscape. Absent from the campaign, however, was any pledge to seek political modernisation.

The Dignity Team incumbents mounted a determined campaign against the insularity of the Unity Team remnants, reminding the society of their concept of economic progress and development. When the results were tabulated, the Dignity Team was victorious and the Unity Team membership further weakened.

Success at the polls brought its own challenges, as a number of newcomers with divergent views soon strained the relationship with the political directorate. When the divergence cost the government its parliamentary majority, a constitutional crisis loomed. The colonial governor, sitting as president of the parliament, saved the political directorate by introducing the controversial Motion 3/90, which allowed the official members to vote with the government in Finance Committee.

This was an unprecedented move that did not go unnoticed by the Caymanian community. Political relations between the government and other members of the Legislative Assembly soured. Encouraged by elements of the Unity Team which had been successful in the 1988 general election, the new elements formed a loose coalition of seven members. These so-called back-benchers challenged the political directorate's every move and staged a continual organised hindrance to the government. The situation crystallised to the point where, in 1991, the opposition was able to wrest the budget away from the government's control. Caymanian politics during these years bore a striking resemblance to a description by Wallace (1977, 18):

> Popular representatives in autocratically governed communities, they tended to form a permanent opposition based not on ideas or principles but simply on the criticism of the establishment ... A fractious attitude of critical, irresponsible and permanent opposition to the administration became accepted as the normal atmosphere of political debate.

Events were not helped by the political directorate's unwise decisions about equipment for the national airline and other topical matters. By the end of the political term, there were several contentious issues which should have served notice to the incumbents that their tenure was in danger.

Amidst all the contention, in November 1990 a private member's motion, number 25/90, called for a review of the constitution. As a result, two commissioners were appointed, and a select committee, comprising all members of the Legislative Assembly, was formed. A series of eight meetings were held in December 1990 and January 1991, followed by more meetings held between January 6 and February 6, 1991. According to the commissioners, a press release invited submissions and visits:

> We also had separate meetings with individual members of the public, held both in George Town in the evenings, and in each of the six electoral districts. Altogether, we met with 92 people representing the 16 organisations; 63 individual members of the public; and a further 120 people attended the public meetings which were held in each district. (Smith and Wallace 1991, 9)

Consider that 20 years earlier, during the constitutional review lasting the same time, 100 people visited the commissioner. While there was some increase in the total number of people visiting the commissioner in 1990–91, it was not proportionate to the rise in population resulting from immigration and the attainment of the age of majority by large numbers of young people. Obviously, questions of constitutional advancement still bore no overriding significance to most Caymanians, compared with economic matters.

In any event, the whole exercise seems to have been ignored by the incoming political directorate when it took office in 1992. It displayed little or no interest in constitutional modernisation. In fact, it became clear early on that this political directorate was more interested in perpetuating itself than in enlightening or informing the electorate.

The proposed instrument which was sent from the Foreign and Commonwealth Office (FCO), marked 'Draft Constitution for the Cayman Islands, July 1992', was a comprehensive document. Prefaced by a chapter on fundamental rights and freedoms of the individual and making provision for a chief minister and a leader of the opposition, it was, comparatively speaking, the most progressive instrument that had been seen in the Cayman Islands to date.

What should have been an effective modern constitution that would have defined a new relationship between the administering power and colony became little more than a useless tool. The National Team political directorate trotted out the usual array of excuses. The chance for modernisation was scuttled by a piecemeal adaptation of the proposed document.[4]

The political directorate rejected the proposal for establishing the posts of chief minister and leader of the opposition. In place of chief minister, the de facto National Team leader persuaded the governor to accept a position called 'leader of government business'. The position carried no constitutional legality and existed in no territory outside of the Cayman Islands.

The position of leader of government business existed as an anomaly until 2003, when the FCO legitimised its existence through an Order-in-Council. That this legitimised position was accepted or even understood by the FCO suggests further confusion concerning the whole idea of the relationship between administering power and colony. Inevitably, too, it calls into question the willingness of the administering power to insist that the constitutional path be one of legitimacy rather than obfuscation and convenience.

Concomitant with this lack of political leadership was the National Team's rejection of fundamental rights and freedoms as an integral part of the proposed draft constitution. By removing the section dealing with freedom of conscience, the National Team set the document up for rejection by the FCO.

Once again, the commitment of the administering power must be called into question, as the FCO made no attempt to entrench fundamental rights in the Cayman Islands. In a clear contradiction of an earlier position, the National Team principals did nothing to promote human rights. In fact, the behaviour mirrored Ryan's description of the behaviour of the parties in the region:

> [P]arties in the Caribbean ... are hardly ever the same when in power as they are in opposition. There seems to be a cycle, an inexorable law which regulates their behaviour. When in opposition, they comprehensively stigmatise and demonise those in power. They tell their supporters and those whom they seek to convert that their rivals are venal, corrupt and in the pay of the highest bidder, whether foreign or local. They also promise to bring affluence, efficiency, order and transparency to the business of governance when they achieve office and to restore pride and dignity to a demoralized, pauperized and alienated people or sections thereof. When in opposition, parties also invariably seek to outbid their rivals. Some do it consciously and cynically, while others do it without making clear how difficult it is to effect the policy changes they espouse. (Ryan 1999, 14)

Intransigence and a lack of progress in moving the bureaucracy forced a leadership change, which brought a former Unity Team member back as leader of government business. Although there was no outward sign of political rancour, the displaced former leader's acceptance of the change was grudging at best.

Constitutional change did not figure prominently in Cayman politics again until 2001, when the then governor appointed three Caymanians to 'conduct a modernisation review'. This review was markedly different from the preceding two, in that it did not result from any motion brought to the Legislative Assembly. Significantly, too, it was carried out not by outsiders but by people from within Cayman appointed by the FCO. This particular constitutional modernisation exercise was extremely important in the political evolution of the Cayman Islands.

The events that followed the general election of 2000 made it clear that the unorganised way of arriving at majority support for the political directorate was no longer appropriate. Casualties of the election included three of the five ministers who had formed the National Team political directorate, two of whom had been original Unity Team members. But it was the way in which the executive council members were chosen that underscored the need for some more effective and logical procedure.

Many Caymanians had anticipated a more sophisticated and clear-cut method of choosing the political directorate, and interest in constitutional modernisation began to appear, if only in the hope that it would bring this about. What transpired was a political marriage of convenience that lasted for one year. The alleged coalition was made up of a number of people whose interests coincided only as far as the defeat of the National Team.

Despite promises of transparency, probity, accountability, and efficiency, glaring differences soon arose. When lack of leadership led the younger members of the group to express a loss of confidence in the leader, a no-confidence vote was taken against him and one other minister. The coalition splintered, and what followed was an exercise in parliamentary practice not hitherto seen in Cayman.

The majority carried the no-confidence vote. While there was some public agitation and a small but vocal demonstration by supporters of the displaced members, politics proceeded as usual, regardless of the characterisation of the change as a 'coup'. Two new ministers were sworn into office and a new political directorate was formed, comprising three previous and two new ministers. The governor accepted the change.

Shortly after November 8, the political directorate along with its supporting Legislative Assembly members announced the launching of the United Democratic Party. Party politics was by this gesture returned to the Caymanian political scene. The operation brought style to the functioning of the political directorate, and the legislative machinery seemed to function more effectively, if not efficiently.

In response to the establishment of the United Democratic Party (UDP), the opposition members announced the launch of their organisation, the People's Progressive Movement (PPM), with the former leader of government business as interim head.

With the formation of these parties, the Cayman Islands had a functioning party system. While there were no apparent major ideological differences, leadership styles varied. The UDP seemed assertive and willing to introduce policies it deemed progressive.

The PPM, on the other hand, with only five opposition members, seemed cautious and defensive, no doubt still adjusting to its relatively new status as a formal political organisation. This being the case, it would have been politically convenient to refrain from proposing any alternative policies at that time. Nonetheless, the presence of the PPM had the effect of galvanising public interest in the 2001 constitutional advancement debate. It appeared that Caymanian society was evolving into a community in which political interests jostled for the place formerly held by economic interests. It would be misleading to leave readers with the impression that party politics at that time meant continuation of the status quo. On the contrary, the resuscitated party politics brought a renewed sense of community, at least partly motivated by the vision of society implicit in the political directorate's philosophy.

Vision 2008 and the quest for a new community

The single most remarkable change in the Cayman Islands during the years 2000–2004 was neither economic nor technological but political. The waning of the historic political community, which had its beginnings in that 'voluntary colonialism' which Caymanians opted for at the demise of federation, is giving way to a sense of community. The 'benevolent guardianship' in which the United Kingdom, as the administering power, and the Cayman Islands, as the colony, existed in a mutually beneficial relationship was based on a metaphorical mother/child relationship. Beginning in the 1990s, there were indications from the administering power that this relationship had to change. It is possible that the relationship had exhausted its natural lifespan some years before, since in three decades there had been no significant political change in the Cayman Islands. In 1998, the governor directed a senior civil servant to develop a broad policy exercise culminating in a strategic plan. This exercise, known as Vision 2008, was the first real attempt to develop a nationally accepted socioeconomic blueprint for a plural society.

When the announcement was made that the Cayman Islands were to embark on a national strategic plan, many elements in the society expressed interest.

Vision 2008 was, for all intents and purposes, the Cayman Islands' first formal exercise in community building. A number of observations can be made regarding the process, but none is more pertinent than the fact that it did not emanate from the political directorate. The foreword contained in the final document explains the philosophical foundations upon which the plan was placed:

> Vision 2008, the planning process which led to the creation of the National Strategic Plan, began in March 1998 with a series of Visioning meetings held with Executive Council and Members of the Legislative Assembly. District meetings were held in every district and in all three Cayman Islands. The purpose of these meetings, and of the interviews, focus groups and public polling exercise that followed was to identify the people's key issues of concern. These were the issues that had to be addressed if we were to plan confidently for a bright future. (*Vision 2008* 1999, 1)

It is an indictment of both the colonial authorities and the then political directorate that an exercise which had the potential to be truly communitarian was largely unsupported by the influential political element. This was particularly problematic in that many of the recommendations had to be implemented as policy by the Legislative Assembly, which lacked the political will to act. The result of this failure to implement the strategies was that in 2000, when the elections brought a change in political directorate, no attempt was made to ensure that the recommendations of Vision 2008 were formally implemented in the policies of the political directorate.

The administering country's policies vis-à-vis the Cayman Islands must also be questioned, since what was implemented at the request of one governor was allowed to become defunct under his successor.

That nothing of national significance came out of the visioning exercise until 2003 is due in large part to the disjointed policies of the FCO. The lack of an effective succession plan accounts for an ineffective transfer of power. Whitehall's briefing of Overseas Territories governors is a throwback to the days of empire. To paraphrase former New York governor Mario Cuomo, they recruit in poetry but govern in prose.

In any case, the society is maturing, and Caymanians now have a sense of jurisdictional pride and community spirit. The Euro Bank debacle and the political imbroglio surrounding the attorney general's departure galvanised Caymanian society into a cohesive entity, which retained its social dynamism until hurricane Ivan made landfall. It is suggested here that even that cohesiveness that manifested itself in the aftermath of the hurricane and into the recovery period is now lost as a result of apprehension over current immigration policies which cloud the position of expatriates living in the Cayman Islands.

The *Cayman Net News* headlines of May 25 and May 29, 2006, respectively 'Expulsion time to change' and 'Banker criticizes rollover', and the accompanying stories point to the issue at hand. The articles delve in some detail into the disappointment and apprehension of expatriate residents in regard to the political directorate's failure to abandon the 'rollover' policy. That policy essentially requires foreign employees to break tenure short of the period required for eligibility to apply for residency. These people have to leave the jurisdiction for a significant period of time before they are again eligible to apply for a work permit.

The practice is viewed by many as onerous, counterproductive, and a hindrance to good business practice in a jurisdiction where competitiveness is critical and expertise the *sine qua non* of success. An editorial in the *Cayman Net News* of May 26, 2006, captures the sentiments of many in the expatriate community. Entitled 'Tinkering is not the answer to the expulsion policy', the column opens with the statement: 'Having been promised a review of the Immigration Law, the first hint of possible changes emerged at this week's Cayman Islands Bankers Association Conference'.

Sadly, though, it will do little to address the problems that are now fully evident throughout our community as a result of the government's insistence on maintaining the rollover policy.

The editorial goes on to capture the policy's contentiousness: 'At present, after an individual holding a work permit is expelled from the country having been used for seven years to sustain this country's viability, they are not allowed to return on another work permit for two years.' The two-year waiting period between work permits (the so-called rollover) may yet be reduced as pressure mounts on the political directorate to scrap the policy in its entirety.

The difficulty stems from the concerns of established Caymanians that they are fast becoming a minority in the society, and, further, that even qualified Caymanians often encounter not only the proverbial glass ceiling but an 'iron door' when seeking employment in some expatriate-owned firms.

The rollover policy seems to be a fait accompli, since the chairman of the Immigration Review Team is on record as stating that there is no alternative to it (*Cayman Net News,* June 7, 2006).

A similar policy was floated in the 1980s but lasted a mere six months before it was scrapped as not feasible. While Caymanians are at least engaged in trying to determine what direction should be followed, there is no constructive debate or social dialogue about why it is in the community's interest to have an inclusive immigration policy.

The situation is compounded by a position paper submitted to the chairman of the Immigration Review Team by several members of the Council of Associations. According to the story headlined 'Rollover changes recommended' (*Caymanian Compass,* June 4, 2006), this group of industry associations is concerned that the rollover policy will have a negative impact on the economy. The associations – the Cayman Islands Bankers' Association, the Cayman Contractors Association, the Cayman Islands Insurance Association, the Cayman Islands Fund Administrators Association, the Association of Architects, Surveyors and Engineers, and the Cayman Islands Tourism Association, supported by their umbrella organisation, the Cayman Islands Chamber of Commerce – recommended consideration of six key actions concerning the seven-year term limit and permanent residency policies.

In the article there are two points which have direct relevance to positions put forward in this chapter. The first has to do with the associations' acknowledgement that 'the term limit [rollover] policy is an effective method of protecting the interest of Caymanians'. This can be interpreted as substantiating the call for some form of protection for established Caymanians in the workplace. The common complaint from established Caymanians, as well as some expatriates who have gained Caymanian citizenship and residency, is that they are often discriminated against by employers who favour new foreign recruits, assuming that such employees will be more amenable to the pressing demands of the workplace owing to their lack of entrenchment and connections in the society.

The second point of interest is found in the Council of Associations' recommendation of 'a reasonable period of consultation so that the industry associations and the general public are given sufficient time to review the document (the proposed new Immigration Law) and to offer input and constructive advice'. The paper ends by suggesting that, if such opportunities are not presented, 'democracy' would be 'removed from the process'.

The problem with accommodating the Council of Associations and the Chamber of Commerce as special-interest groups is that they have always had the power to make such demands on political directorates, unlike the rest of the society. Concessions won by this group almost invariably exclude the interests of people who work just as diligently to make the economy and society function, though they are not often found working in multinational banks, business houses, or law firms. The successful solution to the immigration dilemma does not lie in the granting of concessions in exclusivity. It must begin with an open national dialogue. Such a dialogue must be comprehensive, in that it should take place in each district and in all three islands; inclusive; and free of political rhetoric and political posturing. The roundtable technique used during the Vision 2008 exercise would seem an excellent model to adopt.

The National Strategic Plan 1999–2008 (Vision 2008) document is a valuable guide and source of direction on many issues which loom as challenges in Caymanian society today. Strategy 16 states the intention to create a 'comprehensive Immigration policy' offering protection to Caymanians and giving 'security to long-term residents' at the same time. Action Plan 1 details the objective of such a strategy: 'To ensure the prioritization of the Immigration Policy within the Government Policy framework and that all such policies be linked with the overall Growth Management Strategy.'

To date, however, there has been no sign of a growth management strategy, and it appears as if immigration and work-permit policies are ad hoc, mutually exclusive, and based on nothing more than the disposition of the political directorate and the demands of the private sector. All this has been allowed to take place in spite of the specifics contained in Action Plan 2, Action Step 3 of the document, which states:

> Establish that after the transitional period no NEW permit holder can aspire to PRC [private residency certification] or Caymanian Status for a period of 5 to 7 years (i.e. that during that period all new permitholders entering the island will be subject to a pure roll-over system for the period of 5 to 7 years), at the end of which time the position will be subject to review, with a view to the implementation of the permitholder PRC–Status graduation (or ladder) system (Phase III), promulgated herein and used during the transitional period, as the main immigration policy of the country (*Vision 2008* 1999, 112).

It is posited here that had these Action Plans been followed, the immigration conundrum we are now facing would not have occurred. It should be obvious to all but the least discerning that immigration, work permit allocation, and the related societal challenge of growth management constitute a matter that Caymanian authorities have not, to date, addressed constructively.

Given that there have been several major Immigration Law reviews over the past two decades (not to mention piecemeal amendments), with no satisfactory legislation to this point, it seems logical to suggest a different approach. Past efforts at reform and amendment seem to have been nothing other than responses to immediate problems, which sacrificed long-term objectives for the short-term glamour of a false success. They have been, in this author's opinion, typical political responses to what is clearly a socioeconomic challenge.

A corollary to any successful conclusion is the issue of voting rights for people legally resident in the society for over five years. This and related issues were raised by one prominent businessman in the *Cayman Net News* on May 29, 2006. Under the headline 'Banker criticizes rollover' were discussed matters of exclusivity in rollovers, length of residency, and voting rights for some residents. It is no understatement to remark that immigration (and its ancillary phenomena of voting, residency, and security of tenure) is potentially the most divisive issue facing the Caymanian community at this time. Democracy, the rule of law, and cordial relations can ill afford to depend upon an ad hoc approach to immigration. A workable solution cannot be arrived at without a constructive and committed national dialogue. For too long, political directorates have placed the moral and democratic obligation to arrive at a balanced immigration law in the hands of a few eminent personalities who have been periodically recycled for purposes of political expediency. In any society where engendering democracy is important, transparency and balance must be the basis of immigration policy.

At a time when Caymanian society is beginning to embrace human rights, freedom of information, and constitutional modernisation, no connection has been made between these three important elements and democracy. It should come as no surprise, then, that in true frontier spirit, many (including those who consider themselves educated) in Caymanian society would have the community benefit from the contribution of outside elements within the Cayman Islands while at the same time excluding these elements from the 'soul' of the society. What is of concern here, however, is the absence of any commentary by influential established Caymanians about the nexus between the economy and immigrants, on the one hand, and political stability, on the other. Democracy will not be engendered in a society in which economic prosperity is under threat.

Through a fortuitous combination of circumstances, the idea of community received a tremendous psychological boost when on January 27, 2003, at the beginning of the Cayman Islands' year-long Quincentennial celebrations, approximately 5,000 people attended a national ceremony in Heroes Square. If there was any doubt about the way Caymanians felt about themselves, it should have been erased on this day.

The unveiling of a wall bearing the names of 500 people, chosen on the basis of their commitment to community, was the first step in modern times toward the forging of a national community. Not only did this gesture evoke criticism from some expatriate quarters but it also had the psychological effect of letting both established Caymanians and those of more recent status realise that national pride and community spirit existed in the Cayman Islands.

In a year in which the Islands celebrated the 500 years since their sighting by Columbus, many were buoyed by the sense of a Caymanian identity. There was as much substance as there was symbolism, and 2003 can be described as a kind of jubilee year, in the sense that Caymanian culture attained a new appreciation. It is worth noting that while the Quincentennial generated both pride and fervour, Caymanians were careful not to be intimidating or hostile to members of the British expatriate community. There are, of course, those who would suggest that differences do not exist. The counter to such an argument is that it is a matter of historical record that the very nature of colonialism is predicated upon the differences between the elements (Osterhammel and Frisch 1997, 108). The fact is, too, that of all the various elements making up Caymanian society, the British expatriate element has had the most trouble accepting challenges to their perceived superiority. An example lies in the contention that it is excellence in the modern financial industry which accounts for Cayman's success. There are those who attribute the growth of the modern Cayman Islands to those seamen whose remittances made a modern banking system necessary.

The need for a new paradigm

In his article 'Islands in Comparative Constitutional Perspective', Ronald Watts, commenting on the need to balance self-government and collaboration, commented:

The dual and seemingly contradictory pressures for both autonomous self-government on the one hand and for political partnership on the other are everywhere prevalent in the world today. But nowhere is the need to balance these two sets of perspectives more pervasive than in the situation of island entities (Watts 2000, 17).

Watts is correct in observing that the major challenge facing the self-governing islands (including the Cayman Islands) is the ability to balance their designed self-government with the United Kingdom's version of political partnership. In the Cayman Islands this balance is becoming more difficult to maintain since the administering power has been laying down strict dictates which preclude a full exploration of self-determination. Commenting on this relationship, the *Caymanian Compass* (July 22, 2003) editorialised under the title 'A Question of Autonomy':

The Cayman Islands are inexorably approaching confrontation with the Government of the United Kingdom.

It is a question of autonomy and how far should a colonial administration go in making decisions on the affairs of a local population. This has to be balanced against a backdrop of the fact that the world is in the 21st century and people want to throw off any shackles of the past.

The fast maturing people of the Cayman Islands are becoming increasingly impatient with London pulling strings on most decisions of importance.

That the *Compass* editors chose such language to describe the Caymanian position vis-á-vis the United Kingdom tells us that times were indeed changing. It has become increasingly obvious that the Cayman Islands will not easily accept every dictate from London. The moral and philosophical divide between the administering power and the colony had its genesis in the Cayman Islands' refusal to legalise consensual sexual intercourse between same-sex adults in private. The administering power was left with no alternative but to impose such legislation on the Cayman Islands through an Order-in-Council.

In a similar situation, the *Caymanian Compass* (July 25, 2003) carried the headline 'House says no to governor's order'. This headline captured the disposition of the Cayman Islands Legislative Assembly when it rejected that section of the Terrorism Bill which would have given the governor the power to order telephones to be tapped and private conversations to be eavesdropped on.

In the article, explaining the government's opposition to the United Kingdom's insistence that this power be vested in the governor, the leader of government business commented:

> Therefore, what we do here today, in all good conscience, and for the best interest of our people, we recognise because of our weak constitutional order which gives no protection against the intrusion of the UK into people's basic human rights to privacy, and as the people's duly elected representatives, we can do more than what we are doing. And that is to say No to the Governor's Order in Cabinet and to the FCO's order to him.

In its editorial in the same issue, entitled 'Sacrosanct rights', the editor commented, 'As members have borne in mind the backdrop for Cayman's fears into allowing tapping of phones ordered directly by the government, albeit as anti-terrorism measures, is the recent Euro Bank Trial. Their fear is that such a measure grants powers that have the potential to be misused.'

The comment, of course, refers to the discovery that the Financial Reporting Unit, with responsibility for investigating financial crimes, was headed by someone who was simultaneously in the employ of British intelligence. According to one commentator,

> It also came to be known that the head of the Financial Reporting Unit employed by our Government was on the payroll of MI6. [It is worth noting that the FRU, which had been a part of the Cayman Islands Police Force, was restructured by the Attorney General to fall directly under the auspices of the Attorney General's Office.] Upon becoming tipped off that a search warrant was to be issued against the head of the FRU (the search warrant resulting from suspicion of interference with the telephones of our judiciary), MI6 instructed him to destroy all evidence that would have implicated the UK Government's involvement. Some brief mention was also made on discovery of the evidence held by the prosecution, of "the London Plan" for the Cayman Islands, which left all in wonder and bewilderment as to the true intentions of the UK Government's relationship with the Cayman Islands. (Harris 2003:4)

That the United Kingdom, the administering power, subverted the Cayman Islands' system and clandestinely operated a spy ring evoked public outcry among all sectors of the Islands' society. In choosing this course of action, the UK government destroyed any belief that the relationship between the Cayman Islands as colony and the United Kingdom as administering power was democratic. In a succinct expression of concern, the *Caymanian Compass* editorial on the Terrorism Bill (July 25, 2003) commented: 'Without an unveiling of all the reasons for the UK Government to pursue this line with the bill, it seems right to endorse that nothing be allowed that might breach further what Cayman has held as sacrosanct – its people's privacy; it does not appear to be paranoia.'

At a time when most British Overseas Territories in the Caribbean are embarking on constitutional reform, it is noteworthy to observe that some aspects of the relationship hardly change. Fergus (2003, 1) put the constitutional modernisation initiatives into perspective when he wrote: 'Over the past 30 years none of the Caribbean British Overseas Territories (BOTS) has made any vigorous or sustained agitation for constitutional modernization which in this paper connotes advancement in self-government and self-determination.'

The situation for the Overseas Territories in the Caribbean has changed in the past decade. In the 1990s, the acknowledged position of the UN Committee on Decolonization was that political independence was the ideal for which colonies should strive. It was generally agreed that developing island countries were to be classed as a new category of territories warranting special attention from the international community (Hintjens 1995, 25–26).

On September 13, 1977, two members of the Cayman Islands Legislative Assembly presented the Cayman Islands' position to a mission from the UN Special Committee on Decolonization. The position was that 'Caymanians are content with the present constitutional state of affairs, and there is a strong feeling of allegiance to England and Her Majesty Queen Elizabeth II' (Lawrence 1977, 12).

That allegiance, elsewhere described as voluntary colonialism, emanated from the Caymanian disposition that power is as much about economic well-being as it is about political sovereignty. Strong evidence of voluntary colonialism is implicit in the statement that 'any contemplation of constitutional change would promote unrest among the Caymanian people and lead to great social problems' (ibid.).

In concluding his contribution, one member of the Cayman Islands Legislative Assembly reaffirmed the loyalty of the Caymanian people to the Queen and categorically reported 'the people's desire to remain a Crown Colony with no constitutional change at this time' (ibid.).

The chairman, in presenting the mission's report to the Special Committee, described the 'no change' view as 'realistic and practical': 'It would seem to me to be a realistic and practical approach when one considers the size of the territory and the paucity of resources notwithstanding the facts that these elements alone should not impede political progress.' In conclusion, he noted:

> The political wisdom and their sensitivity to political developments in the region and, indeed, far beyond, did not pass unnoticed. In outlining their views, as the Report indicates in numerous instances, the people and their elected representatives informed the mission of their happy relationship with the administering power (the United Kingdom) and explained how their current links had endured over the years. (Ibid.)

Voluntary colonialism was forged at the breakup of the West Indies Federation, when Jamaica opted for independence in 1962, and it was the informed choice of the Cayman Islands. Out of this concept emerged a metaphorical relationship between 'mother' (the administering power) and 'child', the Cayman Islands.

Given that the relationship has had some disadvantages, it was the persistence of the Caymanian legislators that enabled the system to work. Initially, there was a reluctance among the Caymanian merchant elite to subscribe to any association in which they stood to lose their advantageous position to unknown outside elements. In addition, as Fergus (2003, 2) states, 'It may not be an exaggeration to say that the relative disinterest in independence stems in some instances partly from lack of trust in local politicians, which can also be interpreted as lack of self-confidence.'

As the instrument of politicisation, this metaphorical mother/child relationship grew out of an unquestioning obedience and deference on the part of the 'native' children to the mother's authority. Such deference is given to a superior entity whose benevolent intentions are interpreted by governors sent from the mother country. It is paradoxical that one man, being a loyal citizen representative of the administering power, whose authority he is sworn to uphold, can be expected to so ably and devotedly represent a minor jurisdiction whose public coffers pay his salary and maintain his residence.

Such a relationship represents a power dynamic which at the best of times is problematic and which in times of challenge and controversy borders on philosophical immorality. Skilfully concocted, this 'maternal' bond has evoked powerful and appealing images – images that revolve around the central idea of the weak, vulnerable young being aided and nurtured in its quest for survival and success by a strong, yet extraordinarily benevolent, force.

It is a metaphor which has served British colonialism well in the Cayman Islands. Metaphorical linkages between colonialism and maternal authority are, of course, as old as colonialism itself. In recent years, however, many politically discerning people have come to realise that a new paradigm is needed, one in which the administering power shares political responsibility and relaxes its financial supremacy and political dominance.

Historically, the most significant occurrence in this metaphorical relationship took place during the British war against Argentina over the Falkland Islands. At that time, in a show of loyalty and devotion to the administering power, a number of influential Caymanians launched a 'Mother Needs Your Help' fund. In short order, this drive netted $1 million, a sum that was contributed to the United Kingdom for the war effort.

Armed with such conceptions of loyalty and generosity in the service of a perceived moral authority and imperialism, it was relatively easy for the leaders of the administering power to cast themselves as filling the role of motherly guardians to immature and weak – but loyal – 'natives'.

In 1996, the UK secretary of state, the Hon. Malcolm Rifkind, sent a letter to Hubert Hughes, Chief Minister of Anguilla. This letter, which became known as the Rifkind letter, was written to deal with two specific problems. It began by saying that 'considerable improvements are being made in the administration of the territories and their good government', and promised 'a more detailed account of HMG's policy in this area and to propose a basis for discussions, should these prove to be necessary'. The secretary clearly articulated the administering power's authority:

Firstly, let me emphasise that for these territories for which independence is an option HMG's position remains that it is for the people of the Dependent Territories to decide whether to become independent or to remain constitutionally dependent. The only change is that in future continued dependence may, in some cases, require that there should be an extension of those reserve powers which may, if necessary, be exercised by the Governor, with my approval. This is because experience has shown that over the years, constitutional advance, particularly in Anguilla, BVI and Montserrat, has meant that as Secretary of State, responsible to the U.K. Parliament for the good government of a Dependent Territory, I no longer have the necessary powers to ensure that I am able to fulfil my undoubted obligations in respect of a Dependent Territory, which have increased considerably, e.g. in respect of the observance of international conventions, the adoption of measures to combat drug trafficking and money laundering and the containment of contingent liabilities which may arise.

Whether extended reserve powers prove to be necessary or not will depend on the acceptability or otherwise of the future conduct of public affairs in the territory concerned. I am confident that it is your aim as well as that of HMG, to provide good government. Only if standards of government and the conduct of public affairs fall below acceptable standards would it be necessary to hold discussions with the government concerned about actions needed. This would include the possibility of restoring to the Governor the power, with my approval, to reject the advice of the Executive Council if he considers it would not be expedient in the interest of public order, public faith or good government to accept such advice; and the power, also with my approval, to pass new or amending legislation if the Legislature refuses to do so and if such legislation is necessary in the interest of the public order, public faith or good government.[5]

The excerpts from the Rifkind letter make it clear that the metaphorical relationship referred to previously exists only to the extent that the 'mother', the administering power, holds the option of acting in the best interest of the 'child', the dependent territory. Such a relationship can never accommodate notions of parity, equality, or democracy to enable true dialogue and participatory decision-making.

The insinuation is that Her Majesty's Government wishes to prepare the governor to intervene at the slightest sign of malfeasance on the part of the elected ministers in the Dependent Territories. Fergus (2003, 1) is instructive in detailing the disposition of the administering power with regard to the constitutional authority given to governors versus that held by elected officials: 'Power is partly about economic control, and therefore whether the Governor or an elected minister commands the international finance portfolio, for instance, becomes an important issue ... HMG insists on colonial subordination 'to its international obligations for combating fraud and money laundering.'

Interestingly, on the issue of constitutional modernisation there have been no significant attempts on the part of the administering power to devolve the powers of the governor. Fergus comments about Montserrat: 'They have left the powers of the Governor virtually intact ... Montserratians are not prepared to give the CM or any other Minister responsibility for the public service and the independence of the judiciary and avoid their politicization' (Fergus 2003, 11).

It appears that the administering power's opinion of the abilities of officials in the Overseas Territories is still moulded by an ethnocentric nineteenth-century perspective marked by distrust and suspicion. Confirmation can be found in the Minutes of the Fifth Ministerial Group on the Dependent Territories, held at the Foreign and Commonwealth Office in May 1994. This meeting is of interest for a number of reasons, not the least of which is the fact that there were no elected representatives present from the Dependent Territories. At that meeting, Mark Lennox-Boyd, parliamentary under-secretary of state, outlined the local constraints in the Dependent Territories as 'a lack of civic awareness'. He went on to remark that 'Talent was limited' and that 'there was a need to engage local people in the political and development process'.[6]

In reference to the Country Policy Plans, one representative from the FCO suggested that 'it was now time to exert more pressure, first of all on DT politicians and then civil servants. No doubt local resistance would be encountered but providing we maintained the partnership approach, we could not press hard. We need to eliminate the dependency culture in the DT.[7]

The foregoing, when taken with the suggestion that 'HMG needed to guard against inculcating high quality Western standards in the DT which could not be sustained', calls into question the sincerity of FCO officials in their dealings with the Dependent Territories' politicians and civil servants. If there was any uncertainty about the intentions of the administering power with respect to the dependency question, it was certainly cleared up by the suggestion that 'It might be possible around 1997 to look at whether the UK should have a permanent and more organic relationship with the Dependent Territories or whether there should be a parting of the ways.'[8]

Several conclusions can be drawn from those suggestions. The first is that democracy, to the extent that it exists, serves only to preserve the administering power's ability to set standards and define the relationship. Second, it seems there was little or no regard in the FCO for elected representatives and some civil servants in the Dependent Territories. It is also clear that, should it prove to be expedient, the administering power will effect a 'parting of the ways', which can only be taken to mean encouraging the Dependent Territory to seek political independence.

In the presence of such attitudes, when the administering power proposes a relationship based on *Partnership for Progress and Prosperity*, the suspicion arises that the administering power's interest is only in its own well-being. 'Democracy', in such a case, exists only to serve the administering power, and any dialogue between the metaphorical mother and child as equals is non-existent or exists only theoretically.

The constitutional advancement exercise which began after the 2000 elections has proven informative if for no other reason than to expose the polity's inability to arrive at a consensus. As of March 2006, no definitive position had been arrived at regarding constitutional modernisation in the Cayman Islands.

The Cayman Islands, in contrast to the other British Overseas Territories in the Caribbean, has displayed no interest in constitutional advancement. Fergus, quoting the National Team, stated: 'Caymanians generally entered the twenty-first century decidedly opposed to constitutional advancement' (2003, 8).

That achieving consensus in the Cayman Islands requires such a laborious effort is the result of several factors, not the least of which is that generations of politicians and representatives have neglected to enlighten their constituents about how the Westminster form of government works. Political behaviour related to constitutional advancement is often characterised by accusation, disingenuousness, and obfuscation. Those proposing constitutional advancement are frequently accused of being power-hungry, seeking independence, and being prone to corruption.

Genuine attempts at necessary reform are hindered by this kind of behaviour, and even where the mechanism for constitutional advancement has been set in place by the governor, as was the case after the general election of 2000, the efforts were hijacked by political duplicity and a failure to put aside partisan differences. The attempts at reform that began after 2000 have been blocked by repeated charges and counter-charges, resulting in no progress whatsoever up until 2006.

Cayman's newspaper headlines provide ample evidence. For instance, the lead story in the *Cayman Net News* on March 20, 2006, was headed 'Constitution talks start'. Three days later, the lead story declared 'Constitution in quandary'. The editorial on March 24 was headed 'Constitutional déjà vu' and asked whether 'political expediency is again running roughshod over the democratic advancement of the Caymanian society'.

Ryan (1999) describes such behaviour as characteristic of Caribbean politics. The accuracy of this observation has over the past two decades been borne out repeatedly on the Caymanian political scene. Far too often, valuable time is lost on political brinkmanship and other non-constructive practices while the electorate languishes in a kind of political wilderness waiting for enlightenment and leadership.

Once again, a furor has erupted over the proposed bill of rights and its placement in relationship to the proposed constitution. A *Caymanian Compass* headline on March 24, 2006, read 'Clergy: Separate Bill of Rights'. The editorial of the same date elaborated: 'It turns out the clergy has a major problem with one of the governing People's Progressive Movement's campaign manifesto undertakings: to support a constitutionally enshrined Bill of Rights'.

The lead story explained that a row had erupted because the opposition had sided with the Cayman Ministers' Association (the clergy) in advocating that the bill of rights be gazetted in a separate law, the rationale being that a constitutionally enshrined bill of rights would ensure that the listed rights could not be easily abrogated.

The Ministers' Association was concerned that the European Union's liberal legislation regarding gay rights and family life (including same-sex marriages) might be foisted upon the Cayman Islands. While such concerns are legitimate, it remains to be seen what position the United Kingdom, as administering power, will adopt. Certainly the United Kingdom will be influenced by its membership in the European Union. The Draft Constitution of 1992 was prefaced by the Fundamental Rights and Freedoms of the Individual. The National Team government removed section 9, 'Protection of Freedom of Conscience' from the document and indicated to the United Kingdom that all else was acceptable. The United Kingdom responded, indicating that it was not prepared to offer any bill of fundamental rights and freedoms that did not include protection of freedom of conscience.

The National Team political directorate was not prepared to change its position; likewise, the UK authorities would not relent. The United Kingdom did not, however, use its authority to impose acceptance. Extrapolating from that history, it seems logical to expect that the United Kingdom will not agree to any bill of fundamental rights and freedoms which can be abrogated by a simple legislative amendment.

As these issues have been accorded wide interpretation by the European Union, it would seem that the People's Progressive Movement political directorate's position vis-á-vis that of the opposition United Democratic Party is logical.

The *Caymanian Compass* (March 27, 2006), in a story headlined 'UK seeks draft Constitution changes', reported on a meeting between FCO representatives and the Cayman Islands Human Rights Committee. According to Minister Alden McLaughlin's report, the United Kingdom suggested more than two dozen changes to the 2003 Draft Constitution, all of which have to do with the fundamental rights and freedoms of the individual. While the minister did not list all of the changes, he was reported as saying, 'The UK is not going to settle for anything less [than a constitutionally enshrined bill of rights] and Cayman should not settle for anything less.'

It is this writer's considered opinion that on this point the United Kingdom will not be prepared to compromise, since their position within the European Union seems to dictate that an expression of individual fundamental rights and freedoms promulgated in any document other than the constitution will be unacceptable.

In the jockeying that often takes place surrounding constitutional talks, the opposition United Democratic Party may have aligned itself with the Cayman Ministers' Association for no other reason than to harness the support of an influential ally. The suggestion of political expediency is borne out by the fact that there is no record of the UDP expressing that fundamental rights and freedoms should be set down in a special law. Since this issue is one of the most controversial in the constitutional advancement debate, if the UDP had been so disposed it certainly would have been aired before now.

If past political debates are any example, one can expect robust argument, political posturing, and island-wide lobbying. By the time the discussions move on to the critical areas of the constitutional talks, the political temperature should have reached fever pitch. The choice may well lie between self-determination with a constitutionally enshrined bill of rights for the bold and a new form of colonialism for the timid and those playing the political expediency game. It is the nature of colonialism to be intransigent; this being the case, one is left to wonder what form democracy will take.

The situation as envisaged by this writer does not preclude the possibility that government and opposition could jettison divisive party positions and work together for an instrument which will serve generations of Caymanians. After such a long hiatus, and with all of the other Overseas Territories having more modern constitutions, the Cayman Islands can ill afford to squander this opportunity.

Colonialism or self-determination: Can democracy be engendered?

When the Caribbean Regional Seminar to Review the Political, Economic, and Social Conditions in the Non-Self-Governing Territories convened in Anguilla on May 20, 2003, it brought renewed enthusiasm and hope. Held under the auspices of the UN Special Committee on the Elimination of Colonialism and attended by ministers representing Overseas Territories governments, members of parliament, representatives from civil society and non-government organisations, and senior FCO officials, it was in the main a representative gathering.

The robust agenda set out the topics to be covered and concluded with recommendations as follows:

(a) Recommendations on advancement of the decolonisation process in the Caribbean and Bermuda; and
(b) Recommendations on the decolonisation process in other Non-Self-Governing Territories.

It was clear that the United Kingdom, as the administering power for the British Overseas Territories present at the conference, placed great importance on the outcome. The fact that it had given consent for the conference to be held in Anguilla, an Overseas Territory, spoke volumes about the administering power's new approach.

That the position of the UN Special Committee on Decolonization had changed since the era of the 1970s, when its agenda was to push for political independence, facilitated the conscientiousness apparent at the conference and, in some respects, the administering power's congeniality. Notwithstanding the appearance of congeniality, however, a certain disequilibrium existed between the United Kingdom, as administering power, and the Cayman Islands, as colony. Harris (2003) articulated this disequilibrium in a presentation given at the seminar. Regarding self-determination (which is interpreted here as the absolute right of the Caymanian people to determine their relationship with the United Kingdom), she stated:

> We [the Caymanian people] have been labouring for generations under the impression that we did not have the absolute right to self-determination as an Overseas Territory. Of particular interest, for example, are the wide ranging powers of the Governor and his appointment of the Attorney General of the Cayman Islands, which we understood from the UK Government to be non-negotiable. This is in contrast to Bermuda which operates as an Associated Jurisdiction with the right to self-determination and thus Self-Government and which includes limited powers of the Governor.

> We have been advised that should we seek a similar constitution, which provides for this level of self-government as an Overseas Territory, we must also take the necessary measures to move towards independence. (Harris 2003, 3)

Harris (2003, 4) went on to mention the position of the United Kingdom and the European Union Tax Savings Directive as it related to the Cayman Islands, and, most current at that time, the roles of the attorney general and the head of the Financial Reporting Unit in the context of the MI6 espionage incident in the Cayman Islands (previously referred to as the Euro Bank debacle).

Any discussion of democracy in that context was clouded by this imbroglio, not to mention the United Kingdom's refusal to give House of Commons representation to its remaining Overseas Territories. According to Harris (ibid.), the Cayman Islands 'now had to take stock of the "Partnership for Progress" that it had with the UK Government'.

If by 'taking stock' she meant that there was a new opportunity to ponder the outcome of such an inflexible association, history informs us that as a colonial people we can expect nothing more. Again I refer to the metaphorical mother/child relationship, in which the 'mother's' ethnocentric arrogance establishes the norms for the relationship. It is the nature of colonialism 'that fundamental decisions affecting the lives of the colonized people (natives) are made and implemented by the colonial rulers in pursuit of interests which are often defined in a distant metropolis' (Osterhammel and Frisch 1997, 15).

Harris (2003, 3) provided further substantiation in reference to the negotiations: 'After lengthy negotiations since 2000 in respect of the OECD, the FATF, FSF and the KPMG report ... the United Kingdom Government then indicated that we were required to implement the EU Tax Savings Directive of the European Community into local legislation.'

Fleming-Banks (2003), commenting on the relationship between the United Kingdom and Anguilla, also categorises the relationship as one of power, in which the administering power 'exercises an unequal authority':

> Call us colony; call us British Dependent Territory; call us British Overseas Territory. The essence of the relationship remains the same – a relationship where there is an unequal exercise of authority by the Administering Power over the Administered Community. The stamp of colonialism is tested against how the governmental relationship works, and not by what name the relationship is described.

> We are of the view that the relationship between Anguilla and the UK is in essence a colonial relationship ... and one from which our right to self-determination entitles us to relief. (Fleming-Banks 2003, 5)

Corbin (2003) acknowledges the constraints of this kind of external control:

> In the case of territories like Bermuda, British Virgin Islands and the Cayman Islands where the economic progress has been steady and sustained, concern for the impact of restrictions from external governance appears more acute. European policy imposed on the offshore sector is the most recent illustration, while provision in the British Territorial policy to the Overseas (Dependent) territories limiting their borrowing authority is another example. (Corbin 2003, 23)

Partnership for Progress and Prosperity is clear in its articulation of the administering power's desire to ensure that borrowing (an important tool in the jurisdiction's ability to maintain expected services) in the

Overseas Territories is done only at its discretion. While acknowledging that 'borrowing is a legitimate tool of government policy ...', the document goes on to say that '... borrowing should only be considered for discrete capital investment projects' (p. 25).

It is this writer's opinion that the financial oversight on the part of the administering power in relation to the Cayman Islands amounts to an intrusion into a realm in which the Cayman Islands have an excellent record. The fact that the Cayman Islands have never been grant-aided makes the intrusion even more difficult to understand and accept.

It would seem that from as early as 1992 the administering power had the financial situation in the Overseas Territories under review, as stated in the document *Contingent Liabilities in the Dependent Territories.*

> In light of the comments made by the Committee of Public Accounts when they took evidence on the contingent liabilities in the Dependent Territories in 1992, the Foreign Office set up a Ministerial Group on the Caribbean Dependent Territories to co-ordinate existing and future activities, and to harness expertise in Whitehall to help their economic, social and political development. (p.1)

For the Cayman Islands, this exercise has culminated in the services of two officers from the FCO who visit the colony periodically for appraisals and consultations with the governor and other bureaucratic and political entities. The work of these officials is not always a useful adjunct to what is being achieved in the Cayman Islands. On the contrary, it sometimes seems more of a distraction than a complement. In a not unusual high-handed and arrogant representation, a communiqué from the FCO to the governor (July 25, 2003) reiterated the applicability of the borrowing guidelines to the Cayman Islands. Further, the communiqué suggested that the Cayman Islands government had no tradition of sound financial management. Its concluding statement amounted to the fact that the recent past showed that fiscal management was clouded by a series of poorly considered decisions.

The communiqué goes on to explain the administering power's position with regard to the charge that a 'rigid framework' has been imposed upon the Cayman Islands. That such impositions are made on the Cayman Islands, which prides itself as 'a responsible financial jurisdiction', calls into question the relationship between the United Kingdom, as administering power, and the Cayman Islands as a responsible Overseas Territory.

There are those who consider this and other similar impositions nothing more than attempts at recolonisation. The inauguration of the *Partnership for Progress and Prosperity* suggests that additional demands are being placed upon the Overseas Territories. Two such demands have bearing on culturally sensitive areas within the Overseas Territories – homosexuality and capital punishment.

As the *Partnership* document outlines:

> Homosexuality:
> We believe that all the Overseas Territories should enact legislation similar to the U.K. Sexual Offences Act 1967 which legalised homosexual acts between consenting adults in private. None of the Caribbean Overseas Territories has brought its legislation into line with the Act ... there is particularly strong opposition to homosexuality, based upon firmly held religious beliefs.

> Capital Punishment:
> In 1991 the U.K. abolished capital punishment for murder in the Caribbean Dependent Territories by Order in Council.

The fact that decriminalisation of homosexuality and abolition of capital punishment had to be imposed on the Caribbean Overseas Territories by Orders-in-Council is evidence of the cultural differences which exist between the administering power and its colonies. That exercise informs us that the administering power will not flinch from exercising its dominance in enforcing what it perceives as being in the best interest of the colonies.

There is widespread resentment of the unilateral actions of the administering power, and Fleming-Banks captures its essence:

> [I]t is from this perspective that we strongly protest against the use of Orders in Council which indicate how we should think and what moral values should stand at our core. We reject Baroness Amos's (the former Under-Secretary of State with responsibility for the Overseas Territories) suggestion that we "should display the best features of being British". Such legislative over-lording by its very nature denies the people of the Territories the highly valued right to self-determination. (Fleming-Banks 2003, 7)

The foregoing should serve to confirm the belief that in the Cayman Islands, as in the other Overseas Territories, an 'island ethos' exists. Such an ethos is related not only to the concerns of continued economic stability but also to the shared quest to operate within a relationship with the administering power that allows for self-determination, in all its ramifications, to be explored.

It is relevant to examine briefly the history of the Cayman Islands' colonial connection. Lewis sets the stage:

> A century of Jamaican tutelage after 1863 produced a hodgepodge of constitutional arrangements deserving of the fullest benthamite scorn. The early spontaneous evolution, as in Belize, of a primitive democracy shaped by a community of stragglers lying outside the sphere of official colonial policy was gradually replaced, after 1898, by a system of government by Jamaican administrative and judicial officials. But it was rarely exercised ... especially by Jamaican Governors who rarely visited the islands despite the odd fact that official contract, by law, was with them ...

> It is significant that changes, when they did come after 1945, were the accidental consequence of constitutional developments ... as well as of the new conditions created by the West Indies Federation. (Lewis 1968, 332)

Caymanian society, owing to its isolation and lack of economic importance, did not benefit from the recognition that the administering power gave to other Caribbean colonies whose existence catered to Britain's needs or wants. Like Belize, the Cayman Islands developed their own version of 'frontier democracy' in the circumstances of benign neglect in which they found themselves.

The Cayman Islands arrived on the threshold of modernity in 1959, when they were granted the first written constitution. With the break up of the short-lived federation in 1962, the Cayman Islands were placed in a precarious position.

The decision to sever connections with Jamaica and to seek a made-in-Cayman path led to voluntary colonialism, or continuing association with the administering power, and an emphasis on economic progress rather than social and political well-being. Over the years, and especially in the past decade or so, there has been growing interest in self-determination among certain elements in Cayman society.

The political directorate that was sworn into office following the 2000 general election bore none of the hallmarks of its predecessor.

After a charged campaign in which modernisation, transparency, education, immigration, and inclusion were the focal points, the newly elected members served notice of their intention to work assiduously. Upon assuming office, the newly formed political directorate made it publicly known that there would be no evading the thorny issue of constitutional modernisation, if that was the wish of the people.

In the recent past, the National Team government of 1996–2000 had refrained from tackling the matter of constitutional modernisation even though the United Kingdom, as administering power, had in 1992 forwarded to the Cayman Islands a draft constitution based on the *Report of the Constitutional Commissioners 1991* (Smith and Wallace 1991).

With its provision for a chief minister and a leader of the opposition as constitutionally entrenched positions, the draft constitution appeared to have the potential to propel the Cayman Islands into the modern era of political administration. In the end, however, the National Team political directorate rejected modernity and opted for several piecemeal amendments to the existing constitution, a description of which is contained in the chapter 'From Columbus to the Present: Caymanian History within the Larger West Indian Complex'. The most significant difference was the identification of the leader of the majority group by the title of 'leader of government business'. Such is the situation which obtains as of March 2006, where the leader of the majority party assumes the position of de facto chief minister but is officially titled only leader of government business.

In discussing the awkwardness that arises when trying to maintain a balance between the pressures for self-government and political partnership, one writer states:

> The dual and seemingly contradictory pressures for both autonomy and self-government on the one hand and for political partnership on the other are everywhere prevalent in the world today. But nowhere is the need to balance these two sets of pressures more pervasive than in the situation of island entities – not just for the islands of the North Atlantic but for the many islands elsewhere. (Watts 2000, 17)

Commenting on the contemporary conditions which have arisen out of this interest in autonomy and partnership, Watts further writes:

A notable trend at the end of the twentieth century affecting not only the islands but all polities has been the increasing recognition of the sovereignty of nation states. More and more, the concept of the sovereign nation state has been coming to be regarded as obsolete. The result has been what some scholars have come to refer to as a paradigm shift from a world of nation states to a world of constitutionally confederal or federal character. (p. 17)

Watts (2000) goes on to mention international trends toward state sovereignty and the 'motivation for smaller, self-governing political units' which have been 'accentuated by the desires to make governments more responsive to the individual citizen and to give expression to primary group attachments such as linguistic and cultural ties ... which provide the distinctive basis for a community's sense of identity and yearning for self-determination' (p. 17).

It is this 'yearning for self-determination' that demands exploration. It is striking that of all the offerings that the United Kingdom has made to the Overseas Territories, none has varied from the traditional continuum of self-government to independence. In other words, British colonialism has not moved far beyond where it was when, at its peak, Lord Curzon was viceroy of India.

Constitutional modernisation must, above all, result in a redefining of colonial relations and the introduction of a new identity. To achieve this, the process must must engage the territories' citizens in a national dialogue on the nature of the relationship and the political paradigms that emanate from such a relationship.

Given the reality of an increasingly informed political elite, more and more people are beginning to sense the need for some form of political partnership that would combine aspects of shared rule for specified common purposes with autonomous self-government for purposes related to maintaining regional or island distinctiveness.

It is obvious from the comments of various figures on the Caymanian political landscape that the 2002 constitutional proposal falls short of expectations (*Caymanian Compass*, June 9, 2003, July 25, 2003; *Cayman Net News*, June 10, 2003). In an editorial published on June 9, 2003, the *Caymanian Compass* stated:

It now seems that the boundaries of autonomy may not be carved in stone as most of us have believed over the years. There may be more fluidity than we previously thought.

It is right that the options should be explored, especially now while we are in the middle of a constitutional modernization process.

Interest in the constitutional modernisation process was renewed in 2003 largely as a result of the Cayman Islands Chamber of Commerce inviting the chairman of the UN Committee on Decolonization to speak. But there has been no corresponding effort on the part of the United Kingdom to inform the Cayman Islands of any options (other than the traditional) which they may wish to exercise. The administering power has never made any attempt to pursue an innovative relationship. Even the much-promoted *Partnership for Progress and Prosperity* document bore no signs of divergent thinking.

That this is so at a time when globalisation has unleashed polarising economic and political forces which influence a jurisdiction such as the Cayman Islands to consider protectionist legislation to shield its citizens from competition is not surprising. The political directorate of the People's Progressive Movement has redrafted the Immigration Law. It remains to be seen how the long-term developmental interests of the Cayman Islands will be served by an insular or xenophobic position. It would be a mistake to respond to the immediate problem by sacrificing long-term ambitions and objectives for the short-term glamour of a false political success. Education and training should be harnessed to empower Caymanians for competition in a globalised world. Such empowerment will also serve Caymanians well when the time comes (as it eventually will) to vote with their feet.

Clearly, the Cayman Islands will have to deal with the phenomenon of globalisation, since its economic umbilical cord is intricately woven into international financial regulatory agencies. Ohmae (1995, 18) writes:

> The temptation for old-fashioned government policy makers is to view such a desegregation of effort as a necessary evil that has to be tolerated. To some extent, this is an entirely predictable response to the loss of control by people used to control – or, at least, to the illusion of control. But it also reflects their suspicion about the true ends towards which the centrifugal forces are being directed.

In many respects, Ohmae has mirrored the Caymanian predicament as reflected in the challenges surrounding globalisation and the role expatriates play in Caymanian society. There are influential established Caymanians who apparently refuse to make the connection between the continuing growth and development of Caymanian society and expatriates as being worthy of consideration for citizenship.

It is a failure which places human rights, moral obligations, ethics, and a willingness to be inclusive in opposition to fundamental prejudices that display an inherent insularity, if not xenophobia, and ignorance of reality. Such intransigence has not gone unnoticed by officialdom at the FCO.

Indeed, it was just such concerns which prompted FCO officials to remark to two visiting members of the Cayman Islands Legislative Assembly in 1996 that the FCO authorities regretted having granted the Cayman Islands control over the Islands' immigration policies.

Writing in *The Borderless World*, Ohmae (1990, 165) presents a clear description of how such misguided patriotism works.

> In the past, when political leaders found themselves bankrupt of effective policy and no longer able to rally their people, they would wave the flag and try to stir up emotions by appeals to patriotic sentiment ... It wins votes. It makes the enemy concrete and reachable and recommends a weapon that lies ready. It promises relief from an adversary that is neither well understood nor felt to be just. As policy, however, it is misguided. And as the official position of leaders, it is irresponsible.

Clearly there is room for improvement if democracy, human rights, and multiculturalism are to be the foundations of Caymanian society. There is, too, the obligation for the United Kingdom as the administering power to bear the brunt of the responsibility in encouraging a constructive social dialogue between the disparate elements in Caymanian society. In the same way that governors can initiate constitutional modernity exercises, so should they be able to initiate mechanisms for a national dialogue on important social issues such as immigration and the need for social harmony.

The relationship between the United Kingdom and the Overseas Territories could be remodelled to be much more favourable for the Overseas Territories. Just as it denied British citizenship to residents of Hong Kong following the colony's reversion to the People's Republic of China, Britain could craft a more meaningful and more democratic relationship with the Overseas Territories.

While there is no simple formula for arriving at a meaningful threshold from which island political autonomy can be identified, there is also no reason that a partnership and collaboration between the

United Kingdom and the Overseas Territories could be constructed enabling the Overseas Territories to retain substantial autonomy and self-governance. Is this not the model to which Jersey, Guernsey, and the Isle of Man subscribe?

Explorations in a new discipline which has come to be known as 'island studies' hold great promise for developing other alternatives. In proposing exploration of one of these alternatives, Watts suggests that, in examining the concept of federal relationships, a biological taxonomy is appropriate:

> In biology, the term "genus" refers to a category of living things closely related in structure and evolutionary origin. Within a "genus" are a variety of "species", each with distinctive characteristics. The term "federal" is increasingly being taken by political scientists as a "broad genus" referring to a whole variety of political relationships combining elements of "self rule" (autonomy) and shared rule (collaborative partnership), but this "genus" encompasses a broad spectrum of species, ranging through unions, constitutionally decentralized unions, federations, confederations, federacies, associated states, condominiums, leagues and intergovernmental functional agencies. There may also be hybrids of the specific forms aimed at creating practicable workable arrangements. (Watts 2000, 23)

Watts's comments serve as a point of departure from the realm of conventional political constructs. Just as in biology, in federal relationships there should be room for the consideration of various 'species' of association or partnership arrangements. This is especially so in reference to the Overseas Territories and their relationship with the United Kingdom.

It is a failing of both Westminster and Whitehall that the model of British colonial administration did not mutate to meet the changing times. Indeed, the British attitude toward the political directorates and players in the Overseas Territories remains one of distrust of the 'natives'. The United Kingdom as administering power had only one model for its colonies. Unlike France, the United Kingdom offered no equality of citizenship with direct representation. Even when citizenship (without direct representation) was offered, it was done in such a way as not to arouse much interest. And it is common knowledge that racial equality is still a sought-after objective in the United Kingdom.

I believe it is fair to say that Her Majesty's Government should have tried harder to explore avenues for achieving self-determination in the remaining Overseas Territories. Without attempting an exhaustive presentation, I propose to explore some of these avenues, particularly as they could relate to islands.

Consider unions. A union is a polity constructed in such a way that the units preserve their respective integrities primarily through their participation in the common organs of general government rather than through dual government structures. The advantage of this form is that it maximises shared rule at the expense of the autonomy of the constituent islands or communities. New Zealand, Trinidad and Tobago, and St Vincent and the Grenadines are prominent examples of this political model.

Federations are compound polities which combine strong constituent units with a strong general government. Each government is characterised by having sovereign powers delegated by the people through a constitution. Further, each government is empowered to deal directly with its citizens in the exercise of its legislative, administrative, and taxing powers, and each government is directly elected by its citizens. Examples of this kind of federation number 24 and include such countries as Argentina, Australia, Belgium, Canada, the Comoros Islands, Germany, India, Nigeria, the United States, St Kitts and Nevis, and South Africa.

The advantages of federation as a form of political partnership are that it permits a relatively decisive form of shared rule which facilitates the carrying out of redistributive policies. Additionally, because the federal institutions are based on direct election by the citizens, this form of government provides all citizens with an opportunity to participate democratically in the legislative and executive operations of shared rule. The political autonomy of the shared units is limited to those powers assigned to them by the constitution. Such a limitation, however, can be overcome by a supreme constitution, not unilaterally amended by the federal government. As was the case with the short-lived West Indies Federation, the main disadvantage of federations is their tendency toward constitutional complexity, legalism, and rigidity.

The third form of polity to be discussed here is that of 'federacies'. Elazar (1995) used this term to describe an asymmetrical federal relationship in which a smaller unit is linked to a larger polity. In this model a former colonial power is taken as the larger unit, but the smaller unit or units retain considerable autonomy though they have a limited role in government. The large polity is exclusively responsible for foreign affairs, defence and security, and currency, while the smaller polities have autonomy over all domestic matters. Such a relationship can only be dissolved by mutual agreement.

This is the kind of relationship which could be applicable to the United Kingdom and the Overseas Territories. It should appeal to both entities, since this is the current relationship between the Isle of Man and the United Kingdom. An asymmetrical federal association exists whereby the smaller territory has complete internal autonomy and self-government, which allows it to share in the benefits of association without being incorporated as a full-fledged constituent unit.

Such a relationship has a further advantage in that mutual agreement is required for dissolution, thus enabling a more stable attachment than in the case of an associated state, where dissolution may result from a unilateral decision.

The French model exemplified by Martinique, Guadeloupe (including St Martin), and French Guiana is a variation on the above models, and is a textbook case of full potential equality and full representation by the overseas department in the French political system. Such a system of integration is done in compliance with UN General Assembly Resolution 1541 (XV). The implication is that the smaller polities participate fully as an integral part of the French state, including in the European Union (Corbin 2003, 10). The United Kingdom, it seems, does not value the ability of certain Overseas Territories to contribute to their well-being in this regard.

Contemporary interpretations of the UN Committee on Decolonization have so fuelled the constitutional debate in the Cayman Islands that it may be to the advantage of the administering power to allow some exploration of these issues.

Hintjens (1995, xx), in a chapter entitled 'Post-Colonial Conundrums: Caribbean Examples', states:

> 1990 was declared the start of the Decade of the Eradication of Colonialism by the United Nations. To mark the thirtieth anniversary of the Declaration on the Granting of Independence to Colonial Countries and People, two regional seminars were held: one in the Caribbean and one in the Pacific. Island developing countries generally were to be regarded as a new category of territories meriting special attention from the international

community. There was nothing new about the UN's commitment to ending colonialism. What was perhaps more surprising was the willingness to consider alternatives to outright independence in the case of the smaller remaining dependencies.

This willingness to consider alternatives to independence and the specific emphasis on the territories' right to self-determination served the interests of the Caymanian establishment during the constitutional modernisation exercise of 2003–04. There is, however, an inability or unwillingness on the part of the administering power to 'think outside the box' when it comes to constitutional relations with the remaining Overseas Territories. The complexity of this relationship is based on a number of factors, not the least of which is a lack of trust on the part of the administering power. The governor, as the United Kingdom's representative, is held sacrosanct, but no more responsibility is given to elected ministers.

In the Cayman Islands this failure is compounded by the present government's immigration rollover policy, under which only in extraordinary circumstances will extensions be granted for employees to remain in the jurisdiction beyond the initial work-permit period of seven years. This policy requires careful analysis. While the government has the responsibility to legislate for the long-term best interests of Caymanians, it also is responsible for ensuring that the synergistic relationship between expatriates and established Caymanians, which has brought economic success, continues.

Throughout history, many countries and societies were built by outside labour. The great empires relied on foreigners, both as immigrants and settlers and as slaves and prisoners, to build their empires. In the modern era the United States stands out as the greatest example of a nation built by immigrant labour. In the Cayman Islands what is needed is an economic development model which takes into account the contribution of expatriates. There has never been a manpower needs assessment conducted in Caymanian society. That being the case, it is difficult to determine the number of people and the various vocations which the society needs to sustain its economic progress.

In the quest for democracy, the social dialogue between established Caymanians and their expatriate counterparts must remain current and dynamic. Mutual interests should take precedence over political debate about to whom the society belongs. The sociology of societies suggests that it takes generations before a heterogeneous society can achieve a genuine balance, where ethnic and national identities become secondary to the social and economic well-being of the community. The social value that the various groups accord each other, and the interpersonal dynamics that develop as a result, is a primary determinant of the orderliness of the society. It is upon this orderliness in human relations that the essence of democracy depends. For if there are people in the society who are marginalised because they can never gain citizenship, how can they feel that they are valued as much as the accepted groups?

In the normal course of events, intermarriage (between Caymanians and new immigrants), business partnerships, joint ventures, churches, schools, service clubs, and other civic organisations serve as agents of socialisation, bringing the various elements together. These are crucial in breaking down barriers and eliminating the more insidious prejudices.

It is understandable that established Caymanians should feel threatened and overwhelmed by an ad hoc, frequently changed, and poorly articulated immigration policy. Expatriates wishing to work or settle in Caymanian society bear a moral obligation to understand and appreciate the established Caymanian. Similarly, established Caymanians should be encouraged to appreciate the diverse experience, cultural richness, and mutuality of interests that the expatriate has to offer. If some satisfactory accommodation is not reached, Caymanian society can expect to be fractious, with social upheaval a distinct possibility. More emphasis needs to be placed on cultural enrichment, social concerns, and the development of education as a tool for improving the community, and less attention given to wealth creation, indulgence, and the expansion of personal incomes.

The connection between democracy, dialogue, and cultural experience seems not to be known or appreciated. This may be a peculiarity of the frontier society which is the Cayman Islands. The observation is that attitudinal differences between established Caymanians and some expatriates are problematic. Included in such an observation are the nuances of the 'new colonialism' which suggest that the expatriates in Cayman bear sole responsibility for the jurisdiction's success as an international financial centre. These nuances, along with the fear of many established Caymanians that they will become a minority in their own society, must be dealt with in a meaningful way.

Such an exercise may be easier said than done, however, since the social boundaries of the community, obviously influenced by the settlement pattern of most British expatriates into almost exclusive enclaves, do not offer much hope of anything other than an artificial integration. As studies of these kinds of settlement patterns show, the tendency is not toward integration but rather toward accentuation of differences among the various elements. That fact should call into question the whole process of awarding citizenship under circumstances in which no attempt is made at cultural assimilation.

The arrangement under which Caymanian residency and status (citizenship) are awarded is in essence subversive, since it extracts a monetary sum from each adult recipient for what should be promoted as a privilege, awarded only to the deserving. The practice of charging money for the privilege of citizenship is an exact reversal of sovereignty's intent, and can be interpreted as a mockery of Caymanian values. The apparent efficiencies are likely to be accompanied by long-term society-wide problems, including persistent demands for empowerment by other than established Caymanians, charges of discrimination, and a decrease in the number of small entrepreneurs, who will find it difficult to expand their business interests. As well, the perception of the Cayman Islands as a society accessible only to the super-rich will have to be navigated if true democratic principles are to be engendered.

The problems that have been discussed are potentially overwhelming because they fit well within the unchanging realities of colonialism – the administering power's disregard for the unique and peculiar constructs of Caymanian society; the apparent lack of trust placed in Cayman's elected ministers and senior civil servants; an increasing interference in governance, particularly in the area of human rights; the imposition of threats and pressures upon the financial industry; and, most significant, the power to impose Orders-in-Council to disallow any local legislation – all serve to highlight the disparity in the relationship. Such power could hardly pass as democratic, unless of course one adopts the most cynical definition of democracy.

The suggestion that the Cayman Islands move to a 'one man, one vote' electoral system, as proposed in the Constitutional Modernization Review (2002), is certainly a valid one which should be embraced by the wider society. To give the impression that democracy begins and ends with this achievement only, however, will be tantamount to betrayal.

At a time when established Caymanians are feeling threatened by rapidly changing economic pressures, population explosion through the absorption of new immigrants, and concomitant social and economic relegation, the United Kingdom has chosen to increase political pressure. All of these pressures serve to push the established Caymanian into a position in which citizenship is viewed as an absolute, guaranteed only to the established Caymanian.

The model taxonomy of political forms of self-determination suggests that some form of partnership, rather than political independence, is the route the Cayman Islands should go. This raises obvious questions about the influence of colonialism and the British expatriate element in Caymanian society.

It must be reiterated that the best way forward for the Cayman Islands is as a plural society espousing its own version of democracy. Despite the drawbacks of the political arrangement with the administering power up to this point, there is one fundamental truth: in the current situation, neither dependence nor outright independence offers the most pragmatic path to follow. Democracy, it is suggested, is not limited to 'one man, one vote' packages but in the ability of a people to determine the kind of system or association which they wish to have with the administering power. Given that we live in a diverse world in which there are varying forms of the democratic ideal, the administering power should accord greater importance to the wish of the Caymanian people to articulate their model of self-determination, free from interference and intimidation.

The skies have been promising a new day for some time now, but each time they have opened into a false dawn. Once again, under the political directorate of the People's Progressive Movement, the political skies are showing signs of activity. There have been several calls for the consideration of constitutional modernisation leading to greater self-determination, with full recognition of the administering power's concern for human rights, good governance, an impartial civil service, and an independent judiciary.

Just how the concerns of the United Kingdom are going to play out against the call by the Caymanian populace for greater self-determination remains to be seen. One thing seems certain: this new Caymanian posture should serve to inform the administering power that the Cayman Islands have matured from a sleeping political backwater to the vanguard of modernity. It is a position finally in congruence with the progressive economic stature of the Islands.

Chapter 4

Banks, Hedge Funds, and Trusts:
The Rise and Fall of the Cayman Islands as an International Financial Centre

This chapter represents the efforts of one who is neither a practitioner nor a theoretician in the field of finance. It is, rather, the offering of an observer whose disposition is neither flawed by proximity to the subject matter nor coloured by the need to impress readers so as to maintain an established reputation.

The writer's objective is to avoid legal and technical jargon and to follow a simple, easily understandable line. What is proposed is to trace the beginnings of the tax-haven concept in the Cayman Islands and to progress to the state of the industry as it is today. In its rise to prominence among international financial centres, the Cayman Islands' rate of ascent has been phenomenal. It was only in the 1950s that the Islands were opened to international banking, and in 1957 Barclays Bank DCO opened its first branch in the Cayman Islands (Crossley and Blanford 1957, 314).

In the years since, the Islands have become home to over 500 banks, including 20 of the world's largest (*Financial Times,* July 16, 2001), numerous mutual-fund management and captive insurance companies, and a much-sought-after market in the creation of hedge funds and the segregated portfolio company (SPC), a vehicle created for the captive insurance business. Not surprisingly, the jurisdiction has received some negative publicity, been associated with major international financial scandals, come into disfavour with the Organisation for Economic Cooperation and Development (OECD) in 1998, and been blacklisted by the Financial Action Task Force (FATF) in 2000.

Despite these setbacks, the Cayman Islands are, at present, one of the best-regulated international financial centres. As an offshore centre, its practices have recently earned accolades following inspections by the International Monetary Fund (2005) and Moody's Investor Service (2004). So meticulous and thorough are the standards in the jurisdiction that it is easier to open a bank account in London or New York than in the Cayman Islands. Concomitant with this strict regulation has been a change in focus from individual to corporate business – including in the banking industry, where private banking is now discouraged unless applicants are established international entities or can provide credible references from internationally accepted referees.

Contrary to what many may think, it is not preposterous to write of the fall of the Cayman Islands as a major international financial centre. Over the course of the past two decades since it emerged as a major financial centre, Cayman has had to make major adjustments to its *modus operandi* to maintain credibility and standing. Each time challenges were encountered, the jurisdiction, like a chameleon, changed operational practices to meet the required criteria.

Consider that each time requirements changed, the jurisdiction sacrificed some of its original appeal. Having met the demands of the OECD and FATF, the Cayman Islands were most recently engaged in a contest with the United Kingdom over the European Union Tax Savings Initiative and other issues.

These are such profound issues that some fear that, should the United Kingdom be less than generous, the Cayman Islands as a major international financial centre will be a spent force. It is unlikely that the jurisdiction will come to a sudden demise, but it may simply become less attractive. Should this be the case, many financial-services firms currently operating in the jurisdiction will move elsewhere.

Many of these large firms, while expanding operations in the Cayman Islands, are also cognisant of the realities of globalisation and are adjusting to meet its contingencies. As a result, most, if not all, of the larger and more prestigious firms now have personnel who specialise in litigation. Formerly, these firms concentrated solely on corporate and financial matters. In addition, these firms have now expanded to overseas jurisdictions such as Hong Kong, Dubai, London, and Jersey.

Such expansion, while seen as an attempt to maintain competitiveness and prestige, can also be interpreted as a hedge against any economic downturn in the Cayman Islands. The provision of prestigious international financial services in Cayman has been monopolised by expatriate legal firms incorporated in the Cayman Islands. Comparatively speaking, there is a conspicuous under-representation of law firms owned by established Caymanians in the field of providing international corporate business services.

While this observation has nothing to do with the quality of service delivered, it does speak volumes about the sensitive situation of established versus expatriate Caymanians. It has been suggested that a barrier exists which prevents established Caymanians from attaining other than token positions in the world of corporate law practice.

If the Cayman Islands are to continue to expand and improve, the jurisdiction's financial operations must be flexible, informed, and capable of reacting very fast. There are, of course, other contingencies that could impinge on Cayman's ability to maintain excellence in a highly competitive world. One such factor has to do with the geopolitics surrounding the European Union and Britain's membership in it. Currently, the United Kingdom is one of a few EU member states that still possesses colonies. France has offered its former colonies the choice of independence or status as a department of the metropolis, as exemplified by Martinique and Guadeloupe.

It is doubtful that the European Union will be so accommodating as to allow the United Kingdom to remain a member and retain the present arrangements regarding its Overseas Territories. What is likely is that other EU members will press the United Kingdom to incorporate its remaining Overseas Territories as France has done or grant them independence. The latter course would relieve the United Kingdom of the need to eliminate them as competitors in the world of international finance.

There are other threats to the jurisdiction's existence, including trafficking in human cargoes, illegal migration, narcotics, terrorism, drugs, criminal gangs and cyber-crime practised by international criminal gangs. Just how safe the Cayman Islands are from international criminals who can tap into the accounts of the financial houses is not publicly known. For years the jurisdiction has been concerned primarily with anti–money laundering measures and has paid little or no attention to cyber-crime and the threat posed by hackers.

Concerns have also been expressed about the impact of globalisation on the Cayman financial centre's ability to maintain its international stature. At the Cayman Business Outlook 2006 many of the presenters referred to the threat of outsourcing and the competitiveness – or lack thereof – of the Caymanian economy. Outsourcing is the practice of having certain non-critical ancillary services performed in jurisdictions where wages and salaries are lower and where there is a ready pool of capable workers.

Given that the excellence of the ancillary services supporting the Cayman Islands' financial industry is essential to the maintenance of a competitive product, it is unlikely that outsourcing of labour from the

Cayman Islands will detrimentally affect the jurisdiction's economy. The financial services industry is so contained that it is strategically important, and necessary for confidentiality and control, for the ancillary services of auditing, accounting, and verifying to be performed in the same jurisdiction as the principal services. Information technology notwithstanding, the financial services industry is based primarily upon confidence, confidentiality, and control.

It therefore is hardly likely that any individual or firm would agree to outsourcing part of a transaction when the entire transaction could be professionally accommodated at the one-stop jurisdiction which is the Cayman Islands. Each time part of a confidential transaction is outsourced, the risk of loss of confidentiality and control is heightened through the possibility of errors in information transfer, negligence in interpretation of data, deliberate actions such as theft or sale of data, missed deadlines caused by communicating across time zones, and sabotage of transactions by computer hackers.

The most convincing evidence that the Cayman Islands will remain an attractive jurisdiction in spite of outsourcing comes from the authoritative *Global Competitiveness Report 2005–2006*. The report, published by the World Economic Forum in Geneva, Switzerland. is immensely informative about economic development. It is interesting to note that, despite their stellar performance in terms of economic development, in the global competitiveness ranking China and India rank only 49th and 50th respectively out of the 117 countries surveyed. These countries, for all their rapid economic progress, have serious institutional weaknesses.

While this writer does not suggest that China and India are not important players, it is far-fetched to think that their emergence as outsourcing centres will detrimentally affect the Cayman Islands' standing as a leading financial centre. The Cayman Islands, however, have to benchmark their performance against Singapore, among other jurisdictions, if they wish to maintain excellence. According to the *Global Competitiveness Report,* Singapore holds the number one position in terms of quality of institutions and technological readiness. Singapore also performs creditably in terms of ethics, protection of property rights, control of corruption, and government efficiency. Among the 117 countries assessed, Singapore is top-rated for its high Internet penetration, high level of technological innovation by firms, and its highly sophisticated information and communications technology environment. Already possessing one of the world's largest shipping registries, Singapore was tipped by *Forbes* magazine (January 2006) to surpass Switzerland as the world's premier banking centre within the next decade.

Given Singapore's Confucian ethic, social engineering, and early start, it is doubtful that a jurisdiction such as the Cayman Islands could equal or surpass its economic development record in the near future. Nonetheless, Cayman does have a competitive advantage over many of its rivals. Regarded as an innovator in the range and sophistication of financial instruments offered, the Cayman Islands also compare well in terms of high-quality institutions, technological innovation, high Internet penetration, government efficiency and an absence of bureaucracy in the financial services sector, a highly regulated business environment, excellent communications, a sound economy, and stable politics.

The most engaging and intellectually challenging developments the Cayman Islands will have to address in the immediate future are the Caribbean Single Market and Economy (CSME) and globalisation. In the case of the CSME, Cayman is currently an associate member of the Caribbean Community (CARICOM), and the political directorate has stated that there is no intention to seek full membership.

Full membership in CARICOM could, however, eventually bring the Cayman Islands new economic advantages. Among CARICOM countries, the Bahamas and the Cayman Islands have the most sophisticated financial centres. With the Bahamas opting out of the CSME, there seems to be a need for a reputable financial centre to absorb the business emanating from the CSME organisation itself. Given the nature of the market, it is unlikely that the membership would route such transactions to a jurisdiction other than one in their own organisation. While there *may* be challenges brought about by the small size of the Cayman Islands and its consequent inability to absorb large numbers of economic migrants, there is no empirical evidence to suggest that such would be the case.

Globalisation poses a quandary for the Cayman Islands. It is posited here that one of the first manifestations of this phenomenon is likely to be that educated and trained Caymanians are going to begin to exercise their option of 'voting with their feet'. In a highly competitive and often prejudicial employment atmosphere like that of the Cayman Islands, it should come as no surprise when Caymanian university graduates on scholarships abroad do not return following graduation. For years the Cayman Islands experienced the success of having 100 per cent of these graduates return. Now, however, in fields such as accounting, management, and information and communications technology, many young people are becoming frustrated with the employment practices of firms in the Cayman Islands. Only a few of these establishments demonstrate willingness to accord Caymanian graduates more than token acceptance. By far the worst record is that of the law firms, with their host of expatriate partners and staff. The daily newspapers provide vivid examples of non-Caymanian preference, with their pictures of ruddy-faced expatriates being called to the bar in the presence of equally ruddy-faced expatriate jurists and senior staff of the sponsoring firm. Only the token Caymanian graduate of the Islands' law school is accorded such privilege. Most, it seems, are left to find their own way to make a livelihood in the highly competitive world of criminal law practice.

This assault by the forces of globalisation on personnel perceived, by those steeped in cultural imperialism, to be poorly trained and prepared leaves the trainees bitter, confused, and disoriented. It should come as no surprise, then, when critics of Cayman's economic development complain of 'foreign capital, orchestrated by foreign expertise and implemented in large measure by foreign labour' (Iton 2006). Other criticisms, expressed by both established Caymanians and expatriates, have to do with erosion of labour rights and rising inequality.

Finally, some significance must be attached to the observation that, for all its sophistication in certain areas, the Cayman Islands as a jurisdiction is woefully inadequate in some legislation. For example, at the time of writing there is no legislation protecting against insider trading, there are no provisions for public disclosure or protection of whistleblowers, and there is no legislated protection against identity theft, intellectual property theft, and similar forms of white-collar crime. In the first-ever economic crimes survey, the Cayman Islands Chamber of Commerce expressed concern that 'business owners and managers still aren't comfortable dealing with economic crimes'. An article headlined 'Economic crime hits Cayman' in the *Caymanian Compass* on June 29, 2006, reported that 'The study covered the areas of asset misappropriation, bribery, cheque and credit card fraud, debit card fraud, identity theft, insurance fraud, insolvency fraud, money laundering and theft.'

While not disclosing the number of respondents, the article stated that the survey was circulated to 525 corporate members. Of these,

'55 per cent were from the financial services sector, 30 per cent from the tourism/retail and 15 per cent from professional services and other firms'.

In a sombre warning, the Chamber's CEO concluded that 'In the worst case scenario, economic crime can have a serious impact on the Cayman Islands' international image and reputation.'

The Chamber's survey, however, for all its good intentions, must be taken with the proverbial grain of salt, for not only was it not scientific, it was also misleading, conveying the impression that certain types of crime in the Cayman Islands go unpunished. It is this kind of misleading information which is used by detractors to sully the reputation of the Cayman Islands.

The Portfolio of Finance and Economics also questioned the survey's validity and reliability. Its critique, appearing in the *Cayman Net News* on July 4, 2006, focused on the validity of the results and questioned the accuracy of the Chamber's interpretations given the limits of the exercise. This commentary also took issue with the Chamber's findings on money laundering, in light of the recent convictions in several high-profile cases. By far, however, the most serious criticism was the charge that the survey's conclusion contradicted the results.

The survey is mentioned here only to indicate the level of concern in the Caymanian business sector with combating white-collar crime, not as evidence that such crime is endemic in Caymanian society. It is due to an unfortunate lack of sophistication that the Chamber published such ambiguous information without proper qualification. Surveys of this nature, when not scientific, should be prefaced by a caveat, and even an organisation as established as the Chamber of Commerce should not feign expertise that it does not possess.

In my opinion, there are two basic jurisdictional weaknesses in the Cayman Islands. One is the absence of any local organisation with expertise and experience in conducting scientific surveys. The second is the lack of legislation and transparency with regard to mergers and acquisitions, liquidation and receivership, and insider trading and similar unethical business practices. In the past there have been many business transactions that in more sophisticated jurisdictions would have been called into question and perhaps been the subject of litigation.

Within the retail banking sector, there is the practice of the so-called clearing banks colluding to set identical rates. This practice renders the system uncompetitive and disadvantageous to the customer and makes these institutions into a virtual cartel. It should be a matter of concern

– and a blight on the reputation of the Cayman Islands, which touts its practices as open – that no mechanisms exist to prevent such an unsavoury practice in the twenty-first century.

Conspicuous by its absence also is legislation covering fair trade and fair competition. In a jurisdiction where competition is keen and there is no shortage of people seeking success, it is no surprise that incestuousness in business practice is often the rule rather than the exception. The recent past has seen a number of critics lamenting the disadvantageous position in which established Caymanians find themselves as clients and patrons. Small wonder, then, that established Caymanians seem to be becoming more cynical about the benefits of economic development as it relates to them.

The most vociferous of these critics say that Cayman's economic development lacks a human face, and that no meaningful social agenda exists. It is a view shared by this writer. However, it is proposed here that, instead of cursing the darkness, ways should be found to light a candle, or candles. While much blame lies at the feet of those who perpetuate a system of 'winner takes all', responsible people must work to ensure that another path becomes visible and available.

Too many people in the professions of law, accounting, management, and information and communications technology fail to grasp that education carries the moral imperative of altruism – that education must be obtained not purely for personal gain but also in the interest of individual and community upliftment and improvement. The Cayman Islands can too accurately be described as 'a BMW and Mercedes society', since it seems that these are the status symbols of the nouveau riche.

Of course, it will take time for the positive effects of education and globalisation to become obvious in the Cayman Islands. It may necessitate legislative changes and social and economic planning. There must, however, be some publicly acceptable timetable for change, in the context of which those described in this book as established Caymanians can feel that they have a vested interest in the society's development.

An article entitled 'Study Launched to Assess Levels of Local Poverty', carried on the front page of the *Cayman Net News* (April 19, 2006), details the intent of the Ministry of Health Services to initiate a comprehensive study of the living conditions of Caymanians. Such an instrument is long overdue. It is crucial to the social dialogue regarding the benefits of development for the lower echelons of established Caymanians.

While many are sceptical of the benefits of globalisation, it is a fact that economic growth in the Cayman Islands is critical to social development and stability, if only because if economic growth is not shared, social stagnation will lead to unrest which will destabilise the society.

The impact of globalisation aside, as far as the Caymanian economy is concerned, it appears as if the policies of the current political directorate will have painful long-term costs. While it is true that the Islands are still recovering from the devastation of hurricane Ivan in September 2004, the economy has shown remarkable resilience.

Now, however, a confusing work-permit policy, rising gasoline prices, an apprehensive populace, and the uncertainties of the proposed constitutional modernisation exercise all cloud the horizon and may impinge on the economic outlook. In any consideration of the Caymanian economy, ignorance of what is happening in the United States is maintained at one's peril; as pundits are fond of saying, 'When the United States sneezes, the Cayman Islands catches a cold.' Should the current trend of skyrocketing oil prices continue, the Cayman Islands will indeed be in jeopardy of 'catching a cold'. High gasoline prices affect everything from airfares to the food Caymanians eat, since the Cayman Islands are totally dependent on imports. This is bound to affect the economy as a whole, in that high airfares could result in fewer stay-over tourists visiting the Islands, and high food costs aggravate an already high cost of living.

Growth in the construction industry has been a stimulus to the Islands' economy over the past few years. While such growth brings considerable advantage to the business houses concerned, the trickle-down effect to rank-and-file Caymanians is negligible. At Cayman Business Outlook 2006 much ado was made about the potential loss to the Cayman Islands' economy through outsourcing, yet there was no mention of the competition that educated and trained Caymanians face from imported white expatriates, who are preferred by the law firms, banks, and accounting houses.

The economic problem is multifaceted, in that there is a high incidence of borrowing – credit-card debt and consumer loans – among middle-class established Caymanians. Many households spend more than they earn. Robust consumer spending boosts GDP growth, but at the cost of a negative personal savings rate, a growing burden of household debt (especially in light of a rising cost of living and higher fuel costs), and a huge current account deficit.

Caycompass.com conducted an online poll to which 291 responses were received. A report in the *Caymanian Compass* newspaper (April 12, 2006) indicated that 64.3 per cent of those polled stated that they are worse off now than they were before hurricane Ivan in 2004. According to the report, 'Higher costs of living since Ivan appear to play a big role in the downturn of economic standing with people.'

The question is to what extent the current economic development is beneficial to established Caymanians, particularly those in the lower socioeconomic strata. In response to such concerns, Andre Iton commented in the *Cayman Net News* (April 24, 2006):

> For the better part of three decades, the Caymanian economy has achieved enviable growth rates on a sustained basis.
>
> Over the same period, the indigenous [*sic*] population has, of its own free will, transferred substantial portions of its patrimony to a select band of wealthy individuals of other nationalities, some of whom have chosen, for economic convenience, to be domiciled here. In the main, the proceeds of the transfer of local ownership of land to others in perpetuity have been converted into lavish dwellings and other ostentatious symbols of success.

Iton goes on to lament the 'material resplendence' and 'insatiable consumption capacity' of the residents. It is the same lament this writer made in 1978. It is a delusion that the Cayman Islands are insulated from the economic shocks experienced periodically by the rest of the world.

Such a delusion is accompanied by an equally pernicious myth: that the Cayman Islands can be preserved by legislating a protectionist path that will ensure that expatriates can never be accepted as Caymanians in Cayman. While there are still issues to be worked out between established Caymanians and their expatriate counterparts, history will judge us harshly if our political classes fail to find the courage to help the society equip itself for the twenty-first century. It is instructive to follow Iton's argument when he cautions that 'a failure to appreciate the relevance of the role of economic self-determination in the process of nation building is done at the peril of those entrusted with the responsibility for management of the state' (Iton 2006).

Past practices have generally been limited to production of economic statistics, which left the public bemused and baffled at the same time. What matters, as many in Caymanian society have come to realise, is the human effect, or what might be called 'Gross National Contentment'. In this regard, nothing matters more than the reduction of poverty and a feeling of belonging to the society. The study proposed by the Ministry of Health Services should provide some indication of the size of the task at hand, providing, as it will, raw data to guide physical improvements.

In spite of skewed development objectives and the fact that the society has been built on banking and financial transactions originating outside of the Cayman Islands, the case can be made for the Cayman Islands to be a textbook model. The argument is enticing; let us explore it in detail.

How did the jurisdiction rise from its rudimentary tax-haven beginning to its current position of financial prominence? Although – as might be expected in any frontier society – there were occasions when large sums of cash were accepted on deposit from the bearers on the shortest of notices, often with an absence of protocol, such is certainly not the case any more. Cayman has volunteered to regulate itself and has an established record of meticulousness and discretion.

Beginning in the 1970s, when the drug trade between South, Central, and North America began to flourish, it is probable that traffickers took advantage of the lack of sophistication of the Islands' authorities. On at least one occasion, a self-proclaimed expert, in testimony before the US Senate Foreign Relations Subcommittee on Terrorism, Narcotics, and International Operations, claimed to have 'bribed military and elected officials in many countries' including the Cayman Islands (Powis 1992, 135).

The Cayman Islands, however, acting as a surrogate of the United Kingdom, once having recognised its vulnerability to international narcotics traffickers and money launderers, entered into a treaty with the United States in 1984. This was the first cooperative exercise in this area, described by Elizabeth Davies:

> The location of the Cayman Islands is such that those involved in the transportation of illegal drugs from South America and Central America into North America may seek to make use of the islands as part of their transshipment routes for these narcotics. ... Further it was learned that drug dealers might be taking advantage of the

Cayman Islands' strict confidentiality laws to conceal evidence of their dealings by using bank accounts in the Cayman Islands. In 1984, in an endeavour to eliminate any such funds from local banks, a Treaty was entered into between the United States and the United Kingdom, including the Cayman Islands, which allows the United States authorities in appropriate cases, to have access to certain evidence which would otherwise be classified as confidential, and thus unattainable. (Davies 1989, 3–4).

The Mutual Legal Assistance Treaty (MLAT), as it was called, was a landmark piece of legislation that served as the precursor to all such legislation since that time. It had the desired effect, since cases brought under its scope took precedence over that bastion of secrecy, the Confidential Relationships (Preservation) Law 1976.

The MLAT did not directly compromise the Confidential Relationships (Preservation) Law 1976 (and later 1979). What the treaty legislation permitted was application for access to certain information, after the applicant had convinced the grand court that there was criminal conduct. However, there was some concern in financial circles that business would be adversely affected.

In the event, the businesses that were at risk through the possibility of such exposure relocated to less meticulous jurisdictions. This undertaking represented the first internationally significant attempt by the Cayman Islands to establish itself as a reputable jurisdiction within the international financial community.

The departing business did not adversely affect Cayman's economic stability. In fact, the flight gave the Cayman Islands an opportunity to draw attention to itself as a jurisdiction prepared to lead the way in establishing standards and practices which were in the best interest of international finance. It also served to inform detractors that Cayman was so firmly entrenched as a financial centre that the withdrawal of shady capital could not threaten its ability to continue.

The success of such a financial centre depended on the ability to provide professional, high-calibre service in the minimum time. An important corollary was that the telecommunications and air travel infrastructure had to facilitate instant access to international markets. It was to these markets that the authorities turned shortly after detailing the agenda to set the Cayman Islands up as a leader in international finance.

The logic of history and some sensationalism

Globalisation has weakened the ability of countries to control their economies. Improvements in communications and information technology mean that with the click of a mouse billions of dollars can be moved around the world and multimillion-dollar trusts can be established. An irrevocable letter of credit can be opened in a Cayman Islands bank on instructions from a corporation in London, to purchase a tanker load of crude oil on a ship leaving the Gulf straits for Philadelphia, without the principals ever having set foot in the Cayman Islands. This scenario is typical of the intricate financial transactions to which an offshore financial centre such as the Cayman Islands is accustomed.

Such sophistication in the Cayman Islands had its genesis in the ability to meet certain prerequisites necessary for the development of the financial market. Beginning in the 1960s it was apparent that the remittances sent home from Caymanian seamen exercised a profound effect on the jurisdiction's economic development. Simultaneous with the decline of merchant-seaman employment, the Caymanian authorities began to seek other avenues to bolster the economic shortfall. The decision was taken to promote the financial industry, which began in the following way:

> Four basic laws were needed at that stage. The first, a Companies Law, had already been passed by the Legislative Assembly in December 1960 and brought into effect in 1961. ... Only another three laws were therefore needed in order to move things along, a bank and trust companies law, a separate trust law and a new exchange control law ... (Johnson 2001, 148)

In the opinion of Richard Blum, a US attorney and expert on offshore tax havens, to emerge as a successful tax haven a jurisdiction must have certain general characteristics. These are '(1) confidentiality of records; (2) low cost of operations, including taxation; and (3) freedom from regulation for activities offshore of the haven itself' (Blum 1984, 6).

Neither Blum nor Johnson articulates the equally important prerequisite of capable corporate attorneys; however, such services are absolutely essential. Before the 1960s the only work for attorneys in the Cayman Islands consisted of land claims cases, incidents of trespass, vandalism, and disorderly conduct, and the occasional wounding, serious assault, or murder. For the more serious trials, attorneys were hired from Jamaica, with a Caymanian 'law agent' (an untrained attorney) instructing the senior counsel. The situation resembled that in any other frontier outpost, with courts being held at specific intervals during the year for serious criminal and civil cases.

Until the 1960s there was an absence of even the most rudimentary corporate law practice. That situation prevailed until Lynden Pindling began to promote his nationalist plans in the Bahamas during the late 1960s and early 1970s. In the wake of the smashing political victory for Pindling and the PLP in 1972, many British expatriate professionals realised that their welcome in the Bahamas had ended.

Some of these expatriates made their way to the Cayman Islands, where their expertise, skin colour, and established contacts allowed them to become the doyens of Caymanian high society. The first influx of expatriate expertise allowed the Cayman Islands to establish the infrastructure necessary to provide offshore financial services.

The expatriate migrants from the Bahamas lost no time in informing colleagues elsewhere of the prospects in their adopted society (Robinson 2003, 67–70). The cordial atmosphere experienced in the Cayman Islands, the relatively conflict-free society, and Mr Pindling's continuing nationalism in the Bahamas allowed these *arrivistes* to promote the Cayman Islands as a jurisdiction of choice for their contacts and clients. Their work and promotion were noteworthy, but the credit for creating the modern economy of the Cayman Islands belonged to those hundreds of sailors whose remittances from work on American ships attracted Barclays and other banks to establish branches in the Cayman Islands (*The Journal (Caymanian Compass)*, December 2005).

What expatriate professionals contributed was sophistication in banking practices and an augmentation and expansion of services offered. By 1976, then, the Cayman Islands exhibited all the qualities of a sophisticated offshore centre that was still referred to as a tax haven.

According to Blum, havens have several defining features, some of which are:

> The provision of secrecy with respect to offshore financial transactions, amounts and holders of accounts, and beneficial ownership of companies and securities. Havens do not tax or have very low taxation on foreign funds locally administered ... typically, havens do not enter into international agreements that would

> override domestic secrecy laws or would signal to foreign clients the likelihood of cooperating in positive ... information exchange ... Havens are typically free from many regulations that govern banking practices ... reserve requirements, loan to asset ratios, or interest rate controls. (Blum 1984, 5)

That description may have described Cayman in the mid-1970s. What exists today, however, is much more sophisticated, better regulated, and astonishingly more transparent. Even with these implied deterrents, the Cayman Islands remain at the top in international financial business. It is instructive to refer to Johnson's explanation of the jurisdiction's development:

> In addition to providing a full range of banking services, a sophisticated offshore financial centre also needs to offer an array of other services, particularly trust, company management, captive insurance services and mutual fund administration.
>
> Any jurisdiction that intends to promote itself as an offshore financial centre needs to attract quality trust companies, which for the most part tend to be subsidiaries or affiliates of the major international banks. (Johnson 2001, 150)

Ingo Walter adds:

> Efforts to become a financial centre can take two forms. One is to become a "functional" centre, where transactions are actually undertaken and value-added is created in the design and delivery of financial services.
>
> The other is to become a "booking" centre, where transactions are recorded but the value-added involved is actually created elsewhere. ... In order to attract financial bookings business, one prerequisite is a highly favourable tax climate alongside a benign regulatory and supervisory environment. Clearly, strict financial secrecy or blocking statutes can play an important part in determining a country's attractiveness as a financial booking centre. The benefits include induced employment, fiscal contributions, and positive linkage effects to firms and industries that service the financial sector. (Walter 1985, 94)

Walter's definition makes it clear that the Cayman Islands has progressed from being a 'booking' centre, which in the early stages held a large number of shell companies and corporations represented by nothing more than plaques on a wall, to a 'functional' centre with an established reputation. Increasing sophistication, the realisation that the jurisdiction must regulate itself, and international regulatory demands all combined to propel this transformation. And Cayman's reputation as a financial centre is now so secure that even Hollywood has recognised it.

Hollywood first acknowledged the Cayman Islands in John Grisham's *The Firm,* which was filmed partially on location. More recently, a young Caymanian film director, Frank Flowers, featured the Cayman Islands as a jurisdiction of questionable repute in his work entitled *Haven.* There are those who advocate censoring such dramatisations, even though the plots are purely fictitious. A countervailing and equally credible position is that for international finance, as for the movie business, 'there's no such thing as bad publicity'.

To date there has been no visible loss of business resulting from the films' release. If the Cayman Islands experienced no significant loss of business after being blacklisted by the Financial Action Task Force in 2000, it is doubtful that two fictitious Hollywood productions would spell doom to their continued success as an offshore centre. In any case, well before Hollywood discovered the Cayman Islands, sensationalist journalists had helped to give them a questionable reputation. There were several so-called exposés on the operations of firms in the Cayman Islands. While irresponsible publications played up the 'frontier' aspects of the Caymanian authorities, respectable journals exercised greater judiciousness in their approach.

In some instances, the operators of financial businesses were their own worst enemies. One such case involved an undercover visit to Guardian Bank and Trust by journalists from the BBC. What resulted was a television exposé entitled *Dirty Money,* which created an international storm and embarrassed Caymanian society. Worse was to follow, since it is widely believed that this documentary was the catalyst which eventually brought down Guardian Bank and Trust.

It should come as no surprise that some of these operators, intoxicated by success, forgot that discretion is the better part of valour. It is these reckless players who provide the justification for detractors to label the Cayman Islands as a non-compliant, pariah jurisdiction operating as a 'peekaboo center' (Naylor 1987, 62). There are far more responsible, meticulous, and honest operators in the Cayman Islands' financial industry than there are characters like those who presided over the affairs of Guardian Bank and Trust.

Caymanian society, despite its sophistication and success, has always displayed a weakness for representatives of white expatriate society. A more detailed account of the fall of John Mathewson and Guardian Bank and Trust is offered elsewhere in this chapter. Suffice it to say here, however, that Mathewson's ability to illegally remove vital government exhibits has never been explained, leaving one to suspect collusion or even corruption on the part of some government personnel.

The question must be asked whether his ease of acceptance into Caymanian high society, including membership in the local Masonic lodge, was an aberration or a representation of the routine. It would be logical to expect that newcomers in frontier societies would be allowed only minimal participation and kept on the periphery until they had earned the trust of influential members of society.

There is no reason to believe that this incident brought an end to the Caymanian affinity for the white expatriate elite. In this regard, Caymanian society diverges from the norm in other frontier societies. One might have thought that history would have served to warn the Caymanians against cultivating cozy relationships with people about whom they knew little or nothing.

Globalisation, geography, and good fortune: The geopolitics of money in the Cayman Islands

It is partly the phenomenon known as globalisation, aided and abetted by an absence of exchange controls on foreign currency, which has allowed the Cayman Islands to become a successful offshore centre. Other factors are related to geography – that is, the jurisdiction's proximity to North America, excellent telecommunications and airline connections, and political association with the United Kingdom, which equates to political stability.

Commentators refer to the 'global market' and the 'global economy' as changing established ideas regarding sovereignty and law. Writers and academics such as Greider (1997), Longworth (1999), and Hart (2000) suggest that money movement has created a new political economy.

Longworth suggests that globalisation has curtailed the ability of governments to control their own economies. He further states: 'But much of the global market, by definition, operates in a global realm that ignores frontiers and scoffs at the abilities of individual governments to regulate it' (Longworth 1999, 254).

It is exactly this phenomenon that has allowed jurisdictions such as the Cayman Islands to craft a strategy which has successfully enticed much of the world's money. The movement of money has caused a significant change in the global economy whereby it is not necessarily the world's most powerful military countries which control the money flow. As Longworth (1999, 63) suggests:

> This process is erasing the concept of space. Over half of all transactions on the fiber-optic cable network in Manhattan involve international deals. These deals, between persons or corporations legally based in two or more countries, take place entirely within Manhattan but lie outside the jurisdiction of American courts. Legal disputes are settled by international arbitrators, also often based in New York. The global economy is thus an economic state within a state, untouchable by the government that holds theoretical sovereignty over the soil where all this happens.

'Onshore' versus 'offshore': is there a significant difference?

> 'Some men worship rank, some worship heroes, some worship God, and over these ideals they dispute and cannot unite – but they all worship money.' (Mark Twain, quoted in Leckey 2000, 57)

If Hammurabi, the Babylonian king, is credited with developing a well-defined banking code, aspects of which are referred to in the New Testament (Chambost 1980), it was the Florentine Medicis who pioneered the concept of 'foreign banking', using their family to cater to the political princes of Europe (Parks 2005). Money was power, and those who controlled the money controlled politics and influenced international dynamics, diplomacy, and war, as indicated by Guttle Rothschild's famous remark in 1847. As the storm clouds appeared to be slowly gathering over Europe, the widow of Meyer Amschel Rothschild remarked: 'There will be no war in Europe; my sons will not provide the money for it' (Elon 1996, 184). And there was no war – so, although this is but one example, it epitomises the universal principle 'money is power'.

Money is the engine that powers movements, makes countries powerful, sends armies to war, and even keeps the peace. It is also a coward, according to Colin Powell, former US Secretary of State. In a speech published in a special edition of the United Nations Environment Programme magazine *Our Planet* (August 12, 2003), he said:

> Money is a coward. It flees from corruption and bad policies, conflict and unpredictability. It shuns ignorance, disease and illiteracy. Money goes where it is welcomed and where investors can be confident of a return on the resources they have put at risk. It goes to countries where women can work, children can read and entrepreneurs can dream.

The term *offshore* was in use long before its appropriation by political economists and bankers. It originated with the idea of offshore ('pirate') radio stations. The first known use of *offshore* to describe an unregulated financial centre appeared in a periodical published in November 1971 entitled *The Banker*. According to this trade journal, the term was used as a description for the Euromarket. At that time it carried the connotation, similar to pirate radio stations, of being regulated lightly or not at all and lacking structure. Since then, *offshore* has been used as shorthand for 'jurisdictions in which transactions with non-residents far outweigh transactions with the domestic economy' (Dixon 2001, 18). It also connotes unregulated international financial markets.

The Bank for International Settlements (BIS) added to the confusion by characterising tax havens as 'offshore financial centres'. More recently, however, jurisdictions have avoided describing themselves as tax havens because the phrase carries a connotation of tax evasion. The Cayman Islands long ago stopped referring to themselves as a tax haven. Offshore centres also go to great lengths to explain that what is being catered to is tax avoidance rather than tax evasion. The distinction escapes this writer, however, and it is posited here that the difference is nothing more than semantic.

It is of some historical interest that the offshore financial centres that generate the most international attention are former colonies of the United Kingdom. This should not be surprising, as the City of London has been a major financial centre since the years following World War II. Under the Exchange Control Act, passed by the UK Parliament in 1947, transactions involving foreign currencies were significantly liberalised from the way they had been during the war years. The foreign-exchange market, however, did not flower until December 1951, when banks were given permission to deal in foreign exchange (Palan 2003, 27).

Crucial to the evolution of the offshore industry is the United Kingdom's attitude towards financial services centres such as the Cayman Islands, the British Virgin Islands, the Bahamas, and Bermuda. It is this writer's belief that the United Kingdom allowed these jurisdictions to establish themselves as financial centres because their existence posed no threat to London. *The Economist* (October 24, 1996, p. 95) went further: 'The Government tolerates the offshore industry on the assumption that it brings more money into Britain by channeling more expatriate and financial wealth into London than is taken out by people working tax dodges.'

What seems to have happened is that, while many jurisdictions started as tax havens, external pressure or internal recognition of the need to reform led to a more refined unit – the offshore financial centre.

Blum adds to our understanding of the difference between the two types of jurisdiction:

> Havens, as opposed to "financial centres", are less developed countries/colonies which, as relatively undiversified economies, are dependent on finding specialized economic niches in order to survive. In consequence, expatriate managerial and technical personnel are required. Depending on local law, work permits may be required from them as well as residential/health/transport facilities. Local government convenience, subject to the winds of politics or threats of extortion, determines whether or not a bank will have the work permits of its expatriate managers renewed. Thus infrastructure adequacy is very much a matter of the nature of the society itself, its politics and practitioners. (Blum 1984, 8)

Blum's description fits the Caymanian situation, where for a long time the major beneficiaries have been the expatriate experts who cater to the specialist service needs of the offshore business. Even in cases emanating strictly from company management, Caymanian participation was not at very high levels.

The state, for its part, received only the nominal company-registration fees and, in the case of banks, the requisite bank-licensing fees. Johnson explains the attraction of the Cayman Islands:

> In the early stages of Cayman's rise to international prominence as
> an offshore centre, it became necessary to study and to grasp quite
> fully the basic needs and requirements to achieve and maintain
> that position. Those fundamental ingredients were political stability,
> excellent telecommunications, reliable air services, relative freedom
> in the movement of international currencies, dependable financial
> services, flexible laws and no form of direct taxes such as income
> tax, corporation tax, estate tax and inheritance tax. (Johnson 2001,
> 10)

Offshore financial centres cater mainly, if not exclusively, to non-residents and handle transactions across many jurisdictions. While it is true that many of the basic services are identical to those offered onshore, it is the way these services are delivered that makes the difference.

Onshore financial centres offer the same services as those available in offshore centres, with the difference that in the offshore centre there are no direct taxes. The notion that offshore centres can be readily recognised by their exploitation by shady characters has been put to rest by financial scandals over the recent years (Byles 2005, 15–16), which have involved all the major onshore centres. This suggests that the distinction between compliant, regulated jurisdictions and loosely regulated ones is becoming more academic than real. Byles substantiates the point:

> The OFCs in this context are simply a part of the international
> financial architecture and so is their banking system. Forty-three
> of the world's top 50 banks are licensed and regulated in the
> Cayman Islands and they operate to no different a standard offshore
> than they do onshore. The suggestion that the offshore banking
> world in the OFCs is somehow remote and different is no more
> than part of an outdated public relations campaign that no longer
> stands scrutiny. (Byles 2005, 21)

In any case, as the following tables indicate, the Cayman Islands are accepted as a leader among the elite jurisdictions of the international financial world.

Table 1. International financial centres ranked by banks' external assets at the end of 2000 (US$ billions)*

United Kingdom	2,094
Japan	1,199
Germany	975
United States	951
Cayman Islands	782
Switzerland	740
France	640
Luxembourg	510
Hong Kong	450
Singapore *(inclusive of the Asian currency market)*	424
Netherlands	290
Belgium	285
Bahamas	276

Source: Bank for International Settlements 2000

Palan (2003, 36) places the evolution of the Cayman Islands from tax haven to financial centre when he says that 'modern tax havens preceded the emergence of the Euromarkets by a century or so, and have grown to serve a great many functions and roles, including money laundering and tax evasion. Some, however, have evolved into veritable financial centers.' While the Cayman Islands' presence in the financial world does not add up to a century, the jurisdiction has leapt over money laundering and tax evasion and, as Table 2 (from Dixon 2001) shows, is accepted as a leading financial centre.

Table 2. Scale of international banking activities in selected financial centers as at the end of 2000*

Financial centre	GDP (US$ billions)	BIS banks location claims	
		US$ (billions)	Multiples of GDP
Cayman Islands	0.9	482	518
British Virgin Islands	0.3	25	86
Crown Dependencies	4.6	234	51
Bahamas	5.6	172	31
Bermuda	2.4	32	13
Luxembourg	19.3	245	13
Singapore	85.0	221	2.6
Hong Kong	159.0	193	1.2
United Kingdom	1,142.0	1,508	1.05
United States	9,152.0	2,096	0.2

*Because of the confusing terminology noted above (in the table), official statistics often identify only tax havens as offshore financial centers. The U.S. and U.K. treasuries, however, increasingly use the concept of the "gross domestic product [GDP] multiple", the ratio of GDP to international banking activities, to demonstrate the scale of offshore operations (see Table 2.). The GDP multiple shows clearly those financial centers, including London, that are employed primarily as entrepôt offshore centers, facilitating financial flows around the world. (Dixon 2001, 110)

Not surprisingly, the so-called onshore jurisdictions like London, New York, and Tokyo did not take kindly to the trespass of offshore centres like the Cayman Islands. Their response was formulated in a document entitled *Harmful Tax Competition: An Emerging Global Issue*. This document was a response to a communiqué issued by the G7 countries at their 1996 summit held in Lyon, France. The communiqué clearly expressed the intention of the G7 leaders to address the issue of harmful tax practices. The assembled ministers called upon the OECD to 'develop measures to counter the distorting effects of harmful tax competition on investment and financing decisions and the consequences for national tax bases and report back in 1998' (OECD 1998, 3).

While the political leaders of the Cayman Islands knew that the G7 countries intended to issue this challenge to the OECD, they seemed nonchalant, apparently expecting that the United Kingdom, through its membership in the G7 and the OECD, would act to safeguard the interests of the Cayman Islands.

No such consideration took place, and when the OECD ministers received the report in April 1998, the die was cast. A flurry of activity ensued in both the private and public sectors. Concern was expressed that procrastination on the part of the political directorate cost the jurisdiction valuable time and thus the opportunity to disengage itself from the mudslinging. Representatives of the political directorate, officialdom, and the private sector hastily assembled to arrive at some strategy to avoid being labelled an international pariah.

The Cayman Islands government, led by the financial secretary, had earlier enlisted the private sector's support, establishing the Private Sector Consultative Committee (PSCC).

It was this group, described later, upon which the Cayman Islands government relied to develop a strategic direction which would guarantee its pre-eminence on the international financial scene. The challenge was formidable, since circumstances within the local financial community were not uniformly stable.

Many of the players in positions of influence were expatriates who sometimes were transferred elsewhere or left the Cayman Islands of their own volition. Second, some organisations within the committee were bitter rivals, and, while survival took precedence over pre-existing rivalry, unity was not always attainable. Third, if the leadership of the political directorate appeared indecisive or apprehensive, private-sector enthusiasm and commitment became lukewarm. Fourth, the Cayman

Islands had no association with the other regional offshore jurisdictions, and it appears that the political directorate of 1996–2000 – the period during which international financial regulatory pressure was most intense – decided to continue operating as a lone entity.

Events took a worse turn when in 2000 the Financial Action Task Force included the Cayman Islands among its blacklisted jurisdictions. An immediate outcome in the Cayman Islands' financial theatre was a series of high-level meetings designed to inform, enlighten, and elevate the level of understanding of the players with regard to the OECD's position on harmful tax competition.

As a counterpoint, the financial community in the Cayman Islands promoted Professor Mason Gaffney's response to the OECD's document *Harmful Tax Competition*. Gaffney suggested that the OECD was ill-informed and that it should have produced a document entitled *Global Erosion of National Tax Bases – An Emerging Issue* (Gaffney 1998, 3). Professor Gaffney offered a précis of what he considered the central thesis of the OECD report. This précis accurately captures the OECD's arguments. It is quoted here in its entirety for the simple reason that it will assist the layman in comprehending what was at stake for jurisdictions like the Cayman Islands.

> In a world moving towards a global free market, the factors capital and labour are increasingly mobile. Such factors will tend (other things being equal) to be attracted away from countries with high tax burdens to countries with low tax burdens. This is the phenomenon of tax competition between states. It can occur between countries and also between states within countries.
>
> The Report concedes that tax competition can be beneficial, in stimulating the simplification of tax systems and reduction of tax rates. What it objects to is what it terms "harmful tax competition". However, when tax competition ceases to be beneficial and starts to be harmful is not clear, and is essentially subjective. This is one of the weaknesses of the Report. A country that is adversely affected by international tax competition may claim that such competition is harmful from its perspective, while it may be neutral or even beneficial from the perspective of the world economy.
>
> What the Report identifies as "harmful" effects of tax competition are two things. First, as mobile capital and labour leave a taxing jurisdiction, in the absence of any reduction in public spending, there will be an increasing burden on the less mobile labour and capital remaining in the jurisdiction, and on local consumption. This is considered to be unfair. Secondly, the Report

objects to countries which specifically target mobile labour and capital in other countries to attract them away, either by operating as a "tax haven" or by offering a "preferential tax regime" to overseas individuals and businesses. This is referred to by some jurisdictions as "poaching the natural tax base" of other countries. (Gaffney 1998, 2)

Gaffney's comments succinctly outline the problems between the OECD and the so-called tax havens. It is suggested here that the problem has its base in globalisation. The challenge posed by globalisation to the Westphalian model of monetary geography is not known or appreciated by the OECD countries.

The notion of sovereign statehood based exclusively on territoriality extends to the era of the Thirty Year's War (1618–48). Geographers and political scientists have began to emphasise the severe limitations introduced by reliance on such a tenuous system of conventional territorial imagery and international relations. Globalisation has further de-emphasised the importance of territorial landscape. The monopolistic power of states has been replaced by the invisible hand of competition.

Surprisingly for the industrialised countries, this competition has not come from other similarly industrialised jurisdictions but from countries which were surrogates or one-time colonies or that, in some instances, still are colonies. The OECD, it seems, realises that there are two ways to deal with the challenges: cooperation or coercion. Under cooperation, errant jurisdictions are not sanctioned and thereby do not appear on OECD's list of harmful taxation jurisdictions. Coercion uses an appearance on such a list as a first step. There were to follow, in the event of non-cooperation, other, more serious sanctions which were not enumerated at the time *Harmful Tax Competition* was published. Whether such sanctions would really come into effect is largely a matter for speculators, since a jurisdiction's appearance on the list of identified harmful tax jurisdictions sends a clear and unequivocal message.

That the Cayman Islands appeared to be unprepared is cause for review of the situation leading up to the publication of OECD's list. If OECD's intentions were being mooted from 1996, how was it that the Cayman Islands' financial industry had no warning? Could it have been that notice was given but the time was spent procrastinating? Whatever the reasons, one certainty exists, and that is that by May 2000 there was a flurry of activity in the financial industry in both public and private sectors. This activity had as its sole purpose ensuring that the Cayman Islands would not appear on the list of harmful tax jurisdictions that the OECD planned to publish in July 2001.

The challenge was compounded by the fact that general elections were scheduled for November 2000. While much of the organisation and decision making was led by the financial secretary with advice and assistance from the private sector, the political directorate had the constitutional authority to determine what the policy would be.

The financial secretary relied heavily upon the private sector, particularly the corporate law firms, for advice in demanding situations. The acknowledged mutual interests led to a symbiotic and synergistic relationship between the public and private sectors, and out of this relationship grew the PSCC and the Strategic Advisory Group, sometimes referred to as the Strategy Group.

The PSCC comprised representatives from the major banks, the larger legal firms specialising in corporate law, trust and estate planners, company management, and the Department of Finance, as well as one or two government ministers and, on occasion, one or two members of the Legislative Assembly. Invariably, meetings were chaired by the financial secretary, and it must have been quite a feat to steer such a seemingly competitive and independent agglomeration into a constructive collective.

The Strategic Advisory Group (SAG) was a subset of the PSCC. This group consisted of the financial secretary, the attorney general, at least two ministers of government, and one member of the Legislative Assembly, representing the government. The private sector representation could vary, depending on the nature of the challenge being confronted. More often than not, however, it included at least one senior attorney from a major law firm, a representative from the Society of Professional Accountants, and a representative from the Society of Trust and Estate Practitioners.

Such was the bureaucratic organisation when Governor Peter Smith spearheaded the initiative to have the OECD accept the so-called Advance Commitment of the Cayman Islands government. Two things are worthy of note. In the first place, the Cayman Islands conducted these negotiations without any significant assistance from the United Kingdom. Second, the negotiations were treated as strictly confidential, with no information reaching the public.

The *Caymanian Compass* (October 19, 2000) carried the headline 'OECD Praises Cayman's Tax Policy'. With that headline it was clear to all that the Cayman Islands had emerged with an exemplary report.

Elaborating on what had transpired, the opening paragraph reported that at the press conference in Paris, the OECD revealed that there was 'no indication that jurisdictions intend to increase tax rates materially in order to avoid the List of Uncooperative Tax Havens. In fact, Cayman Islands and Bermuda (both already having committed to eliminate any harmful tax practices) have made clear that they will maintain their zero tax systems.' This was the position which the Cayman Islands had taken in their so-called Advance Commitment letter of May 2000. In essence, what happened at the OECD meeting in Paris turned out to be 'much ado about nothing'. Questioning the publicity and apprehension surrounding the announcement, the editorial in the *Caymanian Compass* (October 19, 2000) wondered 'whether the whole thing has not been something of a storm in a teacup'.

The OECD, in an explanation of what triggered the furore, stated that it had been a serious misunderstanding in the world's financial centres to expect jurisdictions to increase tax rates as a reaction to the OECD's initiative.

This historical underpinning provides a clear insight into the conservative disposition which controls financial activity amongst the world's players. If the Cayman Islands received OECD's approval, it was manifestly unlucky in its dealing with the Financial Action Task Force (FATF).

The jurisdiction appeared on the FATF's so-called blacklist when it was published in mid-2000. Fortunately, Cayman was able to extricate itself from that list after being on it for only a year. It is one of the enduring characteristics of the Cayman Islands as a frontier society that its expatriate expertise always seems ready to circle the wagons and come to the jurisdiction's defense when necessary – whether in the service of expatriates' own economic interests or Caymanian society in general is not clear. However, the private sector, in tandem with its public-sector partners, has managed to surmount all of the external challenges which impinged on its existence up to this point. Such a partnership is as beneficial to the expatriates' personal future as it is to the continuation of the Cayman Islands as a major international financial centre.

The specific reference to external challenges is intended to highlight for the reader the fact that internal pressures are also mounting on the jurisdiction. One such pressure, the result of globalisation and worldwide economic migration, has to do with population issues and the makeup of Caymanian society. While these issues are more thoroughly dealt with elsewhere in this book, this is an appropriate place to introduce a brief discussion on globalisation as it relates to international financial markets.

Globalisation is a phenomenon based upon power, just as military strength is based on power. Three currencies have emerged as the most important in the world: the US dollar, the euro, and the yen. Although these are far from the only currencies in the world, they are the ones that have the most significance on world markets at this time.

Important currencies in the context of this chapter are limited to those of the G8 countries. Within this group, discussions most commonly concern the pound sterling, the Swiss franc, the French franc, the deutschmark, and the US and Canadian dollars, with the yen and the Russian ruble less frequently linked to Western monetary transactions and markets.

At the time of writing there is a worldwide savings glut which is not dampened by the high price of oil (*Business Week,* July 11, 2005, pp. 50–66). According to the story, 'For now, most of this money is being recycled to the global financial markets as savings rather than as investments in oil exploration and production or other productive uses' (p. 62).

It is posited here that a significant portion of this money will find its way to no-tax jurisdictions like the Cayman Islands, particularly in instances where it is not being invested for 'other productive uses'. Herein lies the major weakness of building an infrastructure on a foundation as unstable as other people's money.

Regardless of the excellent reputation of the Cayman Islands, what is going to be the result when market trends and international politics or other expediencies force such money to move away from offshore jurisdictions? There is nothing wrong with building an economy on the offering of financial services and banking practice. But if the money does not belong to the Caymanian economy, there is nothing to stop it from relocating to other jurisdictions.

Serendipity may have smiled on the Cayman Islands in the early 1960s when the laws facilitating the development of a tax haven were passed. In the twenty-first century's international money market, however, the Cayman Islands cannot escape their history – or their vulnerability to market volatility and emerging and established global issues. It is to one of these issues, money laundering, that some attention will now be given.

Washers, dryers, calculators, and computers: Money laundering and beyond

It is a typical mid-morning in downtown George Town. Somewhere in the business district a telephone rings in an attorney's office. It is an international call from a client who will be flying in that afternoon by private aircraft with $3 million in cash. The money is to be counted and deposited until it can be placed in a yet unnamed and unregistered company, all within two days.

At approximately 3 o'clock a taxi pulls up in front of the office. Three men, casually dressed, climb out of the cab and, after settling the fare, retrieve an assortment of boxes, rucksacks, and a couple of overnight bags. After securing the baggage in the foyer of the attorney's office and engaging the receptionist in a discreet conversation, two of the visitors remain seated in the reception area, while the third goes into conference in an attorney's office.

After a brief interval, attorney and client emerge from the office and quietly pass on the information that the baggage will need to be taken to a bank just across the road from their current address. Once that transaction is completed, the two men who accompanied the principal traveller are free to depart and do so with a minimum of ceremony.

The remaining traveller remains in the company of the attorney for the rest of the business day. On the morning of the second day he returns to the downtown office for the processing of the requisite documentation.

With the proper arrangements in place, a company has been formed and registered by close of business on that afternoon. The entire process has taken less than two days, with a minimum of questions being asked. The attorney extracts his office fees; the bank receives 1 per cent for staff time counting the cash; the government receives its company registration fee; and the courier, as per instructions, leaves the island early the next morning by commercial carrier with no records of any of the transactions that took place during his visit.

Such an occurrence was not atypical in the late 1970s, up to 1980, before strict regulations and international obligations led the Cayman Islands to become one of the most effectively regulated international financial jurisdictions in the world.

Undoubtedly there will be those who will argue vehemently that such scenarios did not go down in the Cayman Islands. The facts are, however, that the Cayman Islands are a frontier society, and as certainly as piracy existed, so did money laundering. There is no shortage of legal cases, both civil and criminal, to attest to the proposition that in the Cayman Islands, as in many other offshore jurisdictions, for a time money laundering was par for the course (Robinson 1996; Blum 1984; Naylor 2002).

Laundering money is not only common but traditional: 'Far from being a present-day blight, money laundering is actually an ancient practice; indeed, it might be more deserving than its many competitors of being called the world's second oldest crime – if anyone in the past had thought it was worth criminalizing' (Naylor 2002, 134). And as far as its prevalence is concerned, 'After foreign exchange and the oil industry, the laundering of dirty money is the world's third largest business' (Robinson 1996, 13).

If one assumes that even in the so-called sophisticated onshore jurisdictions, screening for money laundering is a daunting exercise, it is logical to conclude that the challenge must be even greater in the jurisdictions that are microstates. The question naturally arises: What was the attraction of money laundering in the first place?

Robinson (1996) explains that money laundering has three distinct stages. The first of these, immersion, has to do with the placement of the money to be laundered so as to be able to funnel the cash into circulation without the transaction being detected. The second step is called *layering*. The subject separates the money from its illicit source by moving it between a series of accounts, usually through several jurisdictions. At this step it is critical to have strict bank secrecy and dependable attorney-client privilege. The final step is repatriation and integration of the money. It is at this point that the washed funds are brought back into circulation as legitimate taxable income (Robinson 1996, 10–11).

Regardless of the source of the money to be laundered, the process has been described as having four simple prerequisites. First, the ownership of the money must be concealed. Second, the form the money takes must be changed. For example, it would be pointless to launder $5 million in $100 bills only to wind up with $5 million in $100 bills. Third, there must be no trail leading to the source of the funds. Finally, absolute control must be maintained over the money laundered. Many of the people handling the money while it is being laundered will realise all this, and if they steal it, the original owner can do very little about it – legally.

The impression is sometimes given that money laundering is an activity that takes place exclusively in the offshore world (Palan 2003, 48). There is no research bearing out this observation. Indeed, laundering of money obtained from political corruption, illicit arms dealing, and the illegal diamond trade, as well as from the global drug trade and from trafficking in human cargoes, is just as likely to be laundered in a large metropolis as in the more laid-back tropical islands. Recent history reminds us that the late Nigerian dictator Sani Abacha had approximately $60 million deposited in UK banks which he had looted from his country's public treasury, and the Russian mafia laundered millions of dollars through the Bank of New York.

What distinguishes the onshore jurisdictions like Switzerland, Luxemburg, and Lichtenstein from the smaller offshore jurisdictions is that their economy of scale and their membership in the major international organisations allow them to play by two sets of rules.

The new structure which has been brought about by globalisation has ushered in a growing disjuncture between some elements in the Caymanian society. In this writer's opinion, this schism threatens the continuing economic prosperity of the Caymanian financial centre as much as do the external forces previously discussed. Immigration-related stresses have political, economic, and cultural ramifications for Caymanian society. Since 1988 there have been several attempts by the Legislative Assembly to reform immigration laws in a way which is fair and equitable to both the established Caymanians and their immigrant/expatriate counterparts. It is accurate to say that on every occasion, the agenda has been hijacked by people playing to the political gallery. The situation is compounded by the failure to adhere to a formula which ensures that there is scope for the recruitment and training of established Caymanians while at the same time making provisions for expatriate expertise.

The situation is exacerbated by the frontier nature of Caymanian society, which is in and of itself attractive to immigrants. While discussions have always centred around the Caymanian/non-Caymanian duality, several recent news reports have again brought the issue to the boiling point.

The editorial columns of the *Cayman Net News* periodically promote the urgency of finding a satisfactory formula for immigration in Caymanian society. In a response to these columns, a former government minister and veteran legislator stirred up controversy. In a letter in the *Cayman Net News* (April 12, 2006) captioned 'Who Is the "Johnny Come Lately" – Politician or Publisher?' the former legislator sliced through the Cayman/non-Caymanian debate without diplomacy, compassion, or sensitivity.

In an almost immediate response, his position was challenged by another former legislator and equally prominent citizen. What has followed from this point-counterpoint display is the revelation of a glaring division in Caymanian society over an issue that has the ability to strain the society beyond easy repair.

A logical outgrowth of this debate is an article which appeared in the *Cayman Observer* (April 20–26, 2006). Entitled 'Population Increases to Record Levels', the article opens with the statement: 'The population of the Cayman Islands grew about 18% between April 2004 and October 2005, thanks in no small part to a massive jump in the number of non-Caymanians.' While detailed information about the population increase is included, what is of most interest to the debate is the following: 'the number of non-Caymanians increased by 19% from 17,383 in April 2004 to 20,678 in October 2005'.

Indications in the article are that, as striking as these figures may appear, the situation is not as grave as some might think: 'The survey found that the unemployment rate for men was 3%, and for women, 4.2% ... The total figure of 1,303 people out of work placed the overall unemployment rate at 3.5%.'

It is this writer's contention that the vilification of expatriates and the impression that it is 'us against them' threaten the continuing cultural, political, and economic development of Caymanian society. For while such polarisation might seem momentarily popular, it offers no constructive formula for the long-term betterment of established-Caymanian youth, nor does it offer practical methods for addressing the growing chasm between the haves and the have-nots.

Xenophobic behaviour, while it may be appealing to some, is in the end counterproductive and nonsensical. If, as Samuel Johnson is said to have remarked, 'Patriotism is the last refuge of a scoundrel', wrapping the development of a society in a mantle of separation, difference, and divergence on the basis of national interest is the declining cottage industry of those who do not understand the knowledge economy, the borderless world, and the symbiotic relationship between established Caymanians and expatriates.

Ohmae expresses the situation succinctly:

> In a borderless economy, the workings of the market's "invisible hand" have a reach and a strength beyond anything that Adam Smith could have ever imagined. In Smith's day, economic activity took place on a landscape largely defined – and circumscribed – by the political borders of nation states: England with its wool, Portugal with its wines. Now, by contrast, it is economic activity that defines the landscape on which all other institutions, including the apparatus of statehood, must operate. (Ohmae 1996, 41)

Nowhere is this phenomenon more obvious than in the international financial markets, where onshore jurisdictions face tough competition from the offshore low- or no-tax jurisdictions with the same level of legal and financial expertise. A jurisdiction like the Cayman Islands therefore has to ensure that transactions conducted within its borders meet the meticulous standards set by the competition. That this is usually the case is more to the credit of the Cayman Islands than of the international community, where the claim is made that the high standards of the Cayman Islands are not always adhered to.

The scope of this paper does not allow for a detailed examination of every case that has grabbed international attention since the Cayman Islands emerged as an offshore jurisdiction. What follows is a selected listing of some of the most controversial of these cases, with commentary explaining the gist of what transpired and how it may have affected the jurisdiction.

The Castle Bank case (1976) was the first indicator that the activities of banks and bankers in the Cayman Islands were being noted by US authorities. Johnson (2001, 155) has indicated that his concern with this case led him to request some form of legislation to protect Caymanian banking officials from future incursions by outside authorities.

This legislation, the Confidential Relationships (Preservation) Law (1976), made it illegal for information about a client of any banking institution in the Cayman Islands to be divulged to anyone. This law was amended in 1979 to state more precisely under what circumstances it would be permissible to seek, obtain, and divulge confidential information which fitted the legal definition. Any foreign entity or individual seeking information regarding crimes other than tax offences would be required to apply to the Governor-in-Council, through the local police.

As noble as this effort appeared, as events were later to prove, it treated only the symptoms. Ideally, concomitant with the legislation should have been some code of practice or know-your-customer guidelines which articulated the appropriate steps to be taken when dealing with clients.

As events were to unfold, the Castle Bank case was the first in a series of confrontations with international authorities resulting from challenges to the banking practices of the Caymanian establishment. Others, of varying magnitude, followed.

A review of the literature, from Richard Blum's *Offshore Haven Banks, Trusts, and Companies* (1984) and Alan Block's *Masters of Paradise* (1991) to Jeffrey Robinson's *The Laundrymen* (1996) and *The Sink* (2003), not to mention numerous magazines and newspapers, shows that Caymanian financial players were singled out for their forays into, and associations with, foreign criminal enterprises and individuals in the financial world.

Many of the individuals and establishments mentioned in these cases and incidents were or still are active players on the Caymanian financial scene. What has yet to be determined is how many of these incidents occurred as a matter of uninformed practice or naivety and how many occurred out of complicity or the desire to promote the jurisdiction or a business enterprise. Regardless, it is difficult if not impossible to argue persuasively – judging by the subsequent displays of wealth and material success – that some personal aggrandisement was not a by-product.

There are those who would suggest that such is a natural corollary of transacting business in a frontier society. That sentiment is countered by the observation that this type of behaviour is not limited to the offshore jurisdictions, and one would be hard pressed to find significant instances of such behaviour benefiting many established Caymanians.

In 1984, another Caymanian entity made the international press when US authorities fined the Bank of Nova Scotia $1.8 million for failing to comply with a grand jury subpoena. The Cayman Islands branch of Scotia Bank gained international notice, as it was really an offshoot of the Bahamian branch and the two worked in close cooperation. If the Cayman Islands escaped this fiasco with a black eye, the next time it experienced international embarrassment would prove to be an unmitigated disaster.

There is no explanation for what John Mathewson did to the Cayman Islands' banking image in 1991, except that he exploited the age-old Caymanian affinity for white expatriates. An imposing figure,

Mathewson was the typical brash American, and in the frontier society that was the Cayman Islands, he played an Oscar-worthy role.

Having ingratiated himself into the upper echelons of Caymanian society, he impressed his hosts by bringing no less controversial a figure than Oliver North to the Islands, about a year after Ronald Reagan left office. The occasion was a $100-per-plate dinner held at the Hyatt Regency Resort, with the movers and shakers in Caymanian society as audience.

If Caymanian officialdom had any reservations about Mathewson, they were dissolved by his ability to bring a player such as Oliver North to the Cayman Islands – although at a time when Reaganism was no longer in vogue. Mathewson gained blue-chip status among the power elite on Grand Cayman. The evening was a sickening display of expatriate arrogance and contempt, and it is fair to remark that such a performance would not have been accepted in any other Caribbean jurisdiction.

For Mathewson, however, it must have been a triumph, in that his organisation, Guardian Bank and Trust, continued to attract a certain offshore clientele and an enviable and distinguished set of correspondents and associates, including Credit Suisse in Guernsey, Smith Barney, Charles Schwab, Butterfield International, and Richardson Greenshield (Robinson 2003, 185–86).

Mathewson, it appears, had his transactions down to a science. He took a personal interest in each of his clients as he shepherded them through his practised routine. The routine included the sale of a shell company with whatever bank or brokerage accounts the client desired. As Robinson describes it:

> Doing business with Mathewson was not cheap. Guardian's charges were $5,000.00 to open an account and $3,000.00 annually to maintain it. Clients paid an additional $5,000.00 for a standard shell company – they only paid Mathewson $500.00 to buy from the local authorities – and $12,000.00–$26,000.00 if they needed an "aged" shell. That's a company incorporated several years before which allowed clients to back date invoices and create fictitious trading records. The required nominee shareholder for each shell was often a Guardian subsidiary, for which there was a fee. Mathewson also supplied company directors – usually another guardian subsidiary – for another fee. On top of those, he charged $100 per wire transfer, sent or received. (Robinson 2003, 186)

It is curious that Mathewson carried on such scams literally under the nose of the Cayman Islands government: Guardian Bank and Trust was located in a complex adjacent to the Government Administration building. The Monetary Authority, the body responsible for policing such entities as Guardian Bank and Trust, was just across the courtyard.

Mathewson's goose was cooked in January 1995 when, against his expectations, the Cayman Islands government ordered the operation shut down. True to form, Mathewson claimed that the bank was closed out of spite when he refused to pay a $250,000 bribe.

John Mathewson came to the frontier; he saw; but he did not conquer. In the end, his fate was no different from that of many other arrogant prospectors. He failed to learn the most fundamental lesson of all – that is, power often finds a way to mock those who seek it. What transpired after Mathewson's fall, however, was for more detrimental to the Cayman Islands than anything that had occurred previously.

Mathewson, in an attempt to avoid being sent to prison at age 70, provided the US authorities with his coded bank records, which not only exposed his clients but also provided information on how the Cayman Islands worked. Following that blow, the court in the United States ruled against the return of the documents, which were turned over to the FBI by Mathewson. In a sense the Bankers' Association got what it deserved. After all, many members of this organisation associated with Mathewson and encouraged him in his quest to establish himself in the Cayman Islands by using his US contacts to bring Oliver North and other questionable characters to Grand Cayman.

As a final blow to the banking establishment in the Cayman Islands, Mathewson assisted the FBI in decrypting the computer tapes from his banking organisation. The banking establishment in the Cayman Islands paid a heavy price for its acceptance of the maverick American financier.

Nothing about this case should be surprising, though, since the banking establishment – not unlike similar professional organisations – consists primarily of white elements (other than established Caymanians) who accept their own kind. Robinson substantiates this writer's suggestion that racism has played and continues to play an important role in the development and continuation of the Cayman Islands as a financial centre:

> As a direct result of Bahamian independence in 1974, some bankers started having second thoughts about the financial sector there. With Britain in charge, they saw the island as safe. But the WASP

[white Anglo-Saxon Protestant – American shorthand for the Establishment] banking world didn't have a particularly high opinion of native politicians, most of whom seemed to have been cut from the same old cloth as Pindling. Some of those WASP bankers decided it might be time to start looking for someplace else to go.

That racism played a part in the development of the offshore world is undeniable. As one person put it "White bankers wouldn't trust a black crook. White crooks okay. But not black crooks." Which is also why nearby ports of call in the Eastern Caribbean didn't land the business. Instead, money began to head westward, past Jamaica to a British Crown colony – which meant it was still acceptable to the white world – called the Cayman Islands. (Robinson 2003, 67)

Since the demise of Guardian Bank and Trust, there has been no other such spectacular bank failure in the Cayman Islands. In the recent past, however, the Cayman Islands as an international financial centre has been linked to the failure of two multinational corporations as a result of fraudulent practices and white-collar crime.

In both cases these companies were represented in the Cayman Islands by top-flight law firms of expatriate ownership. While the Cayman Islands as a jurisdiction did not bear the full brunt of the Parmalat and Enron scandals, the fact that these companies had significant business interests in the Cayman Islands was sufficient to fuel the suspicion that the jurisdiction still permits shady practices.

The truth is that often the Cayman Islands government and regulatory authorities are uninformed about the details of private-sector involvement in such relationships. For example, one of the firms named by New York District Attorney Robert Morgenthau as a responsible party in the Parmalat scam was willing to make available to the District Attorney's office its client's private files, apparently to preserve its own reputation; yet the company's principals did not have sufficient regard for the Cayman authorities, whose jurisdictional reputation was being tarnished, to explain its relationship with Parmalat.

It is no wonder, then, that many informed Caymanians are suggesting that the whole idea of a financial centre was configured so as to benefit the vested commercial interests exponentially while established Caymanians received only the most grudging of considerations. In a

1978 article, this writer suggested that 'the façade is impressive, however when the surface is scratched it soon becomes obvious that all is not what it is cracked up to be' (Bodden 1978, 14).

External and internal forces sometimes combine to pressure the system so that its practices appear to be roguish and sensational by international standards. When this occurs, no relief is provided by the Cayman Islands' colonial relationship with the United Kingdom.

This was the case in the early 1990s, when the financial crimes unit of the Royal Cayman Islands Police, headed by an expatriate English officer, conducted a 'fishing expedition' which resulted in the prosecution of a banker called John Rea, who took the matter all the way to the Privy Council. The result was an exoneration of Rea and an indictment of the practices used to garner evidence by the financial arm of the police force. The reckless actions of the investigating officer, Brian Gibbs, obliged the Cayman Islands to pay not only the costs of the Privy Council hearing but also personal damages to John Rea for what amounted to the destruction of his career as a banker. Rea was appropriately compensated by the government, and Brian Gibbs was placed in an ideal position to continue his reckless and duplicitous career.

It was the Euro Bank Corporation which would ultimately prove Gibbs's undoing. Registered in the Cayman Islands in 1981, the institution established itself from the outset as an 'ask no questions' receiver of cash from all clients.

Over the years there were numerous incidents of business involvement between Euro Bank and any number of suspicious individuals and organisations, from Adnan Khashoggi to BCCI (Robinson 2003, 252–58). Euro Bank was a source of embarrassment to the banking establishment in the Cayman Islands for years, and it was common knowledge among government circles that the institution flaunted the rules and operated as a law unto itself.

It was the bank's association with Ken Taves, an American client who bilked credit card holders out of millions of dollars and then laundered that money through Euro Bank on Grand Cayman, which brought things to a head. Taves first got into trouble with US authorities, and when it seemed inevitable that the Cayman Islands would once again be linked to a money-laundering scandal of enormous proportions, the Cayman authorities closed Euro Bank's operations.

As a consequence of this closure, several officers of the bank were charged with criminal breaches of the financial regulations law. Two of the people charged were former bankers with significant experience at reputable financial institutions in the Cayman Islands.

Leading the investigation and preparing the case files was none other than Detective Inspector Brian Gibbs of John Rea fame, only he was now in a much more powerful position.

In compliance with the requirements of the Financial Action Task Force, the Cayman Islands had been required to establish a Financial Reporting Unit in 2000. This unit primarily held responsibility for reporting on money laundering. Oddly, it was not operated under the auspices of the police commissioner and by extension the Police Law. Instead it was removed from within the framework of the Royal Cayman Islands Police and placed under the authority of the attorney general.

How such a move escaped public comment by the Bankers' Association and the political establishment is still a matter for conjecture. As events unfolded, however, it turned out that Brian Gibbs, the attorney general, and at least one highly placed officer in Euro Bank were involved in an espionage conspiracy of major international proportions. The revelations came during the now infamous Euro Bank trial of 2002. The case, *Regina* vs. *Donald Stewart, Brian Cunha, Ivan Burgess, and Judith Donegan,* sparked intense interest in Caymanian financial circles and beyond.

This case, one of the most high-profile in Caymanian legal history, was argued by a battery of top-notch UK attorneys, instructed by counsel from the local legal fraternity. The presiding judge was Chief Justice Anthony Smellie, QC, and it was clear from the outset that he would need all his legal acumen and court experience to preside over the trial in such a way as to leave no doubt as to the impartiality of the court. There have never been any aspersions cast on the integrity and conduct of the court in this case, but considering that so much was riding on its outcome, it was critical to ensure that any appeal would be strictly on an evidentiary basis.

While it was not precedent-setting, the attorney general himself appeared on several occasions to bolster the prosecution's team. Later it became clear why he may have had more than a professional commitment to ensure that the alleged perpetrators were convicted.

As the case unfolded, it became apparent that there were records and documents held by the prosecution to which the defense was not privy. Upon further investigation it was revealed that, if found to be factual, this was a serious breach that could lead to a mistrial. Upon examination, the court not only ascertained that it was factual but uncovered evidence of a conspiracy involving the so-called London Plan. As it turned out, the prosecution's reluctance to make Brian Gibbs available as a witness and its rueful admission regarding the documents in its possession and the sanitising of evidence led to the discovery of a cover-up conspiracy of unprecedented proportions.

It was revealed that Brian Gibbs, the head of the Financial Reporting Unit in the Cayman Islands, was also an agent of the UK espionage agency MI6. His handler operated out of the agency's headquarters in England. Gibbs, in turn, had recruited Edward Warwick, a senior manager of the Euro Bank Corporation, as an informant, and this relationship had existed for some considerable time.

The conspiracy was further complicated when it was realised that the attorney general, to whom Gibbs reported locally, must have had knowledge of the conspiracy and may even have sanctioned the relationship with MI6. It is not farfetched to suggest that the trail probably led all the way to the governor's office. The governor would have had access to the coded communication between the parties in London and the Cayman Islands and most likely would have been briefed by Gibbs, since such matters as money-laundering investigations fall under the his reserve powers.

Events came to a head on January 13, 2003, when the attorney general, realising that the Crown's case had been irreparably compromised, announced that the Crown would be offering no further evidence. The next day the jury foreman informed the court that the jury had registered unanimous not-guilty verdicts for all 15 charges to which the defendants were required to answer.

In his discharge of the defendants, the chief justice explained that the outcome should be viewed only as a 'technical matter' and further stated, 'I think it is owed to the defendants that the public be made aware that, so far as this court is concerned, this represents the proper and fair verdict.'

With that seemingly fitting commentary, what was described by one of the defendants as an 'ordeal' came to an end. While the attorney general was attending to the task of cleaning up the legal detritus, a virtual political hurricane was blowing his way.

On the morning of January 16, 2003, the elected ministers of Executive Council (now the cabinet) hand-delivered a letter to the governor. The letter complained of the serious setback dealt to the Cayman financial community as a result of the failed Euro Bank trial.

It suggested that the clandestine operations by an agency of Her Majesty's Government based in London was intended to bring down Cayman's financial industry.

The letter went on to raise the matter of court costs and indemnification of the defendants, and other liabilities which might arise. It also informed the governor that the five elected ministers would not be sitting in ExCo meetings or in the Legislative Assembly with the attorney general and recommended that the governor terminate his employment and commission the solicitor general to act until a suitable replacement could be found. Additionally, the letter demanded the immediate termination of the employment of Brian Gibbs. The letter concluded thus:

> As you are no doubt aware, Members of the Legislative Assembly and the public are increasingly calling upon the Government to give a full explanation of various matters which have come to light over the last week and the actions which the elected Members of Government propose to take as a result of these revelations.

> The elected Members of Government will have to deal with these matters as best they can and to discharge in a democratic manner, the duties which have been entrusted to them by the public.

The elected ministers of government, along with their back-bench supporters in the United Democratic Party, held a public meeting on the evening of January 20, 2003. The opposition was invited to share the platform but demurred. Later it was learnt that at least one prominent member of the opposition party held a clandestine meeting with the embattled attorney general.

If the opposition was aiming at political expediency by hedging their bets, they must have received a rude awakening. As public criticism intensified following the official announcement of the trial's collapse, the two legal associations registered their position publicly. In a lead story in the *Cayman Net News* (January 27, 2003), both the Cayman Islands Law Society and the Caymanian Bar Association called for the retirement of the attorney general on the grounds that it was in the best interest of the Cayman Islands. The publicly expressed displeasure of both these associations, coupled with the position taken by the elected ministers, placed considerable pressure on the attorney general and the governor.

The governor could rely on the support of the United Kingdom and Baroness Amos, whose responsibilities included the Overseas Territories. The baroness did try to intimidate the leader of government business into recanting the elected ministers' stated position, but her efforts were in vain.

It was, for the elected ministers, a matter of principle, and they once more conveyed to the governor that they would not accept a compromise. As discussions took place, the attorney general continued to occupy his chambers, but the ministers, true to their pledge, had no official or unofficial dealings with him. On this they had support from the financial secretary and the chief secretary, who held the view that what had occurred jeopardised the Cayman Islands' ability to remain economically prosperous.

Pressure had also been building around Brian Gibbs, and it was well recognised that his position was the more vulnerable. Gibbs extricated himself from embarrassment, and possibly arrest, when he apparently heeded the warning from his handler in the United Kingdom and illegally departed the Cayman Islands. Given the structure of the service and the relationship between such a sensitive department and the governor's office, it is hard to believe that this high-level operative, assigned to such an important mission, could have left the jurisdiction without the express written permission of the governor.

It is a fact of colonialism, and British colonialism is no exception, that certain activities are conducted with the utmost discretion. The fundamental principle has always centred on not sharing with the 'natives' certain sensitive information. The success of colonialism was based upon the old practice of 'divide and rule', which meant that there were two systems: one for the 'natives' and the other consisting of strategies for the advancement of the whites from the colonial power. Even among the 'natives' there were those who were favoured by the colonisers and enjoyed certain confidences, as opposed to those who were identified as potential troublemakers and kept out of the loop. Osterhammer (1997) explains the characteristics well:

> The principal traits of a colonial state are its dual character, subordinate and yet nearly omnipotent, its autocratic centralization of power at the top while pursuing "divide and conquer" at the bottom, its self-perception as neutral authority over the parties, and, last but not least, the unbridgeable cultural gap between rulers and ruled. The fact that the fundamental loyalty of the colonial

state lay outside its sphere of activity ultimately rendered it unstable or illegitimate, even if it strove for fair exercise of rule in particular cases. In the final analysis, the common good it claimed to represent was not that of the political structure over which it presided, but that of empire. (Osterhammer 1997, 58)

In that quotation are found the operating principles of this still influential phenomenon. All this influence came into play in the Cayman Islands during the mid- to late 1990s. The upshot was the Euro Bank fiasco and a strained relationship between the Cayman Islands as colony and the United Kingdom as administering power.

The explanation offered by officialdom and carried in the *Caymanian Compass* (January 20, 2003) must be accepted as 'plausible denial'. No self-respecting officer would let himself be caught in a deliberate lie, but an admission of complicity would have left the Office of the Governor open to slander, innuendo, and worse.

The *Cayman Net News* editorial (January 20, 2003) poignantly expressed the Caymanian position: 'In the face of adversity which was brought on by the trial's controversial collapse, the Cayman Islands' head is bloody but unbowed.'

The editorial, aptly titled 'Euro Bank's shame is Britain's blame', went on to suggest:

> There can be no doubt that the UK, despite the Cayman Islands being its dependent, overstepped its boundaries and exceeded the four corners of propriety through its special agents and certain other people.

> Coming on the heels of its attitude towards this country with respect to the European Union's Draft Initiative of the Tax of Savings Initiative, the relationship between "Mother" and sibling needs to be revisited, reexamined and reviewed.

> Indeed, it may cause many to conclude that the present state of affairs presents reasons why this country should pursue a firm date for self-determination.

The more conservative *Caymanian Compass* began its editorial, entitled 'Broken trust' (January 20, 2003): 'An unprecedented situation has emerged with the elected arm of ExCo having lost faith in an Official Member of government following the Euro Bank trial debacle.'

This editorial, while not as stinging as the one in the *Cayman Net News*, nevertheless captured the disquiet expressed by the elected ministers of government. It reminded its readers of two important facts. The first was that the Euro Bank liquidation in 1999 was contrived by elements within certain government circles, based upon evidence emanating from the Brian Gibbs and the FRU. And it reiterated that there was no acceptable recourse for the attorney general who had abused his authority but to relinquish his post.

Eventually, the attorney general did agree to resign his post, though only after the UK government succeeded in extracting an enviable financial settlement and a face-saving exit from the Cayman Islands.

In the course of the Euro Bank debacle, it was learnt that Attorney General David Ballantyne had had to leave his previous posting in the Turks and Caicos Islands prematurely because of his involvement in an illegal wiretapping operation. It is in the nature of colonial administration that the administering power would not make such a damaging admission to an overseas territory. Indeed, if the colony succeeded in having such a charge opened for discussion, it would be glossed over, ignored, or denied by the administering power. Such an action then could offer little hope of getting the officer's posting changed.

As for Ballantyne's departure from the Cayman Islands, an important codicil was the United Kingdom's insistence that there should be no recriminations, no lawsuits, and no smear campaign against him by the Cayman Islands government.

Since the Euro Bank debacle there have been a few cases of lesser importance. One of these, Cash 4 Titles, ended in the acquittal of one person charged and the retrial of a second person on technical grounds. The Segoes investigation into the alleged fraud and bilking of investors' funds by the company founder and CEO seems to be in a lull at the time of writing – largely, it seems, because the alleged perpetrator is no longer residing in the Cayman Islands. Another alleged fraudster, Brian Kuhn, has been convicted. Most recently (April 2006), Raymond Creed, an acquaintance and neighbour of the convicted credit card fraudster, Ken Taves, has been convicted.

These prosecutions and the continuing pursuit of those who transgress the law underscore this writer's contention that the jurisdiction remains committed to its pursuit of excellence in financial dealings. There are, however, some potentially damaging matters still unresolved. In both the Enron and Parmalat cases it is expected that the Cayman Islands will receive some negative publicity. According to the *New York Times* (January 18, 2002), Enron had 881 subsidiaries in offshore jurisdictions, 692 of which were reported to be in the Cayman Islands. Additionally, it appears that another scandal may be looming, since the weekly business section of the *Cayman Net News* (April 24, 2006) carried the story that Deloitte Cayman and Deloitte UK have been accused of a 'farce' in their role as liquidators in a multimillion-dollar case. The story, headlined 'Liquidators involved in "farce" case in UK', alleges that the liquidators 'ran-up a tally of 256 days in court bills for time costs exceeded £100 million and sullied some 42 bank officials' names'.

In many respects, this case is indicative of the need for Cayman Islands authorities to exercise more discretion over the conduct of receivers and liquidators in the jurisdiction. From the era of the Interbank liquidation in the 1970s up to the present time, it seems that once an organisation goes into receivership or liquidation in the Cayman Islands, all hope of restitution and revitalisation is lost. Past practice in this area represents a lurid case history in which many owners of these businesses suffered crippling legal fees in addition to losing their life's investment. It remains to be seen what will become of the recent allegations and subsequent 'investigation' by the House of Commons Constitutional Affairs Committee.

Obligations of the territory

There are certain obligations placed upon the Cayman Islands and other Overseas Territories by the administering power. One such obligation is known as the European Union Savings Directive or the EU Tax Savings Initiative.

After a considerable period of stalemate, argument, and a lawsuit, the Cayman Islands government acceded to pressure from the UK government and agreed to the European Union Savings Directive. The United Democratic Party's political directorate had held a hard line for approximately two years. Similarly, the financial establishments in the Cayman Islands adopted a reactionary position and, perhaps led by the government, did not really analyse what the directive was seeking to achieve. In February 2004, however, the Cayman Islands government, after a series of negotiations, discontinued its objections.

The jurisdiction gained a few concessions, including the United Kingdom's recognition of the Cayman Islands Stock Exchange and permission for the Cayman Islands to become a Designated Investment

Exchange. This will be positive for the stock exchange, since it will allow for easier growth and complement the promotional work undertaken by local law firms, listing agents, and fund administrators.

Despite the belief at one stage that the Savings Directive would result in a tax on all interest, including interest accruing on individual accounts, in fact it applies only where an interest payment is made by an economic entity, namely a bank or mutual fund operator, to an individual EU resident. Assuming that the majority of commerce originating in the European Union and involving the Cayman Islands is institutional, there should be negligible effects on the Caymanian economy. Most offshore accounts in the Cayman Islands are corporate rather than individual accounts.

Before the general election of May 2005 the United Democratic Party seemed to have softened its stance toward the directive (*Caymanian Compass,* February 22, 2005). Almost immediately after being sworn into office, the succeeding People's Progressive Movement announced its intention to bring the matter to a conclusion by acceding to the principles of the directive.

There are several lessons to be learnt from the events leading to the settlement of the EU Savings Directive. In the first place, it seems obvious that it is critically important for the Cayman Islands, as a sophisticated jurisdiction, to develop a financial intelligence mechanism that can deliver accurate first-hand information about obligations and requirements in the international arena.

Secondly, there must be a well-developed and informed strategy for dealing with international obligations and requirements of a financial nature. The National Team political directorate of the 1990s took the attitude of benign neglect, more or less ignoring such obligations or requirements when they seemed ominous. The United Democratic Party leader's operational style was confrontational, adversarial, and combative. During both administrations complaints arose about 'shifting goalposts' and the absence of a level playing field. Unfortunately, given what is at stake, the administering power is under no obligation to tailor its colonial relations to offer the Cayman Islands competitive advantage. The phenomenon of globalisation and the mobility of money have enabled the Cayman Islands to become a player of significance. What is important now is for the jurisdiction to maintain its stature among the jurisdictions regarded as leaders in international financial services by employing its own initiatives through home-grown strategies.

In this writer's opinion, the origin of the Cayman Islands as a successful financial centre owed as much to geography and a fortuitous combination of circumstances as to any deliberate planning. While this combination worked to develop the jurisdiction, it cannot now be relied upon to maintain its position of leadership.

It is surprising that neither the private sector nor the various political directorates over the years have seen fit to develop a local institution to provide training and experience so as to turn out a cadre of Caymanians with financial expertise. It was even more surprising to learn that many of the people working in financial circles in both public and private sectors are unfamiliar with Michael Porter's work (1980, 1985, 1990) on competitive advantage and competitive strategy.

The characterisation of the Cayman Islands as a frontier society is as applicable for its provision of excellence in the financial services sector as for its historical and political evolution. The financial services sector is dominated by an expatriate elite who seem unable or unwilling to engage and train Caymanian successors, to share their expertise, or to offer the opportunity for genuine partnerships. It is a world of glass ceilings and double standards except for a few token cases where a 'safe' Caymanian is elevated as a concession.

Occasionally complaints of discrimination against Caymanians are aired on local radio talk shows. Regrettably, to date this avenue has not proven effective in having complaints satisfactorily addressed. Political directorates have placed other challenges ahead of developing the kind of social dialogue which would elevate Caymanians in more than token numbers. In many instances, genuine attempts to eliminate such discrimination are thwarted by an alliance of special-interest groups and political elements that are disingenuous and insincere. During debate on the Employment Bill 2004, for instance, a majority of the members of the governing United Democratic Party absented themselves from the parliamentary proceedings rather than support reformist efforts by some of their members.

One reason that more Caymanians have not succeeded in breaking through the glass ceiling in the legal and financial sectors is that certain individuals in these arenas have, in their own interest, been able to establish 'unholy alliances' with politicians. Such alliances have done little except promote tokenism, which flatters the unwitting while halting progress for the majority.

Each time efforts have been made to set some standards and to raise the bar, they have been circumvented by a powerful cabal of self-interested players, who are quick to refer to the Bahamas in the early 1970s.

The fall of the Cayman Islands as a financial centre is not going to occur solely as a result of external pressure from competing onshore jurisdictions or international regulatory bodies. Internal dynamics will contribute equally to the jurisdiction's demise. One has only to read the papers each week to realise that the numbers of foreign professionals recruited to work in the legal and ancillary professions must mean less employment for qualified established Caymanians.

Has anyone conscientiously analysed why there are no firms with international branches owned by established Caymanians? Or where the established-Caymanian partners are in the major law firms? Why is there not more established-Caymanian expertise in mutual funds, special-purpose vehicles, and hedge funds?

A major failing has been the absence of a system to continually select and train those with aptitude in specialised financial areas. Why is there no directorate or similar organisation to ensure that there is a constant supply of young Caymanians to train and equip for sensitive and important positions in the financial sector? Should there not be some defined policy for educating and training Caymanians for public-sector positions now held by expatriates? Or do the powers that be think that the 'ad hocracy' will forever be good enough?

In a jurisdiction where the majority are not established Caymanians, what provision is there for cultivating an interest in the maintenance of excellence among Caymanians? It is not inappropriate to conclude that we shall have to ask ourselves, when the chickens have come home to roost, whether we have not ourselves perpetuated as much pressure, injustice, and unfairness on the jurisdiction's development as the United Kingdom, the European Union, the Financial Action Task Force, and myriad other external forces. For if the Caymanian financial centre is not to be developed for the benefit of established Caymanians, for whom should it be developed?

There is much to be said for the development of a reputation as bankers to the world. However, the ideal situation has to be one in which the Cayman Islands are less prone to the winds of change which occasionally bring more than a seasonal hurricane. Drucker, writing in *Post-Capitalist Society* (1993), stated that the primary resource in post-capitalist society would be 'knowledge' and the leading social groups would be 'knowledge workers'. It makes good sense to have strategies in place that promote the 'knowledge economy', since, as Drucker

(1993, 205–9) states, 'the forces that are creating post-capitalist society and post-capitalist polity originate in the developed world. They are the product and result of its development. Answers to the challenges of post-capitalist society and post-capitalist polity will not be found in the Third World.'

One might logically ask, 'Of what relevance is Drucker's observation to the rise and fall of the Cayman Islands as an international financial centre?' Simply put, the Cayman Islands is a developing society. Many persons mistakenly describe the Cayman Islands as a country. This is an unacceptable error, since, by its most rudimentary definition, a country has to have self-determination.

Their status as a colony administered by the United Kingdom precludes the Cayman Islands from individual membership in most international organisations. Even in the Commonwealth Parliamentary Association, that body comprised almost exclusively of the United Kingdom and its former and present colonies, the Cayman Islands are included as part of the United Kingdom, with 'the other Overseas Territories'. In such a position, the Cayman Islands will always be vulnerable to certain realities, both social and geopolitical. This vulnerability is the best argument for the Islands to receive special and differential treatment from both the administering power and the international organisations.

As islands unconnected with a nearby mainland, the Cayman Islands are dependent on international transport by both air and sea. The Islands are susceptible to severe environmental and ecological threats, and hurricane Ivan starkly reminded Caymanians that unbridled development has brought about an ecological disaster. Ivan also showed that there is relatively weak public and private institutional capacity to respond to domestic physical disasters, although the jurisdiction performed excellently in carrying on its international financial services obligations. Even more stark was the reminder that the jurisdiction would be well advised not to have any expectations of relief from the United Kingdom. Finally, the disaster exposed the jurisdiction's dependence on external business which is almost exclusively controlled by Cayman-based multinational institutions with largely expatriate expertise.

As a result of this last fact, per capita income figures are grossly misleading, and the Cayman Islands' reputation as a jurisdiction where the populace is wealthy is seriously inaccurate. The fragility of the situation becomes clear when one realises that investors often regard small islands as a risk because of their vulnerability in all spheres.

Since small islands have higher income vulnerability than most large states by as much as 25 per cent, they (small islands) consequently have higher levels of income inequality. This should come as no surprise in the case of small islands which are offshore centres. In the case of the Cayman Islands, consider that challenges span the spectrum from seasonal storms to international regulatory obligations. The situation is aggravated by the difference in salaries between the metropolis and small islands. It should not be forgotten that one of the main drawing cards of small islands is the level of sophistication available at a premium price. Many of these jurisdictions – the Cayman Islands, Jersey, and Guernsey, for example – have to send students overseas for education and training. While the majority of Caymanian students return, the same is not the case for some other jurisdictions. Such a situation sets up an expensive reliance on imported expertise and labour, thus placing additional strain on the economy.

Academics have recognised these vulnerabilities, and the new discipline of island studies is emerging at some North Atlantic academic institutions.

Income inequality is one area to which little other than lip service has been paid over the decades since the Cayman Islands' development as a leading international financial centre. A jurisdiction in which the monthly income of the working majority is widely accepted as being between CI$1,500 and CI$2,000 per month can hardly characterise itself as a prosperous community and a developed society.

There is no agenda for sustainable development and no programme for the attainment of an economic standard with which all Caymanians can identify. No attention has been given to Millennium Development Goals, and there is an absence of comprehensive planning. The political establishment has failed to use Vision 2008 as an instrument with which to establish a new and more comprehensive social dialogue. It is one of its most signal failures that the United Democratic Party's political directorate did not use its tenure to promote a comprehensive social agenda which would have eased much of the socioeconomic pressure experienced by the lower end of Caymanian society.

The opportunity for the Cayman Islands to launch itself into a sustainable-development mode still exists. The response should not take an eternity to fall into place. History will judge us harshly if it turns out that the Cayman Islands were developed only for the benefit of the people described by American sociologist C. Wright Mills (2000, 4–6) as the 'power elite'.

It is widely anticipated that 2007 will usher in efforts towards constitutional modernisation. A corollary of any modernisation exercise will be a re-examination of the constitutional relationship between the Cayman Islands and the United Kingdom. These possibilities were more fully explored in chapter 3, 'Engendering Democracy: An Analysis of the Relationship Between Administering Power and Colony'. It is appropriate to record here, however, that even that most talked-about pillar of attraction, the jurisdiction's colonial association with the United Kingdom, seems slated for an examination. There is an inclination toward self-determination on the part of many in the society. Exactly what this entails has not yet been articulated. It is, however, doubtful that such a gesture will involve political independence. It may well be that 'self-determination' is a euphemism for a continuation of the status quo.

The disposition of most Caymanians, both established and expatriate, towards voluntary colonialism is that the formalisation of the post of chief minister and some inconsequential amendments dealing with political administration are all that is necessary. Elsewhere, as previously indicated, there may be human rights conventions that may have some impact on the economy and society, but it is inadvisable to speculate as to what effects, if any, such instruments would have on the operations of the financial centre.

It is the studied position of this writer that while there are improvements to be made in the relationship between administering power and colony, political independence at this time would not serve any constructive purpose. The Cayman Islands' association with the United Kingdom is an attraction for much foreign financial business. To risk losing this market would be to sacrifice a promising long-term economic market for the short-term glamour of a false political success. After the initial euphoria of the sovereignty celebrations wore off and sobriety set in, Caymanians could well awaken to the prospect of political independence minus a thriving financial centre, since some businesses would opt to leave, at least until the new entity proved it was stable. And one must not forget the attitude of WASP investors.

Finally, what of cultural imperialism? Where are established Caymanians in an industry dominated by WASPs? Where are the provisions for Caymanians of all classes and colours to benefit from more than tokenism? It should be recognised that resorting to restrictive work-permit policies without ensuring that qualified Caymanians are being placed in position to acquire the necessary experience is neither appropriate nor effective.

To perpetuate the system currently in existence by ignoring the tensions and challenges facing it is fraught with danger. All colonised societies must eventually exorcise old ghosts such as prejudice, arrogance, and snobbery. In the Cayman Islands, there are many who have been dodging this responsibility for decades.

Then, too, the jurisdiction's ability to adjust to the demands of globalisation and the 'knowledge economy' must be examined. Let us take hedge funds, for example. Created more than a half century ago as a hedge against risk, these funds have risen to prominence in the Cayman Islands.

Hedge funds are vehicles which require the expertise of the fund manager to anticipate the market. Using talent and skill, the fund manager must make trades which outsmart the market. According to the *New York Times*, many managers have found striking ways to extract profits from all kinds of markets and market conditions. These practices are referred to as 'exploiting market inefficiencies' and are taken to mean not only trading in stocks, bonds, and commodities but also dealing in innumerable types of arbitrage (Dunleavy 2005).

Knowledgeable sources fear that some managers may be courting too many risks with their investment strategies – thus adding to rather than hedging a fund's overall risk. Of some concern, too, is the large number of hedge funds, attracted by the promise of few restrictions and attractive fees. Over the years, the drive for large returns has led managers to develop varying strategies, and the large-investment field has led to even more pressure to bring in mega-profits.

According to Hedge Fund Research, a database that tracks hedge fund performance, the number of hedge funds in the United Sates is in the vicinity of 8,000, with approximately $1 trillion invested. What should be of concern is that there has traditionally been an accepted lack of transparency on the part of both investors and federal regulators in the United States.

At the time of writing, there are two scandals, involving the Bayou Group in Connecticut and the K.L. Group in Florida, in which millions of dollars are unaccounted for. While new regulations in 2006 will require some funds to register with the Securities and Exchange Commission, the opaque nature of the hedge business means that it still pays for the investor to have a basic knowledge of how hedge funds work.

It would be interesting to ascertain just how widely the various financial vehicles are used by Caymanians. Have a significant number of Caymanians availed themselves of opportunities for investment beyond the traditional sources?

Dubai has now established itself as an international financial centre. Part of the United Arab Emirates, this jurisdiction seems eminently attractive to the oil-rich countries which are close by. Singapore is likely to rival Switzerland as the next great international financial centre, poised as it is to service China's financial growth. How will the development of these offshore centres affect the Cayman Islands, which, according to the literature, have been frequented by some wealthy Middle Eastern and Asian entrepreneurs? While it makes sense to prepare for the knowledge economy, it is foolish to concentrate all efforts on development which benefits almost exclusively one segment of the population.

Money still comes to the Cayman Islands; indeed, money has been coming to the Cayman Islands since their earliest days as an international financial centre. Will money keep coming to the Cayman Islands? That is, literally, the multimillion-dollar question. The situation in the Cayman Islands is not unlike that described by Alexis de Tocqueville (2000, 50) when he observed in 1835:

> Indeed I do not know a country where the love of money holds a larger place in the hearts of men, and where they profess a more profound scorn for the theory of the permanent equality of goods. But fortune turns there with incredible rapidity and experience teaches that it is rare to see two generations collect its favours.

Chapter 5

From Frontier Society to International Financial Centre:
A Nuanced View

The modern Cayman Islands offer large scope for a comparative study in colonial developments. Such a study should naturally have as a focal point the years which followed World War II. This is not to say that the years prior to this point held no interest; rather, for purposes of this exploration, it is most convenient to examine developments from the 1950s until the present day.

Ulf Hannerz provides some insight into the early evolution of the Islands. His work, which was published in the first decade of what can be described as the 'coming of age' of the Cayman Islands, still bears some relevance in this, the twenty-first century, and sets the tone for what is offered in this chapter.

> For the greater part of the twentieth century, the Cayman Islands, a small British Colony in the Western Caribbean with a population of some 10,000, were best known to the outside world for their postage stamps. More recently, their claim to fame has come to rest to a great extent with their status as a tax haven, and to a somewhat lesser extent with the attractions they hold for North American tourist. (Hannerz 1974, 57–58)

Beginning in the days of sailing ships, Caymanian men gained a reputation for their knowledge of the waters surrounding the Islands and their proficiency in the turtle trade (Duncan 1943). At the end of World War II, when the great industrial expansion came to the United States, the Islands became a primary recruiting jurisdiction for the shipping companies, especially National Bulk Carriers, a shipping conglomerate owned by American multimillionaire Daniel K. Ludwig. Caymanians, it later turned out, had a friend in Ludwig's agent, Captain

Southwell, who ensured that within the NBC organisation, Caymanians were the preferred seamen.

Lewis (1968, 331–32) provides a brief background to the developments which led to Caymanian men progressing from sailors, crewing and fishing turtle schooners owned by local merchant/ shipowners, to world-renowned seamen, captaining and crewing some of the largest behemoths to ply the oceans.

This chapter examines some of the major events that accompanied the evolution from 'the islands Time forgot' to the modern Cayman Islands. It is important to establish at this juncture that although some important players are mentioned by name, the chapter is not intended to focus on personalities. It is intended, rather, as a nuanced examination of the influences of the Cayman Islands' association with the colonial policies of the United Kingdom. More important, it is an attempt to interpret how the implementation of such policies influences current development trends. Until recently, Caymanians appeared to be concerned primarily with economic success. Now, however, the society is transforming itself into a multicultural mosaic consisting of many different ethnic and national groups. The Cayman Islands emerged as a 'total colonial society', according to the definition of Professor Ken Tracey in a lecture entitled 'The Colonial Heritage of the English-Speaking Caribbean'. This lecture, given at Trent University on December 5, 1977, suggested that the early settlers in much of the British Caribbean were either slaves – predominantly African, and brought involuntarily – or colonists – Europeans who were contracted as managers, overseers, or caretakers of the plantations, settlers seeking a fortune in a hostile Caribbean environment, or indentured servants. In the British Caribbean, this agglomeration of Europeans and their African slaves settled mainly on the more fertile and accessible islands. The Cayman Islands, while not fitting this norm, provide a textbook example of a frontier society, and while the Cayman Islands were not a slave society, the Islands were a society with slaves, as argued in chapter 1.

In examining the relationships between neighbouring jurisdictions, it is necessary to keep in mind that geopolitics have now changed since the original article was published. In 1978, Cuba was excluded from political or business dealings with the Cayman Islands. This was not mandated by the United Kingdom, since that country has always retained diplomatic and economic relations with Cuba, but was a policy adopted by the then political directorate. Currently, however, the Cayman Islands have air links to Cuba, and there are regular contacts, cultural and otherwise, between Caymanians and Cuban society.

Hannerz, in analysing the earlier Caymanian attitude toward Cuba, cites the following reasons for hostility:

> In the early 1960s, Caymanians were strongly concerned about the situation in Cuba ... Generally they were, and still remain, vehemently anti-Castro. Throughout their past the people of the islands had been in contact with Spanish-speaking territories and often enough these contacts had involved some antagonism. ...
>
> Another reason was the strong ties to the United States. As anti-Castro feelings grew among Americans, Caymanians quickly followed with a kind of vigilante action which seems to borrow traits from other frontier communities. (Hannerz 1974, 55)

Relations between the Cayman Islands and the other British and former British West Indian islands of the Eastern Caribbean were almost non-existent, possibly owing to the distance between them. So acute were the differences between the various islands that not even Britain's external stimulus and help in the immediate post-colonial period could persuade the former British territories to form a West Indian Federation (De Kadt 1972, 36–37; Lewis 1968, 368–86).

Integration came via the establishment of the Caribbean Community (CARICOM) in 1973. The Cayman Islands displayed no interest in this organisation until the United Democratic Party government accepted associate membership in 2002. Until the integration movement matured into the community of nations that it is today, the British Caribbean islands were a disparate and challenging collection of states. Although forced to confront the realities of globalisation – the World Trade Organisation, the Free Trade Area of the Americas (FTAA), and the General Agreement on Trade and Services (GATS) – the islands' prospects for economic survival remain daunting.

The Cayman Islands have until recently remained isolated from those developments which have impinged on the mainly agricultural economies of the other formerly British islands. As a booming financial centre, however, the Cayman Islands have experienced increasing pressures. International obligations brought on by the Organization for Economic Cooperation and Development, the Financial Action Task Force, the European Union, and the United Kingdom itself have forced a continuous evolution of this sector of the Caymanian economy.

Tourism, which constitutes the other sector of the economy, has likewise experienced a transformation. Apart from their reputation as an expensive destination, the Cayman Islands, like other Caribbean destinations, now face increasing competition from Cuba. Once dubbed 'the playground of the Americas', Cuba has great attraction as a vast, beautiful, unspoiled island with abundant cultural and historical sites, and which is safe for visitors.

The phenomenon of Cayman's development is not all positive: many Caymanians express frustration at congested roads, excessively crowded streets and sidewalks on cruise-ship days, and the stresses on the Islands' natural environment. Also, there is the question of who really benefits from Grand Cayman's overdevelopment. With real estate prices out of reach for most ordinary Caymanians and a proliferation of imported workers, the tourism industry is not as beneficial to the Caymanian economy and society as it could be.

The society is affected in other ways as well, and while tourism as an important contributor to the Islands' economy is discussed elsewhere in this chapter, it is appropriate to make a few cursory observations here. The most important one is that tourism in the Cayman Islands is in its infancy, compared with other Caribbean islands, and Cayman as a tourist destination has never achieved the captivating and colourful distinctiveness that marks many other island destinations. Whether the explanation lies in Cayman's specific history or whether it is a simple matter of economics remains to be ascertained.

One thing seems obvious from a comparative development perspective, and that is that Caymanian society is more akin to that of South Florida than to that of any other West Indian island. With its proliferation of North American fast-food chains and with the more upscale restaurants offering European or North American cuisine, there is no great choice of establishments offering local and West Indian dishes. The same is applicable to entertainment and nightlife: there are no popular centres featuring local music and floor shows which are typically Caymanian or even Caribbean. It should come as no surprise, then, when informed critics suggest that, outside of its safety, the Cayman Islands have little that is unique to offer the stay-over visitor.

The economics of survival: Turtling, thatch rope, and subsistence agriculture

The Cayman Islands were a simple society in 1950. For the most part, the Islands remained isolated, mosquito-infested, and economically sluggish. There was limited contact with the outside world, and certainly there was no reason to believe that anything like the current level of international communication could have bloomed out of the rudimentary infrastructure which existed at that time.

What passed as the economy could be divided into two categories, the local economy and the limited export/import economy. The local economy consisted mainly of the turtle and thatch-rope industries. The manufacture of thatch rope was controlled by the merchant establishment, which purchased the rope by the 'coil' from ropemakers in the districts of East End, North Side, and, to a lesser degree, Bodden Town and West Bay.

The simple production system, from cutting 'tops' (gathering the unopened sheaves of the thatch palms) and drying them to splicing and twisting into ropes, involved whole families, and it was not uncommon for more than one family to team up to produce larger amounts. Since payment was based on the number of coils produced, such an arrangement made good economic sense.

Transport from the centres of production was by truck. The merchant in George Town would have as his agent some person in the district who was responsible for selecting the rope, ensuring the number of coils, and arranging for delivery in George Town. At the port, there was a final inspection and counting before the rope was loaded onto one of the motor vessels plying the waters between Jamaica and the Cayman Islands. The main export point for Caymanian thatch rope was Jamaica, where it was used primarily by local fisherman. The thatch-rope industry continued until the early 1970s, when the development of cheaper, mass-produced rope of synthetic fibre made the Caymanian product uncompetitive.

During the 1950s and 1960s, trade was mainly between Grand Cayman, Kingston, and Tampa, Florida. This triangular trade was dominated by the merchant houses of H.O. Merren and Company and R.E. McTaggart and Brother. Every aspect of import commerce fell into the orbit of one or both of these establishments. It was difficult, if not impossible, for competing merchants to eclipse these two commercial giants, since they were able to keep control of all transactions including shipping – they owned most of the ships, contracted the labour force, and controlled the capital.

The 'House of Merren' had a fleet of motor vessels and steamships, including the *Merco* and the *Mizpah,* captained and crewed by Caymanians, most of whom had gained their skills on many voyages to the Miskito Cays, San Andres and Old Providence (Providencia), and Cuba's Isle of Pines. The *Rembro* (an acronym for R.E. McTaggart and Brother), the flagship of the McTaggart merchant house, plied the popular trade route between Tampa and Grand Cayman and provided competition to other vessels sailing this route. It was logical that the merchants would equip themselves to cater to the needs of travelling Caymanians, so their vessels accommodated some passengers in addition to cargo.

Additionally, the two merchant houses were the appointed representatives, distributors, and agents for a variety of popular products and consumer items. For example, H.O. Merren and Company was the exclusive distributor of Libby, McNeil and Libby (Chicago) products. The McTaggarts, for their part, held sole distributorship for the products of the R.J. Reynolds Tobacco Company, in addition to other popular consumer items. Such associations spawned the Caymanian monopolistic system and the unfair trade practice of wholesale and retailing at the same time.

Complementing the large (by Caymanian standards) merchant houses was an assortment of smaller merchants who operated in association with, and were reliant upon, the established merchant houses. This reliance took the form of credit, and in a cash-strapped society, the ability to negotiate a flexible payment arrangement dictated solvency or insolvency.

Such, then, was the system which existed between the two classes of merchants – it was symbiosis at its Caymanian best. And the relationship extended to the point where, in some cases, the petty merchants were the political surrogates (vestrymen) of the more powerful justices from these merchant houses.

In terms of overall wealth, power, and privilege, H.O. Merren and Company was the leader. Along with branch stores in George Town, Savannah, and North Side as well as the main department store in the downtown area, this business house owned cattle, land, and the Pageant Beach and Bayview hotels, in addition to their shipping interests. Even by standards elsewhere in the British Caribbean, such an asset base was impressive, and yet failure to propagate their wealth and increase the assets led to the demise of this first Caymanian business house. The Merrens monopolised business until the 1960s, when members of the Kirkconnell family, originally from the island of Cayman Brac but with considerable business interests in Jamaica, moved to Grand Cayman after the Jamaican political climate soured.

Within a few years, the Kirkconnell family superseded the House of Merren as the premier merchant family in the Cayman Islands. Holding a more diverse asset base than that of the Merrens, this family also displayed greater business acumen. Interestingly, it was not their practice to embark on joint ventures with outside capital. At one time, the Kirkconnell family's holdings included a hotel on Grand Cayman, ships, and significant property on both Grand Cayman and Cayman Brac. Later, one brother embarked upon a very successful duty-free retail business; this enterprise is currently one of the two leading free-port conglomerates in the Cayman Islands.

The period from the 1950s until about the mid-1980s saw a proliferation of small and medium-sized mercantile establishments in George Town. Most of these businesses apparently realised sufficient returns on their investments to remain in operation until the 1980s, when the significant increase in international finance and offshore business necessitated the expansion of office-space capacity in George Town. Many of the small merchants sold their properties to the moneyed interests, some of whom were recent immigrants, mainly from Europe and North America.

While the merchant houses monopolised commerce and dominated the export of thatch rope to Jamaica, that other trade staple, turtle and its by-products, was handled by merchants and traders primarily from West Bay. Most of the principals in this trade were experienced mariners who either owned their own schooners, were co-owners or shareholders in schooners, or were investors in a voyage. Experienced mariners were often addressed as 'Captain', a term of respect connoting that the person, while not necessarily holding formal qualifications, was a successful navigator and knowledgeable mariner of the waters around the Cayman Islands and, in some instances, the northwest Caribbean. It was not unusual for Caymanian seamen to have sailed in international waters, and there is reason to believe that some mariners from the Cayman Islands traded as far north as Nova Scotia.

In contrast to the thatch-rope industry, the turtling industry was fraught with unavoidable risks. In the first place, payment depended upon the successful outcome of the voyage. Simply put, no turtles caught meant no wages paid. At the end of a voyage, a complicated system of calculating shares went into effect, in which the boat received shares separate and apart from the captain, even if he was the boat's owner. Expenses came out next, and what was left was shared among the crew according to a ranking system in which the cook ranked among the highest-paid.

It was turtling that prepared many Caymanian sailors to become seamen capable of crewing the largest and most sophisticated bulk carriers and cargo ships. Equally important socially and culturally, it was this call to turtling and later to the merchant marine that became a rite of passage from boyhood to manhood.

The turtling industry reached its greatest significance in 1951 when a turtle canning factory was built with funds from the Colonial Development Corporation. In 1952 the processing of turtle began. So popular was this product that at the Lord Mayor of London's banquet, the menu was deemed incomplete if it did not offer turtle soup from the Cayman Islands. The product was not as popular in the closer US markets of Tampa and Key West. Largely as a result of poor marketing arrangements in these two cities, commercial operations became unprofitable, and within five years of its inception the factory had to be closed.

Aside from turtling and ropemaking, most Caymanians practised subsistence farming to meet their daily food needs. It was commonplace for every household to have access to its own plot of land or 'ground' for the purpose of producing its own food. Subsistence farming was supplemented by fishing, and Caymanian society at that time relied almost exclusively on local food. Red meat was a rarity, and when it was available, it was strictly locally raised and usually eaten only on special occasions, mainly at Christmas and New Year's celebrations.

The reliance on subsistence farming and the sea made for an active lifestyle for the Caymanians of the day. Most families, accustomed to this kind of existence, accepted the demanding and frugal lifestyle as an important part of their upbringing. It has been suggested that the moulding of the Caymanian psyche and culture through hardship and hard work contributed to the uniqueness of the Caymanian male in comparison to his West Indian counterparts. While there are no empirical studies to substantiate this suggestion, experienced Caymanian seamen were noted for their mastery of geography, sound common sense, and apparent contentment with the political status quo.

Be that as it may, change was soon to manifest itself. In 1953 Barclays Bank DCO opened its first operation in the Cayman Islands. A colonial bank, Barclays came to the Cayman Islands from Jamaica. Its arrival in the Cayman Islands was brought about by the need for a financial institution to service the increasing business generated by the remittances sent home by Caymanian merchant seaman.

Before Barclays, there was only the Government Savings Bank. This bank was a peculiar institution, and its management and eventual closure demonstrated a lack of vision and foresight not only on the part of the local government and bureaucrats but also on the part of the colonial administration. Not allowing the Government Savings Bank to expand to meet the needs of the growing Caymanian economy was one of a series of ill-advised decisions made by Colonial Office policymakers and bureaucrats between the 1950s and 1970s.

That a decision was taken to shut down the Government Savings Bank at a time when there was an opportunity to expand it into a commercially viable national bank speaks eloquently to the self-serving colonial policies of the administering power. It is logical to assume that the closure of the Government Savings Bank benefited Barclays Bank, the colonial flagship and symbol of British commerce from the early twentieth century on (Crossley and Blanford 1975). The closure of the Government Savings Bank and its replacement by Barclays no doubt suited the Colonial Office, since this bastion of empire signified the English presence.

Among the myopic decisions made by local policymakers and sanctioned by the imperial power, this one ranks a close second to encouraging the sale of land by Caymanians to outsiders who held an altogether different view of private property than the Caymanian people. The practice has turned out to be inimical to the interests of established Caymanians, who in the twenty-first century are finding themselves a landless people in a society where wealth equates to an ability to develop property either for residential or commercial uses.

The role of land in the evolution of the modern Cayman Islands

In most frontier societies, land assumes a critical importance, and its ownership or lack thereof exercises an important influence upon the local economy. Up to and shortly after the end of World War II, land ownership among established Caymanians was common in the Cayman

Islands. Indeed, it is accurate to describe many Caymanians residents as 'land rich' – so much so that they had no use for beach land, other than as a secure place for their livestock during periods of acute mosquito infestation and for their catboats, canoes, and other vessels during the bad-weather months or when the boat was not in regular use.

Established Caymanians did not normally build their houses on beach land or near the water as is the practice nowadays. Mindful of hurricanes and the accompanying high waves, and the possibility of being cut off from the rest of the island, as were Prospect's residents during the 1932 storm, established Caymanians always sought the high ground for their house sites.

North Americans, arriving in the years following World War II, were so interested in beach land that many local landowners realised that it was a desirable commodity. It was at this time that G.H. Smith, a white American, established himself in George Town as one of the earliest realtors.

From his base in George Town, this pioneer would hire an equally well-known Caymanian taxi driver, Ira Thompson, to ferry him anywhere on the island that was accessible. It was an island characteristic at that time that land in which he exhibited a interest bore his hallmark identification: 'FOR SALE SEE G.H. SMITH GEORGE TOWN'.

It was an incredibly simple system, for it was easy to find G.H. Smith, a white North American, on Grand Cayman, which at that time had fewer than 50 foreign residents. Certainly there was only one realtor by that name. Indeed, there is no available evidence to show that there was any other realtor on the island at that time.

G.H. Smith maintained his monopoly until the boom of the 1960s. The arrival of international banks, an increasing number of investors and speculators, and the opportunities generated by the remittances of Caymanian seamen meant that by the end of that decade, land on Grand Cayman had taken on a wholly new importance.

While it took G. H. Smith, an American with off-island appeal, to open the market, the next entrepreneurs would be of an entirely different genre. Robert Selkirk Watler was a white Bodden Towner with family connections to Cayman's original settlers. Self-taught and honest, with a personable disposition and a winning smile, Watler gained the confidence of Caymanian landowners. Within 10 years this conscientious young man of humble origins had gained such a favourable reputation as a real estate agent, speculator, and confidant that he was sought after by anyone who had an interest in property – buyer or seller, local or foreign.

Watler's gregariousness and fairness propelled him to the forefront of Caymanian real estate circles and enabled him to achieve a level of wealth equal to that of the most affluent foreign residents. His Caymanian roots ensured that this now prominent Bodden Towner retained the confidence of the local people, unlike wealthy outsiders of whom Caymanians felt suspicious. It was characteristic of his upbringing that, while not betraying this confidence, he was also respected by his non-Caymanian clientele as a savvy and scrupulous businessman. Robert Selkirk Watler, entrepreneur from Bodden Town, set the standard for real estate practice in the Cayman Islands and left a legacy of honesty, integrity, and fair play in land dealings.

Caymanians, not unlike other Caribbean people, are excellent imitators, and several other Caymanians followed Selkirk Watler into the land market. Prominent among these were the late James Manoah (Jim) Bodden and Rex Crighton. While it was Watler who opened the market and set the standard, it fell to Jim Bodden and others to revolutionise land dealings and to open the islands to mass transactions.

A Caymanian who had emigrated to the United States, Jim Bodden returned to the Cayman Islands at a time when the real estate market was poised to explode. This articulate man, with his adopted southern style and native salesmanship, soon won a seat in the Legislative Assembly. Despite some controversy over his election, in 1972 he was able to solidify his seat as one of two representatives for Bodden Town. His ability to successfully marry his private career as an entrepreneur and real estate magnate with his public career as a Legislative Assembly member made him popular with both locals and foreigners, many of whom considered him a visionary. By the mid-1970s Jim Bodden's real-estate operation was the largest on the island.

He was not, however, without his critics: many in the Caymanian establishment objected to his outspoken nationalism, his interest in the humbler classes of Caymanians, and his frustration with the fact that the society suffered from its inability to determine its own political direction.

Land sales had reached new dimensions by 1976. Jim Bodden reached the peak of his political ambitions when his Unity Team swept the incumbent political directorate from power. He became, in essence, the de facto chief minister of the Cayman Islands. The demands of political office and people's expectation that he would assume the role of a benevolent godfather meant that he had to divest himself of the routine responsibilities of his by now extensive real estate interests.

Whether his divestment was the root cause of the problems later experienced by his real estate company is a question to be answered in a different book. What is clear is that such an intricate and successful organisation should have survived without his daily presence. Nonetheless, by the time of his death in 1988, there was little or nothing left of the once-dominant real estate empire built by this flamboyant initiator, now a National Hero.

There were, of course, other realtors of merit in the evolution of the land market in the Cayman Islands. While this is not a history of the emergence of land as a commodity, the intent of this chapter is to illustrate its importance to the larger scene of the development of the modern Cayman Islands. It is in this regard that the following observations are made.

It is curious that there were no prominent black real estate developers of the calibre of Watler and Bodden. Their absence becomes more striking when one considers that in the Cayman Islands at that time there were black landowners of significance in almost all districts. Could there have been a different sense of the value of land between Caymanians of colour and other Caymanians? Or is it possible that large landholdings held by Caymanians of colour were in undesirable areas? Whatever the reasons, to this day there is no significant number of Caymanians of colour in the real estate business. Indeed, the entire business has changed. Foreign franchises with foreign salespeople, many on work permits, now dominate the market, and those agents are almost exclusively North American or European and cater mainly to their compatriots.

As alarming as such a transformation is, what is of concern here are the origin and consequences of the idea that Caymanians should sell absolute title to their land to outsiders who have a different notion of private property than do Caymanians. To grasp the significance of this, one must remember that in a Cayman where land ownership was common and where geography dictated that many people had close neighbours, until the mid-twentieth century land had little or no commercial value.

The Caymanian concept of private property did not extend to the land grabs and range wars that were common on the North American frontier in the nineteenth and early twentieth centuries. To the Caymanian, 'private property' did not mean denial of access or refusal of passage across. The political directorate should have assumed responsibility for ensuring that Caymanians understood the full ramifications of selling their land with absolute title to foreigners. More important, since the government pioneered the leasing of land on a large scale in the Cayman Islands, someone should have had the foresight to propose that private individuals follow that model.

It was a serious oversight for the political directorate not to have legislated against outsiders having absolute entitlement to Caymanian landholdings. Precedent was set by an agreement between the government and Benson Greenall concerning property along the West Bay road. This development deserves further elaboration since, in this writer's opinion, it highlights the failure of the political directorate and the colonial administration to safeguard the interests of the colonised by encouraging them to limit the sale of leaseholds. Leaseholds were a familiar concept to Europeans and North Americans, and there is no credible argument to suggest that such a concept could not have become the norm in Caymanian society. British colonialism, however, was predicated upon ownership of land as a means to the natural resources, and – whether the land was in Africa, with its vast array of natural resources, the larger West Indian islands, with their sugar acreage, or the minuscule Cayman Islands – the colonial authorities had no history of preserving the land interests of the local population.

An opportunity to establish a precedent which would have ensured that established Caymanian landholders maintained advantage presented itself when Benson Greenall indicated an interest in leasing land along what is now Seven Mile Beach.

Benson Greenall and the making of Seven Mile Beach

Even at this early stage in the development of the Islands, the pristine nature of the West Bay beach area (later called Seven Mile Beach) was recognised. Credit Benson Greenall with realising its potential and acting to procure it. According to correspondence from the Commissioner's Office dated June 20, 1957, there was no objection to the proposal by Benson Greenall to sublet lands along Seven Mile Beach (file 95/49). Earlier, in 1952, a lease had been agreed upon between Benson Greenall and Sir Hugh Mackintosh Foot, representing the Cayman Islands.

The lease, according to documents examined at Cayman Islands National Archive, was for 99 years commencing on April 11, 1950. The annual rate of £100 was 'payable in advance by equal half yearly payments to be made on the Eleventh Day of each of the months of April and October'.

There were, of course, other covenants, some of which were:

a) To build a hotel on and develop the demised lands as a holiday resort;

b) Within a period of eighteen months from the date of these presents to commence the work of building the said hotel and of developing the demised lands as a holiday resort and within a period of five years from the date of these presents to extend a sum of not less than Fifty Thousand Pounds in building the said hotel and developing the demised lands as a holiday resort and thereafter to maintain operate and keep open on the demised lands (to the extent thereinafter provided) a hotel suitable for the accommodation of visitors to the island of Grand Cayman.

c) To make available to the residents of the island of Grand Cayman and the general public at all times a portion of sea beach not less than five hundred feet in length and extending in depth from the high water mark to the existing road at a place to be approved by the Lessor either on the Southern side of the demised lands or on other land acquired by the Lessee between George Town and West Bay and to the South of the demised lands and to permit the residents of the Islands of Grand Cayman and the general public at all times to have access to and from such portions of sea beach.

The lease was recorded in the Cayman Islands by the Public Recorder, William Simpson Coe, on May 6, 1950.

The proposal by the entrepreneur Benson Greenall regarding leasing Crown lands on Grand Cayman led to the modernisation of the system of the acquisition and disposal of Crown properties. Prior to this time no legislation existed whereby the Commissioner could vest Crown lands. In Jamaica up to 1863 such authority was held by the Executive Committee. In 1866, however, the Colonial Secretary (Vesting of Lands) Law Chap. 368 was passed, transferring all such authority to the Colonial Secretary of Jamaica.

Although the Cayman Islands were a dependency of Jamaica, this legislation did not extend to them. What related to the Cayman Islands was found in the Imperial Act 31, which was issued under Queen Victoria's seal on June 22, 1863, and called An Act for the Government of the Cayman Islands. Section Three of this instrument provided that:

> Until it shall be otherwise provided by the said Legislature, it shall be lawful for the said Justices and Vestry, in their accustomed matter, or in such other manner as shall be prescribed, in writing, under the hand and seal of the Governor of Jamaica, to make such regulations as to them shall seem fit for the following purposes, that is to say, inter alia, "Respecting the management, occupation and disposal of the public property, or common land."

There seems to have been confusion as to what course of action should be followed, and, as a footnote to the above correspondence, the Clerk of the Court remarked to the Commissioner that the leasing and purchase of lands involving the government was done in the name of the 'Officer Administering the Government'.

A slew of correspondence on the matter of land lease, land purchases, and management of Crown property passed between the various officials on Grand Cayman and Jamaica. However, it was not until some years later that the matter was resolved. In a document entitled 'Message from His Honour the Commissioner to the Assembly of Justices & Vestry', Commissioner Gerrard wrote:

> The present position is most unsatisfactory, where on one hand, lands purchased are purchased in the name of the Commissioner as an individual (for instance "William Bodden to A.M. Gerrard, Commissioner of the Cayman Islands") and where, when it comes to the sale or lease of Government lands there is considerable doubt as to the correct legal procedure, whether lands should be conveyed or leased by His Excellency the Governor, or by the Commissioner, and there is no doubt as to the precise position of the Justices and Vestry. In regard to this latter, the Imperial Act for the Government of the Cayman Islands empowers the Justices and Vestry to make regulation, inter alia, for the management, occupation and disposal of public property or common land, but legal doubts have arisen whether in fact these are, or are not vested in the Justices and Vestry.

The document ended with a recommendation to Justices and Vestrymen to support the accompanying bill, which dealt with the clarification of the legal position regarding the vesting of public lands. As a result of the government's decision to lease land to Greenall, it was discovered that no legal mechanism was in place to transfer the land to the lessee. After a protracted exchange of correspondence between the commissioner in the Cayman Islands and the authorities in Jamaica, it was decided to bring a bill to the Assembly in the Cayman Islands, authorising a law. That law has now come to be known as the Governor Vesting of Lands Law, and it authorises the governor, upon the advice of cabinet, to dispense with the lease, sale, or gift of public property.

While public lands were protected somewhat against acquisition by speculators and outsiders, no such consideration was encouraged among private landholders. There were certain peculiarities about privately owned land in Cayman. Settlement was mainly along the island's coasts, so many established Caymanian families owned beach land. Such land, however, held little or no commercial value to its owners. Early Caymanian settlers soon learnt the dangers of building close to the sea on hurricane-prone islands. Foreigners who purchased such lands, believing they had received the better of the bargain, have realised since the passing of hurricane Ivan, if not before, that the early Caymanians were a practical people.

In short, there was little or no beach land bought and sold among established Caymanians until the beginning of the real-estate boom. When foreigners – particularly North Americans – came, however, beach land was the real estate that attracted their interest. Lacking a culture of land transactions and lacking any vision of the Islands' future development potential, in most instances the Caymanians sold their land at what later proved to be disadvantageous prices.

In Caymanian society up to the 1960s, cash was always at a premium. Considering that before the 1950s there was no commercial bank for depositing savings, borrowing money, or carrying out even the most rudimentary financial transactions, it is not surprising that Caymanians were awed when apparently rich foreigners offered them a few hundred pounds for land which, until that point, had had no commercial value.

Speculators, developers, and so-called investors thrived throughout the 1970s until the mid-1980s, aided and abetted by Caymanian real-estate salesmen. Few Caymanians realised the folly of selling absolute title to outsiders whose notion of private property was more exclusionary and more absolute than that of a society of extended families, close neighbours, and mainly docile inhabitants.

Along with the interest by apparently wealthy foreigners came the erosion of the traditional *laissez faire* attitude to land ownership. Land sales increased significantly, and while speculators, realtors, and developers benefited, the Caymanians derived no tangible long-term benefit. Indeed, it is indisputable that their sale of absolute title brought them almost immediate disadvantage and eventual deprivation.

Alarmed at the obvious failure of the political directorate or the wider society to envisage the social changes this practice would eventually bring about, one Caymanian cautioned against it. In an article in a Caymanian newsmagazine (Bodden 1978, 35), this writer warned of the danger of encouraging Caymanians to dispose of what amounted to their only asset in this way. Several years earlier, another commentator had raised the matter of land sales to outsiders when he posed questions regarding tourism and development in Cayman (Hannerz 1974, 18).

In the article, it was suggested that it was a bad idea for established Caymanians to sell absolute title to their land to rich foreigners (mainly Europeans and North Americans) whose notion of private property was significantly different from that of the Caymanians. It was suggested that Caymanians should instead be encouraged to sell leaseholds of 50 and 99 years' duration. The article intimated that the transaction between the Cayman Islands government and Benson Greenall could have served as a model.

The article was widely misunderstood by the uninformed white establishment, who saw the ideas as a trespass upon what they deemed an unchallengeable right. The matter was taken so far that one minister of government took it upon himself to castigate the author as a 'Castro sympathiser' in a scathing diatribe recorded in the Legislative Assembly (Hansard, April 11, 1979).

It should come as no surprise that an informative article published for the edification of the public met such a hostile reception. Caymanian politics for some time had been largely influenced by a white merchant elite of the type best described by American sociologist C. Wright Mills:

> ... men whose positions enable them to transcend ordinary environments of ordinary men and women; they are in positions to make decisions having major consequences. ... They rule the big corporations. They run the machinery of the state and claim its prerogatives. ... They occupy the strategic command post of

the social structure, in which are centered the effective means of power and the wealth and celebrity which they enjoy. (Mills 2000, 3–4)

Caymanians have continued to sell their land to outsiders, not realising that the fundamental principle is not just to sell but to use some of the returns to acquire other property. The result is just as was predicted in the 1978 article: there is a growing number of young Caymanians, the sons and daughters of those same people who were so misguidedly encouraged to sell to foreigners absolute title to their land, who are landless with no hope of even acquiring a house. Their progeny will have to spend the rest of their lives landless, residing in one of the many apartment complexes which seem to be the newest speculative fad to come to this frontier society.

Even the promised benefits which were to be derived from the construction of condominiums have not materialised, since many of the foreign owners prefer to have their properties managed by their white compatriots.

Established Caymanians are, then, for the most part, left to salvage the detritus of the tourist economy. It is a distressing denouement to what should have been a robust and secure landholding future for the established Caymanian. Few Caribbean countries have gone this route. And one must ask why the Caymanian political directorate chose this way, when the lease agreement between Benson Greenall and the government could have served as a template for future land sales, both public and private, where foreigners were involved.

Since Hannerz (1974) and Bodden (1978) recorded their concerns about land sales to outsiders, there has been no significant decrease in transactions. Matters have been compounded by large-scale acquisitions by at least one outsider. These acquisitions and subsequent large developments have caused disquiet among some sectors in Caymanian society and were mentioned by two members of the Legislative Assembly meeting with officials at the Foreign and Commonwealth Office in 1995. Economic pressures brought on by rapid commercial development and an accompanying increase in the immigrant population have meant that for many Caymanians, the only way to progress is to sell off their land.

It must be understood that land is still a valuable commodity, and in a frontier society such as the Cayman Islands it plays a pivotal role in economic development. It is therefore alarming that land which should be used for food production is so valuable and so much in demand that it is sold for housing estates and commercial developments. To many, it seems more sensible and, one could argue, less costly to import food.

The result is that Caymanian society is totally dependent upon imported foods. The vulnerability of such a position has thus far not manifested itself, and geographical proximity to the North American continent serves to lessen Caymanian concerns, but this situation cannot be expected to continue forever. The Cayman Islands are today in a much less fortunate position than they were during the late nineteenth and early twentieth centuries, when land was used optimally for agricultural purposes and the Islands exported beef cattle to nearby jurisdictions.

As in most frontier societies, there were always land-claim disputes in the Grand Court of the Cayman Islands. In 1971 the Cayman Islands government initiated the regional cadastral survey and land registration process, which culminated in the mapping and registration of every plot of land on the three islands. At the conclusion of this process in 1977, there was a documented land ownership system. In addition to eliminating contention over ownership and legal entitlement, the cadastral survey aided in land sales by permitting less contentious transfer of titles. It also revolutionised the way titles and deeds were kept: the Department of Lands and Survey began keeping all original titles in its land information system.

In contrast with some other colonial and former colonial enclaves in the Caribbean, land ownership by foreigners is not restricted in the Cayman Islands. As a result, many foreign landowners are under the impression that they can deny access to beaches and other areas at will. From time to time there are confrontations when landowners or hotel managers try to enforce the exclusivity of 'their' beaches. Such confrontations lead to letters to the editor, complaints on radio talk shows, debates in the Legislative Assembly, and occasionally police intervention. Evidently the same misunderstanding exists elsewhere, as the Barbadian kaiso artist Gabby chronicles the islanders' defiant response in his refrain, 'Jack, this beach is mine! I will bathe here anytime.'

The energy derived from land speculation found its way into other areas of the economy, attracting many financial houses and law offices. By the 1980s Cayman was attracting serious numbers of expatriate workers and economic migrants whose primary purpose was to service this growing economy. Many of these people were the displaced employees of banks, trust companies, and merchant houses in former colonial outposts like the Bahamas. Following their arrival in the Cayman Islands, a symbiotic relationship developed between them and the established Caymanians. There was, however, a less acknowledged side to their arrival, since in many cases they brought prejudices and idiosyncrasies which had not been openly encountered in Caymanian society prior to their arrival.

Les nouveaux arrivants: Banks, business, and bonanza

No account of the rise of the Cayman Islands from a frontier society on the periphery of what was the British Empire to a world-class financial centre would be complete without comment on the genesis of its banking industry.

To begin with, it is no longer acceptable to describe the industry as 'the banking industry'. The Cayman Islands are referred to as a financial centre. It is this transformation that is discussed in this section.

While there were established commercial banks on Grand Cayman and at least one on Cayman Brac, no competitive atmosphere in banking existed until Jean Doucet established his business on Grand Cayman. Nor, for that matter has any existed since the demise of Interbank. A French Canadian with a flair for the cocktail circuit, this newcomer soon proved to be a popular person, a personable businessman, and a friend to the established Caymanians. He cultivated Caymanian society by hosting cocktail parties, and this white Canadian with his black wife so captivated polite Caymanian society that the local business elite were soon speaking of him warmly.

Whether his activities were a calculated assault on the established banks or whether he was a genuinely brilliant entrepreneur is a matter for conjecture. There is, to this writer's knowledge, no evidence to suggest anything other than that his banking acumen was founded on utilitarian but misguided principles – principles which in the end allowed the establishment to exploit the demise of his business empire.

Be that as it may, his initial efforts were so successful that within a few years of his original venture, Sterling Bank, another bank, the International Bank (later called Interbank), was formed, with the former Sterling Bank assuming the role of a trust company.

The advertising literature for the Interbank group indicated that in addition to the establishments in the Cayman Islands, there were bank branches in London, Buenos Aires, and other international centres. There were also other investments, including a hotel in the Virgin Islands, a cattle ranch in Quebec, and a vaccine that prevented tooth decay (Chodos 1977, 105).

Jean Doucet represented a liberalism that had not previously existed among Caymanian bankers and which was instrumental in attracting Caymanians in the middle and lower economic strata. The apparent generosity of his banking practices attracted the common labourer as well as the emerging middle class. Interbank offered personalised banking in private surroundings with female tellers – whose attire certainly did not fit the conservative mould of the established banks. Indeed, there were those who considered it suggestive, which certainly would have been in keeping with the operating psychology of the bank. It appeared that normal protocols governing fraternisation with clients were ignored when the clients were wealthy, influential, and international.

M. Doucet cultivated the persona of a benevolent *padrone,* and his foray into real-estate development led many to believe that he was wealthy beyond his interests in Cayman. Numerous accounts of his generosity pervaded Caymanian society, and the dispossessed and disenfranchised who could not normally obtain loans and mortgages held high hopes of benefiting from his largesse.

As it turned out, many of these accounts were apocryphal – wishful thinking. While there was a certain similarity between Jean Doucet and Jim Bodden in terms of their operational flair, Doucet lacked Bodden's ability to take on the establishment.

In April 1974 both local and international investors were buoyed by the announcement that investments in the Interbank group totalled a phenomenal US$74 million. The fall of Interbank came as a great surprise to many in Caymanian society. It was also one of those rare events genuinely worthy of Tennysonian high diction. In other Caribbean societies, this fall would have been lampooned by poets, calypsonians, and parodists. In Cayman, however, Jean Doucet was pursued, prosecuted, and imprisoned. There are those who believe that his greatest shortcoming may have been his desire to spread economic prosperity among the middle and lower echelons of Caymanian society. This idea is interesting and bears further exploration.

Fate, fractiousness, and finality: Doucet meets his demise

There is no convincing evidence to establish Doucet's association with the events leading up to the demonstration which took place in George Town in April 1970 as anything other than a coincidence. As it turned out, however, Doucet was inextricably linked to this event in a way that, conspiracy theorists in Cayman claim, brought about his demise, and from which only history can offer ultimate exoneration. The story is an intriguing one.

It happened that the political directorate introduced new planning regulations and a Statistics Law in 1970. The Islands had previously had a Statistics Law, but it was inadvertently omitted during a law review. There were sections in the new planning regulations which seemed unreasonable and unacceptable for the development of the Islands. One such regulation had to do with the size of lots required for constructing houses and the zoning of residential areas.

Intransigence and obstinacy by the political directorate ruled out any compromise, and by the middle of April 1970 the community on Grand Cayman was so restive that there was talk of a demonstration. Johnson (2001) offers a vivid description of what followed, including how Doucet became caught up in the subsequent events:

> The situation eventually led to a demonstration by political opposition members of the Legislative Assembly and their public support group, joined by a number of "black power" troublemakers, which immediately began to scare tourists, visitors and local business persons. In spite of the demonstration, the government moved on with the Bills through the Legislative Assembly amid the tension and the fury. The demonstrators, while under close police vigilance, ended up at the Beach Club Colony. This was just across the road from Interbank House and where Jean Doucet lived as well. It was reported that Doucet was seen with some of the demonstrators at Beach Club and that he also had the group to dinner at his home. People around town, including other bankers, called me, in my position as Bank Inspector, to complain about Doucet's involvement with the demonstrators. (Johnson 2001, 159)

Hannerz (1974), another chronicler of this event, offers more insight into the demonstrators and the demonstration than does Johnson. His description is equally informative:

The marchers walked four by four. There were perhaps around five hundred of them with spectators standing on the sides of the streets, often finally deciding to drift along. In a car in front of the march drove Jim Bodden, the real estate man, with Annie Bodden (no relation) in the seat next to him. Leading the march were Ira Walton and Berkley Bush, with two other men who had taken a part in organizing it, Bert Watler and Gilbert McLean. The marchers carried a variety of flags and placards, some of which read:

> Caymanians united – repeal all unjust laws now
> Stop Communism
> We have lost faith in our representatives
> We want to live in the future as we have done in the past
> Say No to the regulation (with a swastika)
> No more foreign policemen – this is not the Congo

This last sign referred to the fact that a conspicuous number of recent new recruits to the Caymanian police had been men from other territories, such as Jamaica, Barbados and British Honduras. (Hannerz 1974, 131)

Hannerz also explains the tensions which remained after the demonstration and clearly describes the participants. Of interest here are those described by Johnson (2001) as '"black power" troublemakers'. Hannerz (1974) explains:

> Much of the speculation centred on the young black and coloured men who had appeared in the march with black "P" letters, and many of whom had also gone around to the public meetings ... They were known locally as "Mathilda's Corner Boys", after the location of the bar which they had long used for a hangout ... Much of the concern over this group was voiced by persons who were, in these days rather quietly, for the Administration, but George Town businessmen who actively supported the protest also began to worry ... The problem was that the "P" mark and other things seemed like overtones of black power ... there was indeed some rather vague evidence that the protest movement had not been altogether united behind the strategy of nonviolence. (Hannerz 1974, 147–48)

When combined, the accounts of Hannerz (1974) and Johnson (2001) provide a comprehensive account of events leading up to the April 1970 demonstration and set the tone for the speculation and various conspiracy theories emanating out of the events. It seems clear that no definitive connection linked any member of the demonstration to any black power movement outside of the Cayman Islands. More important, there is no evidence to suggest that any black power group had existed in the Cayman Islands since the island's settlement.

As Hannerz (1974, 148–49) shows, there was no shortage of guesswork and speculation about who may have been involved. While the messages on some of the placards may suggest issues other than the planning regulations, it would be far-fetched to speculate that there was any attempt to hijack this peaceful demonstration and turn it into an armed black power confrontation. If this was the objective, where were the organisers? Who spearheaded such a plot? And, most important, what was to be gained? Was this part of a greater conspiracy?

Similarly, it seems ill-advised and unfounded to conclude that Jean Doucet would be acting out of any other motive than altruism in associating with some of the demonstrators after the march. Johnson (2001) admits that Doucet's explanation of this association was credible and acknowledges that he accepted the explanation (p. 159).

Hannerz (1974), commenting on the allegation of Doucet's involvement with the black power fringe or the Mathilda's Corner Boys, stated: 'One apparently rather fanciful theory pointed to a foreign banker who had been more ready than most of the expatriates to mix with the local people; it would seem more probable that whatever influence he could exercise was in the direction of restraint (p. 148).

It is in keeping with the nature of frontier societies that perceived enemies and troublemakers are dispatched in callous and unorthodox ways. In Doucet's case there was not so much as a fitting public epitaph. At the conclusion of the case against him, public expression was divided between vilification on the part of detractors and conspiracy theories floated by admirers and well-wishers. Little by way of appreciation flowed from anyone of consequence until Sir Vassel Johnson admitted:

> Doucet undoubtedly did much to assist many local residents with loans and mortgage financing to build and repair their homes and improve their little businesses, much of which financing would not normally have been available elsewhere. He also did much in the way of promoting Cayman's offshore business. (Johnson 2001, 160)

It is left to history to ultimately untangle Doucet's reputation from the exigencies of frontier events. His efforts to introduce competitive banking and consideration for the proverbial 'little man', however have not gone unnoticed by enlightened residents of the Cayman Islands.

Amid the intricate details that Johnson offers about the Interbank saga, one cannot but note the solemn remarks that provide a fitting conclusion to this episode in Caymanian financial history: 'It was felt that the false rumour on the streets indicated that somebody wanted Sterling Bank out of the way and that false accusations both against Doucet and his bank were the only recourse available' (ibid.).

In view of the circumstances, it is logical to conclude that some conspiracy was hatched to bring ruin to this perceived intruder as a punishment for his association with 'black troublemakers'. The action of an invisible hand in Caymanian financial affairs set a dangerous precedent. While no entity was so bold as to admit direct intervention, suspicion was rife that it was a conspiracy motivated by efforts to preserve the status quo. Those seeking examples of vindictiveness in a frontier society need look no further, for this action spoke eloquently. To this day there are reactionary elements eager to dismiss any political or cultural organisation of black Caymanians as some kind of evil entity inimical to their version of a pure society.

The Interbank debacle took years to settle. It was a weakness of the Cayman Islands government's financial regulatory regime that at the end of the liquidation process, the creditors received little or nothing on their investments, while the court-appointed liquidators received enormous fees and were not subject to any court-determined liquidation schedule. It was for many Caymanians a most distressing end to widespread local dreams, and one can argue that it derailed the hopes of many small investors and businesspersons for at least a decade.

To this day, there exists little or no legislation spelling out the responsibilities, schedules, professional fees, and conduct of receivers and liquidators, which would provide protection for all parties in the wind-up process. The absence of such critical legislation attests to the fact that in this premier financial jurisdiction there are challenges yet to be met, even though the Cayman Islands remain among the best-regulated jurisdictions in the international finance business.

After a few years clearing the financial detritus and surviving the worldwide recession, the Cayman Islands rebounded significantly. The society and the economy developed with a renewed vigour, and from 1976, with the election of the Unity Team political directorate, an unprecedented economic boom, based primarily on land sales and speculation, took hold.

The failure of the Interbank enterprise acted, it seems, as a magnet for other institutions. While those expatriates closely associated with Doucet found it convenient to leave the Cayman Islands, others representing other institutions made their appearance. This human flotsam and jetsam came from several jurisdictions and found not only immediate employment but a warm welcome in their own expatriate circles. These newcomers, representing as they did the more negative aspects of empire, did not necessarily associate with Caymanians. Indeed, the association may have been limited to the weekly matches of the local amateur football league, where it was not unusual to have expatriates and established Caymanians on the same team. Elsewhere in this book, it has been posited that this association formed the basis for a symbiotic relationship, even though many of the newcomers brought with them an imperial attitude that would certainly have been unwelcome in former colonies like Jamaica, Barbados, and many of the African countries. The veil of cultural superiority worn by many new arrivals did not, however, fool those Caymanians whose knowledge of colonialism and experience living abroad enabled them to be equally contemptuous of the newcomers, who were, after all, economic migrants despite their white skin and inflated sense of importance.

Many established Caymanians reject the way that some of these imperialistic newcomers even today discount the contributions of Caymanian merchant seamen to the economic development of Caymanian society. They also reject the fantasy that Caymanians are not capable of authoring their own success.

One cannot be sanguine about how such a rancorous situation will unfold, especially in light of the fact that so many of these people choose to leave the Cayman Islands in times of discomfort and inconvenience. The exodus of such people before and immediately after hurricane Ivan in September 2004 is indicative of their loyalty to the jurisdiction. It is all too obvious that the primary motivation of many of these people is economic rather than any desire to make a meaningful contribution to the society's advancement.

There are other forms of insult as well. Some expatriate law firms assume that only they can map out the legal and intellectual strategies necessary for Cayman's success. The following memo, dated February 17, 2004, was circulated to his expatriate colleagues by a principal of one of those firms: 'Very often we propose legislation in draft. This does no more than ensure alignment of the Cayman Islands legislative and regulatory system to the expectation of a client base that we resolved we would promote in the 1990s.'

It is a remarkable coincidence that this acknowledgement confirms the impression of some bureaucrats in the section of the Foreign and Commonwealth Office with responsibility for the Cayman Islands. In 1995, the author and another Caymanian legislator were told by two FCO staff members that it was common knowledge in the section that the Cayman Islands were run by 'The Firm'. 'The Firm' was, of course, a reference to the film of the same name, which starred Gene Hackman and Tom Cruise and a segment of which was shot in the Cayman Islands. In Caymanian society, however, 'The Firm' refers to the one of the law firms that popular opinion associates with the firm in the movie. It seems that there was indeed close association between some members of this organisation and some people in government over a number of years. There is, however, no evidence to suggest that it was anything other than the incestuous relationship that is accepted as normal in this frontier society. The firm would use its perceived 'most favoured position' to convey the impression among its competitors that it could exercise some influence over the political directorate.

In November 2001 a new political directorate emerged, and while such connections still appeared to exist, they were not as pronounced as before. Indeed, there seemed to be no clearly favoured expatriate legal entity until the aftermath of hurricane Ivan. Immediately following the passage of Ivan, a state of emergency was declared. During this time the functions of cabinet and the powers of the Legislative Assembly were suspended, over objections from the elected ministers of government who, in the main, wished to maintain a healthy distance from the self-aggrandising motives of the more blatant business houses.

The British governor was in control, under emergency powers granted in the constitution. Oddly, meetings that the governor held with various public-sector authorities and private-sector representatives did not take place at any government offices or neutral location. They were held at the offices of one of the major legal firms, allegedly because the amenities and conveniences available there made it a logical venue for critical decision making when so many structures had been badly damaged.

What any perceptive governor should have realised as awkward turned almost farcical. It appeared that agendas were being set by self-serving entities and that the early recovery effort was being dictated by elements other than the elected representatives of the people. When the state of emergency was declared, the governor suspended the parliament and ruled by decree without consultation with the elected members.

Such examples of subtle control by powerful expatriate British interests to protect their economic stake are far more routine than they are aberrant. Of course, the disposition and abilities of the governor to a large extent determine the acceptable level of manipulation. Assertive governors will have drawn a line early on, indicating what is acceptable from intrusive expatriate private-sector elements. Those who lack ability or clarity of vision regarding the direction the territory should take would not necessarily accept private-sector overtures without suspicion or resentment. In September 2004, it seemed obvious that Governor Dinwiddy welcomed such assistance, since he did not demonstrate the supreme self-confidence characteristic of a capable crisis manager.

It is difficult not to perceive some of the actions of the expatriate British governors and their compatriots who hold influential positions in the Cayman Islands as a form of collusion with their private-sector colleagues, where such collusion maintains the status quo. Observers of colonial developments will not be surprised that such an incestuous relationship exists. Indeed, it is often his compatriots who hold carte blanche privileges to the governor's residence and also to his ears. As might be expected, it is frequently the same people who are rewarded with the remaining trappings of a long-dead empire, in the form of honours and awards.

In the Cayman Islands it is common knowledge that those who seek to ingratiate themselves with the occupants of Government House see themselves as the upper crust in Caymanian society. While, strictly speaking, the Cayman Islands cannot accurately be cast as a racist society, established Caymanians know perfectly well that WASPs from England and North America consider themselves culturally superior to the islanders. This notion fits in with Caribbean history and settlement practices, which are well established and have been documented by historians and commentators from Eric Williams to Frantz Fanon.

Interestingly, there are people who suggest that, since the dismantling of the Colonial Office, which used to prepare colonial officers through a series of postings throughout the colonies, the quality of governors has declined. In the Cayman Islands, for example, people say that the administrative style of Thomas Russell and Alan Scott was markedly more efficient and expedient than those of their successors, largely as a result of experiences gained in various jurisdictions when the Colonial

Office was operational. To the relief of many, the more ridiculous trappings of a colonial past, like the governor's military-style uniforms, have now been done away with.

Whether these observations are popular is beyond the scope of this work. What is indisputable, however, is that people drawn from relatively low levels in the diplomatic service lack the experience and background knowledge that would be available to officers rising through the ranks of the colonial service – or even to movers and shakers in the business world. Among past governors, Caymanians unanimously hold the greatest respect for Thomas Russell.

Alan Scott's tenure as governor was fraught with challenges and controversy. First it was hurricane Gilbert and the recovery and clean-up process; then there was his controversial decision to review the Cayman Islands' constitution, which was followed by a Private Member's Motion to replace Governor Scott as president of the Legislative Assembly with a Speaker.

Governor Scott was accused by the opposition members of the Legislative Assembly of breaching protocol and departing from convention by dabbling in politics. When the political directorate lost its majority vote in Finance Committee, it was realised that the precedent-setting move to have the official members vote in Finance Committee was Governor Scott's idea. While this breach of convention took place while Governor Scott was on leave, there is reason to believe that it could not have taken place without his approval and that of the FCO authorities. Motion 3/90, as this motion was officially designated, haunted the tenure of both the political directorate and Scott's governorship.

Not even the crash of the Bank of Credit and Commerce International (BCCI), the Cayman Airways accident in which a Boeing 737 overshot the runway and ended up in the North Sound, nor the protest march against the adoption of Motion 3/90 could distract the electorate from its anger. The abolition of the death penalty for murder was another controversial development which generated robust debate and divisiveness, and further contributed to the public contempt for Governor Scott.

Shortly before his retirement in 1992, it was revealed that Governor Scott had been carrying on a torrid extramarital affair. There were sordid accusations and revelations of a daughter resulting from this relationship. Alan Scott left the jurisdiction amidst as much controversy as he brought. His no-nonsense approach at the political level had brought tempers to the boiling point. In the general elections that followed his departure, the political directorate lost its majority, and the society breathed a collective sigh of relief, eagerly anticipating more politically sedate times.

Alan Scott's tenure as governor was bracketed by two historically significant occurrences. In the first place, the Legislative Assembly took an important step towards achieving true parliamentary democracy by having an independent professional Speaker. Second, Governor Scott was the last Cayman Islands governor with a colonial background and experience. In the future, governors would be recruited from the ranks of the British diplomatic service.

This practice was made necessary by reorganisation in the Foreign and Commonwealth Office. Circumstances dictated that the Colonial Office (which to a large extent became obsolete when most of the former colonies gained independence) be replaced with a more modern and relevant organisation. This meant a new type of governor, lacking the experience gained on the colonial circuit. These new governors seemed more diplomatic, less assertive, and more willing to yield to the political directorate.

Most recently, the official white military-style uniform with plumed helmet and sword has been discarded in favour of a dark-grey business suit and hat on formal occasions. Many people welcome this reflection of changing times, since the old Victorian-era uniform served no purpose other than to remind audiences of a time many would prefer to forget. Even some British Members of Parliament admit that a uniformed and plumed representative from the United Kingdom is an irrelevant relic from a bygone colonial era. The preferred model, according to these pundits, should be someone who can perform as an enlightened and visionary CEO managing a developing society's economy in the twenty-first century.

While the change in formal regalia has been welcomed, it is more cosmetic than substantive, since the governor has been divested of none of his powers. If divestment of these powers does not result from the anticipated constitutional advancement, then the change in official dress is of no significance.

Modernity, money, and materialism: The revolution of rising expectations

In his address to the Legislative Assembly of Justices and Vestry on March 16, 1955, Commissioner Andrew Morris Gerrard said:

> The Cayman Islands today is an uncommonly prosperous community, and it is cause for satisfaction that it is so. The people of the Dependency are better fed than they have ever been before, they are better dressed than they have ever been before; they have greater opportunities for social and cultural relaxation than they have ever had before. Some members of the community have, indeed, become astonishingly rich.

The foundation had been laid by a number of fortuitous circumstances, not the least of which was the worldwide economic boom which manifested itself first in the United States, then in Europe, and finally in Japan, following the end of World War II. Remittances sent home by Caymanian seamen allowed the Caymanian economy to rise to unprecedented levels. Caymanian seamen were introduced to consumerism and the conveniences of modern society, and it was inevitable that much of this would become ingrained. In short order air travel, modern communications, and mail-order catalogues made it possible for Caymanian people with money to obtain all the latest products available from North America. So obvious were the new developments that Gerrard continued:

> I am not sure that the people of the Dependency, better fed, better housed, better clothed as they are, and richer as a great many are, are any happier as a result. The curse of Grand Cayman today is an alarming materialism – an unthinking covetousness, a desire for money and for the material things that money can buy, and a growing contempt for the things of the mind, for education, for culture, and for the domestic virtues. It is not a healthy state of affairs and Cayman is not the first community which has sold its birthright for a mess of pottage and regretted the bargain when it was too late.

In the Cayman Islands, then, the stage had been set for the 'revolution of rising expectations' from the mid-1950s. It is worthwhile to explore the origins of this expression and articulate its underlying significance.

The term 'revolution of rising expectations' originated with the American academic Harlan Cleveland, who used it as the title of a speech he delivered at Colgate University in 1949. The phrase has since been attributed to almost every American of literate or political repute.

In the context of this chapter, the term is used to denote the phenomenon, common among developing societies, of an increasing desire for material and consumer goods to the point of opulence and extravagance. Such desires invariably are indulged to the detriment of more sound investments such as education, health, the arts, and the environment.

The phenomenon is significant on both the personal and national levels. Many jurisdictions in the so-called third world, or developing world, invest in prestige projects such as stadiums, airlines, armed forces, and grandiose capital cities with superhighways rather than in improved health systems, housing, and education for their people. On the personal level, there is no greater example than young people who, once employed in their first job, fulfil their dream by purchasing a luxury car or SUV instead of enrolling in advanced-study courses or buying a home and investing their money for the future. In the Cayman Islands, the phenomenon is particularly evident as people attempt to acquire the luxuries that they believe define the 'leisure class'. Sadly, many do not realise that credit and debit cards require discipline, and personal indebtedness has become a serious problem.

The revolution of rising expectations is not peculiar to the Cayman Islands or to developing societies, but it is affecting the evolution of Caymanian society. The advent of the 500-channel television universe, proximity to the United States, the relative ease with which Caymanians can access personal and consumer loans, and the absence of foreign exchange regulations make it easy for all but the most wary to become victims of the revolution of rising expectations, by discouraging temperance and frugality when it comes to personal money management.

The situation is exacerbated by the absence of a national savings strategy and the fact that financial institutions do not encourage personal investment plans. Only the Cayman Islands Civil Service Credit Union promotes thrift and savings. Caymanian society is falsely recording its progress and prosperity by publishing skewed figures for its gross national product and per capita income. The published numbers, based on the salaries of a few expatriate CEOs and managing directors, mask the reality that most people in the workforce earn wages and salaries below CI$2,000 per month.

The Cayman Islands government, which provides public education, health services, and social services, derives its revenue from import duties, hotel room tax, real estate sales tax, bank and corporate licence fees, and the like. No financial assistance comes from the administering power, and the Cayman Islands has the enviable reputation of never having been grant-aided. This in itself is remarkable enough; when taken in tandem with the United Kingdom's cavalier disregard towards the Islands' lack of access to development aid from international agencies and the United Kingdom's own Department for International Development (DFID), it is nothing short of astounding.

One does not have to look any further than the aftermath of hurricane Ivan to realise that the interests of the United Kingdom and those of the Cayman Islands do not coincide. While the DFID gave millions of pounds in aid to Haiti and Grenada, the Cayman Islands received no such consideration. Nor, for that matter, did the Cayman Islands receive any significant assistance from the Foreign and Commonwealth Office. What assistance was promised should have come from the Euopean Union. The situation was precedent-setting, as it represented the first time any Caymanian political directorate had presented itself as a supplicant. In fact, the *Cayman Net News* on January 18, 2007, published an editorial titled 'Have we become a beggar nation?' It must be a source of embarrassment to the PPM government that as of January 2007 no funds from the EU have been received.

What the Cayman Islands did receive from the United Kingdom was a visit from a member of the Royal Family, who good-naturedly expressed royal empathy and wished the society a speedy recovery. Any hopes of large-scale relief from the outside world were dashed by the reluctance of the Caymanian authorities to publicise the plight of the Cayman Islands, and by the reticence of the United Kingdom and international donor agencies. In many respects, the position in which the Cayman Islands found itself was not entirely unfamiliar.

In his *Notes on the History of the Cayman Islands* (1910), Hirst wrote: 'After each hurricane the inhabitants lost no time in pulling themselves together and I am informed that on no single occasion did they seek alms from abroad. This speaks highly for the independence of the people and I believe the same characteristic would be found in their dependants today' (p. 246).

The devastation visited on Cayman by hurricane Ivan was not as confidently dealt with as past disasters apparently were. This was so for a number of reasons, not the least of which is that Ivan was one of the most destructive hurricanes in Caymanian history. Damage to vital communications and infrastructural links necessary for the operations of the finance industry alone would have caused a crippling effect that would not have been witnessed previously, when such links did not exist. Then, too, there were other jurisdictions that suffered devastation from Ivan and 'competed' with the Cayman Islands for outside assistance. Compare, for example, the United Kingdom's attitude towards Grenada, an independent country and former colony, with that towards Cayman, which is still constitutionally tied to the United Kingdom and which was severely damaged by the same hurricane.

Ivan and its aftermath were instructive in other ways as well, for the destruction of coastal properties served to remind islanders why Caymanians in former times did not build their homes along the coast. It was a lesson many had failed to grasp. The result was widespread devastation, particularly of the luxurious residences lining the South Sound coastline. More important is what Ivan taught us about the insurance industry in the Cayman Islands. In the absence of empirical data, it would be unwise to offer conjecture on exactly what percentage of buildings were underinsured, but informal reports indicate that the number was significant for both private dwellings and commercial buildings.

There is, however, a distinct difference between the insurance coverage carried on properties owned by middle-class Caymanian entrepreneurs, multinational corporations, and wealthy expatriates and the coverage carried by Caymanians of more modest means. The former, with experience and knowledge of the insurance industry, more than likely had adequate coverage, whereas many of the latter apparently did not.

The experience of Ivan brought an added dimension to the concept of a revolution of rising expectations: that of an apparent dependence on the state to provide relief in times of dire need and hardship. The expectation arises from the mistaken idea that in a society such as the Cayman Islands the government can accept responsibility for every failed enterprise and every experienced misfortune. In light of such an expectation, it would seem appropriate and wise for the state to establish a disaster-management agency with funds earmarked exclusively for disaster relief.

Caymanian governments have traditionally offered assistance to individuals where it was deemed necessary and advisable. In recent years, however, certain people have been able to obtain rather ill-advised assistance from the public purse in controversial circumstances. This practice leads to the false expectation that the state will be responsible for mitigating every individual loss, even those resulting from business failure. Experience gained in the aftermath of hurricane Ivan has highlighted the danger of this expectation, revealing both the existence of a significant impoverished underclass on Grand Cayman and the public assumption that after island-wide natural disasters the government will bear the brunt of recovery costs.

It is this writer's contention that in any jurisdiction with a small and somewhat limited revenue base, such as the Cayman Islands, no sensible political directorate will use state funds for disaster relief in other than the most desperate of cases. There is a need for a state agency, free of political influence, to manage the distribution of emergency aid.

Ivan also uncovered the fact that the high standard of living of which many islanders boast has not spread to all members of society. In the absence of a statistically sound survey (underway at the time of writing), it is unwise to assume that no abject poverty exists in Cayman.

There are, then, in the Cayman Islands two dimensions to the revolution of rising expectations. The first is the conventional dimension, in which both the state and the individual use precious financial resources to acquire luxury items, mainly for the prestige that accompanies ownership. Such behaviour is not entirely uncommon in – though it is not exclusive to – developing societies.

The second dimension poses a more dangerous problem. This is when the state, using state funds, wishes to present itself as a benevolent godfather figure. In these circumstances, people are led to believe that the state bears a legal obligation to bail out all those who experience economic misfortune in any of its myriad forms. Obviously, this sort of expectation has an influence on political behaviour.

Politics, populism, and parties: The more things change, the more they remain the same

Politics in the Cayman Islands has changed little since the days of the Cayman Vanguard Progressive Party of 1958 and Ormond Panton's National Democratic Party of 1960. Indeed, it seems as though every time a group not of the merchant establishment agitates for political change and advancement, regressive elements organise to form a countervailing force.

Invariably these groups are spearheaded by those who see themselves as the establishment. In a society in which many proclaim that no colour prejudice exists, it is a striking coincidence that on every occasion since the launching of the Cayman Vanguard Progressive Party in 1958, the opposition was led by members of the white merchant establishment, even when co-opted black people appeared in the front lines.

While this chapter will delve into several political developments, readers are cautioned that it is not intended to provide a general introduction to Caymanian politics. What is offered here is merely a corollary to other significant developments since the 1990s.

With the death of Jim Bodden in 1988 and the subsequent crumbling of the Unity Team organisation, the Caymanian political scene became comparatively quiet. For one thing, there was no flamboyant, dominant personality around whom the people could gather. Secondly, the society became preoccupied with its economic well-being, and politics reverted to a quieter vocation.

The elections of November 1988 did bring new, younger members into the Legislative Assembly. While it was not perceived as such at the time, the general elections of 1988 were to be the watershed of change in Caymanian politics.

For the first time in the history of the Legislative Assembly, there were enough members with post-secondary education to make their presence felt. Some of the younger members gravitated together, seeing themselves as professional politicians, in that they had no business ties to the merchant establishment, they represented constituencies other than George Town, and they had little or no formal allegiance to their established colleagues.

It did not take long for the political dynamics to change, and when the Dignity Team, which had succeeded the Unity Team, took a step back towards traditional establishment politics, some of the younger members in its ranks resorted to open dissension. The older members' inflexibility, arrogance, and unwillingness to mentor younger, ambitious members eventually led to a split within the Dignity Team. It is a commonplace of the old Caymanian political establishment that assertive behaviour by younger aspirants should be treated with contempt. As a result, a glorious opportunity was squandered, and no serious effort was made to try to re-engage the disgruntled younger members of the party. Instead, a tenuous arrangement was entered into which allowed the political directorate to operate with a one-vote majority. This arrangement required the collusion of the administering power's representative, and so smug were the members of the political directorate that they did not recognise its detrimental effect on the political advancement of the jurisdiction.

To ensure a majority in the Finance Committee, the governor allowed Legislative Assembly Motion 3/90, by which the official members (that is, the appointed civil servants) were made members of the Finance Committee. This retrograde step made a joke of the political process and aroused such indignation in the electorate that relations between the populace and the government remained strained until the general elections of 1992.

During that interim period, new members gravitated to the remainder of the Unity Team. With the addition of the breakaway faction from the Dignity Team, this new collective, comprising seven members, presented a robust challenge to the political directorate.

For all its apparent success, this new agglomeration known as the back-benchers was an unholy alliance. While its members, all relatively young, were capable legislators, there were hidden agendas and differing political styles. Be that as it may, in the general elections of November 1992 the team was successful and during the course of events the agglomeration took the form of a new political entity. The election victory transformed this entity into what became known as the National Team.

Any hope of an extended political honeymoon was dashed with the choosing of the Executive Council. There was no attempt to bring in new, dynamic members, and, despite the pretensions of the occasion, sensible people realised that this was nothing but a false dawn.

Several legislative controversies arose and were defused without serious incident. The most controversial was an attempt to dismantle the health-care system administration put in place by the Dignity Team. The National Team survived this harrowing experience, but then there were charges of misconduct in ministerial administration and weaknesses in the political directorate. In spite of this, the National Team managed to perform and appeared strong until the general elections of 1996.

In the time leading up to the election, new political forces had organised themselves. Team Cayman, consisting of a varied membership of Dignity Team leftovers, newcomers, and at least two former National Team members, presented a united opposition.

Complete with party headquarters, an administrative office, constitution, and manifesto, Team Cayman was the most organised party Cayman had yet seen. With a complement of nine candidates and a high-profile campaign, Team Cayman had high expectations of success against the National Team.

Election night, however, brought defeat and demoralisation. Only one Team Cayman candidate, an incumbent from Bodden Town, retained his seat. The National Team won near-total victory, since there was only one new member elected, from George Town, who was not part of its organisation.

At the swearing-in of the new Legislative Assembly, the celebrations were muted compared with four years earlier. Many in Caymanian political circles did not realise that the National Team had won a hollow victory. Within the first year of the new term, divisions began to show, and in the face of relentless opposition from the third elected member from Bodden Town and the first and third elected members from George Town, the National Team sometimes seemed politically impotent. Charges of political malfeasance and a banking scandal involving a National Team member sent this once formidable political team into its death throes. To buy time and distance itself from the political meltdown, it jettisoned the member. It was a move which proved to be counterproductive, for by this time at least one other disgruntled member was preparing to change sides, and the banking scandal for which the member was sacrificed did not have the devastating results that were widely expected.

On the contrary, a significant element saw the punishment of the party member as a kind of victimisation. Popular sentiment changed, with a majority believing that a conspiracy had taken place and that the National Team minister involved was duped into playing a pivotal role in the bank's affairs. Indeed, it was suggested that the real culprit was another National Team minister. This conflation of events showed the National Team for the dinosaur it was rather than the dynamic political organisation it pretended to be.

In the remaining months of its term the National Team blundered from one crisis to the next. There was no cohesive policy in any ministry; rather, there were a number of questionable and inappropriate actions by several ministers. Many of these carried charges of political malfeasance, and several serious motions against National Team ministers were brought to the Legislative Assembly.

In the general elections of 2000, the National Team reaped what it had sowed, as the voters unceremoniously turned its members out of office. Two ministers failed to get elected, and those members who were elected were happy to fade into obscurity and dodged any association with their now-defunct organisation.

It is the nature of Caribbean politics that those who commit political suicide are seldom raised from the dead. And so it was that with the passing into history of the National Team, new alliances were made, and the public was called upon to witness yet another marriage of political convenience where, as it turned out, 'pirate politics' were the order of the day. The political directorate was literally chosen after a big cookout of breadfruit and turtle meat. The first elected member for George Town, unofficially the most popular of the members-elect, gathered a majority of the newly elected at his home. After the better part of a day of negotiating and bickering, a new political directorate was agreed upon.

It came as no surprise to anyone that, at the swearing-in ceremony for the new Legislative Assembly, the first elected member for George Town was the popular choice to lead the new political directorate. But other decisions were not arrived at as easily. As it turned out, the victors agreed unanimously on only one objective, and that had been accomplished with the demise of the former leader of government business and the destruction of the National Team. That having been achieved, it was literally every man (and woman) for himself, and there was no shortage of political manoeuvring. Those holding out hope for the emergence of a civil and dignified political directorate were in for a distressing disappointment.

Accounts vary as to how the incoming political directorate was ultimately set up. Various versions were formed at different venues, only to be quashed when a particular member or members did not realise their ambitions. After several abortive attempts, consensus was reached when the first elected member from George Town was chosen leader by a majority of elected members and four other ministers – one each from George Town, North Side, Bodden Town, and West Bay – were selected.

Although there were still some disgruntled members, the choice of the first elected member from Cayman Brac, a woman, as Speaker quieted the malcontents to a degree. The peace was destined to be short-lived, however, because a bland leadership style, lack of a clear sense of direction, and the absence of a plan to remediate the government's inherited bleak financial position threw the leadership into crisis.

In fairness, all the blame should not be placed upon the leader, although he failed in not demonstrating the resolve necessary to move the economy forward. The demands of the administering power for more stringent financial management and the national questions regarding international financial obligations also served as distractions. Nonetheless, an opportunity was squandered when the government did not call upon the financial community of bankers, accountants, and lawyers to bear a greater share of the costs of running the jurisdiction. The leader's lack of direction was made clear when the government raised a loan of CI$52 million to meet, among other things, recurrent expenditure needs – the first time in history that recurrent expenditure was to be serviced by a loan. Many became alarmed at this, and there was widespread public disquiet. What became obvious much later is that there was also behind-the-scenes agitation for a change in leadership.

An implosion occurred in the Legislative Assembly on November 8, 2001. A motion of no confidence removed the leader of government business and his close colleague, the Minister of Youth, Sports, Community and Women's Affairs, and paved the way for a new political directorate.

With these two ministers gone, two new ministers were sworn in as replacements. When the political dust had settled, there was still some rumbling and disquiet in the wider community. Supporters of the two former ministers accused the new political directorate of fomenting a coup and threatened disruption.

The political directorate, for its part, tried to settle down to the business of government. An ambitious agenda of ministerial actions was adopted, and considerable efforts were expended in developing the new group and its supporters into a formal organisation. It was a historic moment when the announcement came that the political directorate, its back-bench supporters, and its community organisations had coalesced into the United Democratic Party. For the first time since the demise of the National Democratic Party, the Cayman Islands had a formal political party.

There were, of course, the usual detractors and sceptics who floated the old concerns about corruption, lack of independence, dishonesty, and nepotism. The political directorate tried not to be distracted and concerned itself with trying to improve the society.

In an effort to become more effective and keep its appeal, before long the opposition announced that it too had formed itself into an organisation which, while not a political party per se, was formed to offer an alternative to the United Democratic Party (UDP). The new grouping was called the People's Progressive Movement (PPM).

The stage was set for the Cayman Islands once more to operate within the realm of modern political practice and to take full advantage of Westminster-style democracy. This system, predicated as it is upon an adversarial government and opposition, operating within clearly defined parameters, is designed to offer the electorate clear choices in political representation.

Irrespective of one's position with regard to the events of November 8, 2001, it can be argued that the electorate in the Cayman Islands is in a much better position to make clear and informed choices as to the type of representation it wants. Clearly defined party lines allowed both government and opposition to focus more intensely on the challenges and problems facing the society.

One pressing problem facing the government was the thousands of expatriates living and working in the Cayman Islands, some for as long as 40 years. They came from many different jurisdictions, but a majority were of Jamaican origin. Previous political directorates had promised to regularise their status in the country, and there had been at least two attempts at immigration-law reform in the preceding 20 years. Each time it appeared that the problem would be addressed, something prompted the political directorate to defer plans.

The situation had become intolerable by 2000, with the UK government applying pressure, human-rights advocates citing violations, and enlightened and fair-minded Caymanians advocating fairness. In fact, it was known that at least one person deemed well qualified to have received Caymanian status – the equivalent of citizenship – was preparing to bring a test case to the courts. Realising the seriousness of the problem, the UDP government decided to act at last.

What followed defied all sense of proper policymaking. Outlining no qualifying criteria and making no provisions for due diligence, the cabinet collected the names of thousands of potential status grantees. The leader of government business was told by some elected cabinet members that to proceed without proper criteria would have disastrous consequences. One minister suggested that the cabinet should have submitted the names on the list to the Immigration Board to carry out the appropriate investigations, and then should have announced that the mass grants of Caymanian status were the result of a special dispensation in connection with the 2003 Quincentennial celebrations.

Following such a procedure would have alleviated fears that there would be future mass status grants awarded by cabinet. It would have denied detractors the opportunity to imply that the UDP had acted corruptly and inappropriately. It would also have enabled cabinet to control the list of names, which were recommended by politicians, civil servants, and even people who had previously been granted status. This being the case, it did not take long to realise that what was intended to be an exercise in fairness was a fiasco, with no control over who suggested names and no procedure for vetting the names that were suggested.

In the end, some 3,000 people of diverse vocations, nationalities, and duration of stay in the Cayman Islands received grants of Caymanian status. So chaotic was the process that pandemonium broke out three days prior to the deadline, when it was announced that all applicants had to submit police records. The police department was overwhelmed, and the government department receiving the applications had to suspend service.

Apprehension about Jamaicans has always existed on the part of some established Caymanians – despite the fact that the Islands were for the most part settled by people who came from Jamaica. There are other historical ties, such as the early Colonial Office practice of administering the Cayman Islands through the Office of the Governor of Jamaica. Before Jamaica gained independence in 1962, the Cayman Islands depended on Jamaica for services in every important facet of its existence. Notwithstanding that these services were paid for by the Cayman Islands government, it is logical to assume that the relationship between the two jurisdictions would be a cordial one.

While cordiality has always existed at the official level, from time to time there have been strains in the societal relationship. Many established Caymanians hold the view that most Jamaicans are aggressive and therefore threatening in a society in which docility, calmness, and consideration for others are the desired characteristics. Caymanians are reluctant to admit that there maybe other reasons for apprehension. In the course of objections to the 2003 status grants, however, it became clear that there were those (not all established

Caymanians) whose concern was that the majority of the grants were made to people of black skin colour and menial vocation. There was some reason to believe that such mischief was spread by people of a different nationality who were themselves recipients of status grants. It was also suggested that the fairer-skinned, wealthier Jamaicans who had emigrated immediately after the Manley era have always sought to distinguish themselves from their darker-skinned compatriots. These 'red' Jamaicans, as Caymanians pejoratively refer to them, have long viewed the Cayman Islands as their secret fiefdom and capitalised on the Caymanian societal attitudes described elsewhere.

Caymanian society has always held hypocritical attitudes towards skin colour and race. Exactly how one rationalises hiring black Jamaicans to cook one's food, care for one's children, and take care of the most private recesses of one's home while at the same time regarding them as being unworthy of citizenship is beyond comprehension.

Naturally, there were no publicly expressed objections to the skin colour of the new Caymanians. Interestingly, though complaining that these status holders were going to take employment from Caymanians, no objector publicly lamented that white expatriates receiving the status grants were even more guilty of the same offence.

There was widespread national objection to the grants, and the parliamentary opposition joined with a proliferation of organisations and individuals to foment national turmoil. Some of the most vehement objections came from people who were themselves earlier beneficiaries of status grants.

One organisation, the Caymanian Bar Association, threatened court action to reverse the process. The UDP government remained firm, defending its action on human-rights, economic, and moral grounds. The parliamentary opposition meanwhile brought a no-confidence motion against the government. With no hope of succeeding, the opposition used the occasion to inflame emotions to the point where one member spoke of 'blood' in his contribution to the debate. The motion failed, but the status grants were to be a theme in the coming general election campaign.

For its part, the government was remiss in not mounting a campaign to inform the public of the beneficial effects of the grants. It should have been widely publicised that millions of dollars trickled down as a result of real-estate sales and of remittances that would have been sent elsewhere had not the status grants taken place.

It is also true that while there were positive aspects, there remained the challenge of providing social services and accommodating school-age children of the new status holders. There are many lessons to be learnt from the experience, not the least of which is that in a fragile society like the Cayman Islands, ad hoc decisions often have serious and unpredictable consequences.

The chickens apparently came home to roost in the election of May 2005, when the PPM campaigned against the status grants, among other things, and won an almost absolute victory. The incumbent UDP suffered a resounding defeat – and while other factors may have been in play, it is safe to assume that the status grants were decisive.

Until recently, no effort has been made to illuminate and inform Caymanian society's understanding of politics, the constitution, and how the Cayman Islands as a developing society can best address the issues of the social contract and the evolution of self-determination. In the past, Caymanian political directorates have failed to recognise that they themselves are individuals with private virtues and prejudices, and those who disagree with them politically are nonetheless worthy and respectable components of the democratic calculus. The national vision of the political process has long been that government works from the top down, from the 'Glass House' – the Government Administration building – to the Legislative Assembly, rather than, as in a true democracy, from the Legislative Assembly to the Glass House.

At a time when Caymanian society is trying so painfully to feel its way through the falsification and suppression of its relationship with the United Kingdom, it is crucial that a political directorate that was swept to power so convincingly be given the opportunity to prove itself. There is a distant bugle sounding the call for an advance to the battle of crafting our own solutions to our unique problems. If progress already achieved is to be preserved and extended, and we are to stamp the 'Caymanian' imprint on our own affairs, this is not the time to be reticent or to retreat.

Andrew Morris Gerrard, that quintessential colonial administrator, described the future in his customary eloquence in his Budget Address to the Legislative Assembly of Justices and Vestry on March 16, 1955:

> If the Dependency does not chart out a realistic course of its own, then there is every likelihood that in the future it will be compelled by force of circumstance to follow a course which may be unacceptable to it, and indeed dangerous to its own interest and way of life. (p. 2)

And so it has come down to this: less than ten years into a new millennium and with a new political directorate in charge, the Cayman Islands still face a myriad of intractable problems. Just as René Dumont wrote in 1962 in his seminal work about Africa, translated from the French as *False Start in Africa,* there is a false start in Cayman.

In this writer's article in the *Nor'wester* magazine (Bodden 1978), a parallel was drawn between what transpired in Dumont's Africa and the developing Cayman Islands. In both cases there has been, in all but the most exceptional circumstances, a succession of paternalistic governors with no relevant local knowledge and little more than a token acquaintance with the development challenges of the jurisdiction. In the recent past, there seemed some signs that the chasm between poverty and wealth was being reduced; but continued cronyism seems to be the order of the day.

Economics, society, and self-determination: Emerging problems in Cayman society

The winds of change which have blown in the former British colonies of the Caribbean, like the meteorological storms, have now begun to affect the Cayman Islands. The financial sector will continue to face challenges brought by international regulatory authorities or by the G8 countries, which view offshore financial centres as little more than tax-dodging jurisdictions whose sole purpose is to lure potentially taxable funds from their rightful owner states. Too, the possibility exists that a rival offshore centre or even one of the onshore centres – London being a prime player – will gain a competitive edge over the Cayman Islands.

In tourism (of which more will be said later), the Cayman Islands must come to grips with its high costs compared with other regional destinations. This challenge is compounded by the Western Hemisphere Travel Initiative (WHTI), which places new requirements on US citizens. According to the US State Department Web site (travel.state.gov/travel/cbpmc/cbpmc_2223.html), the Intelligence Reform and Terrorism Prevention Act of 2004 requires that by 23 January 2007, US citizens travelling by air between the United States and the Caribbean must present a passport or other citizenship document to enter the United States. Just how much of a deterrent this will be to US citizens wishing to visit the Cayman Islands remains to be seen. The Caribbean Tourism Organisation has expressed serious concern that the initiative will result in reduced visitor arrivals and significant loss of income to Caribbean destinations. Such an eventuality is a reminder of the fragile nature of one of Cayman's principal economic pillars, tourism.

While Caymanians like to tout their sound economy and high standard of living – which is cavalierly reported as being 'among the highest in the Western Hemisphere' – immigration offers increasing challenges, the solutions to which seem elusive to the Caymanian authorities. The current quandary had its genesis in the short-sighted policies of previous political administrations. A state of uncertainty and apprehension prevails in the Cayman Islands as a result of the so-called rollover policy, involving a fixed term of residence for work permit holders and much more stringent enforcement of term limits. While it is too early to ascertain just how the policy will affect the economy, there are Jeremiahs who assert that its effects will be disastrous.

Writing of immigration and population growth, Bodden (1978, 40–41) posed the following questions: 'What will be the ratio of immigrants to that of "established" Caymanians? Where are these immigrants coming from? Will such an open immigration policy [as proposed in the Development Plan of 1975] not create resentment on the part of Caymanians who might, justifiably, feel their status threatened? What guarantees do Caymanians have that such an immigration policy will not lead to a significant fall in the standard of living? Until all of these questions can be satisfactorily answered Caymanians should object in the most vehement and vociferous way to an open immigration policy.'

The question to pose now, therefore, is 'How can we fix the problem?' An examination of the records reveals that the Development Plan proposed by the political directorate in 1975, while it would have regulated unbridled development, would also have discouraged property development by the less well off. It became irrelevant, in any case, when the incumbent political directorate was swept from power in 1976 as a result of its failure to address the stagnant economy and the complaints of the working class.

The succeeding Unity Team political directorate jettisoned the entire Development Plan of 1975 and replaced it with a wide-open development policy, which, coming in at the end of the recession in the United States, fuelled an economic explosion. The explosion continued for the four years of the Unity Team's first term. There were no attempts during this time to impress upon the authorities the necessity for planned development. In any case, the Unity Team leaders dismissed a call for five-year development plans as socialist, claiming that only countries of the so-called eastern bloc resorted to such exercises.

In true frontier spirit, the doors of the Cayman Islands were swung wide open, and while there was obvious economic growth, no attention was paid to increasing immigration and its associated challenges. Consumed by Texas-style development, no one in the political directorate took the time to assess the situation.

As a result of these past policies, Caymanian society may never be able to achieve a sustainable balance, since the Islands are now on an economic treadmill from which there is no easy alighting. In taking the action it did, the Unity Team political directorate sacrificed the long-term prospects of the Cayman Islands for short-term economic success. Land sales were encouraged, condominium projects flourished, and money flowed, while education, training, and human resource development were relegated to the back burner or ignored. It was a recipe guaranteed to produce the untenable position in which the society now finds itself. Much of the remaining available land is out of the price range of middle- and lower-income Caymanians. This fact, coupled with rising utility costs and ever-increasing prices for basic necessities, all of which have to be imported, ensures that most Caymanians are caught in an economic vortex over which they have no control.

Few realised that the thrill of economic prosperity overrode the concerns of an earlier generation of politicians and leaders who were always vigilant and alert to the possibility of the Cayman Islands being dominated by more populous outside elements. While there have been several attempts at immigration reform, political circumstances have, until now, masked the true magnitude of this challenge.

The *Caymanian Compass* on 8 October 2006 ran the headline 'Jamaican dilemma detailed'. Using the term 'sobering warning', the article reported that 'The need for the rollover policy in the face of possibly thousands of Jamaicans becoming Caymanian was discussed at the Council of Associations' Immigration Forum on Friday afternoon. It was revealed at that forum, that out of 24,134 foreign workers in the Cayman Islands, 11,391 were Jamaican nationals.' In a society in which ambivalence about the Jamaican influence has been a defining factor for well over two centuries, many Caymanians are again expressing concern – unfortunately, primarily in biased and non-constructive ways.

The immigration situation is made more complex by the growing numbers of Filipinos who were brought in to reduce the society's dependence on Jamaican labourers. The *Compass* article stated that there were over 2,000 Filipino work-permit holders. What is more alarming is that in the previous nine months, the number of Filipino workers in the Cayman Islands had increased by 25 per cent. Assuming that Filipinos were encouraged to apply for work permits to enable a reduction in the disproportionate numbers of Jamaican workers so as to achieve a better social balance, it is becoming increasingly clear that the strategy was flawed.

The proposal, in the rollover policy, to create a category of 'exempt persons' glosses over the fact that it is white-collar professionals who have created the glass ceiling blocking Caymanian university graduates from the top of the corporate ladder. In their enthusiasm to play to the gallery, rollover proponents have failed to realise that Caymanians' concerns are not exclusively about being outnumbered. Caymanians – especially young, college-educated Caymanians – expect fair and equal access to positions for which they are trained. There is no convincing evidence that mechanisms are in place to make this an achievable objective in the near future, and blue-collar workers, regardless of nationality, are not the major problem.

With construction still booming and several business complexes, including the mega-community of Camana Bay, coming on line, the question arises: where will the employees needed for the future come from? The Cayman Islands are still being developed without an economic development plan, without environmental impact studies, and without a human-resource needs assessment. It is unquestionably a recipe for disaster. There is a glaring need to establish a clear link between the economy, immigration, the interests of established Caymanians, constitutional modernisation, and human rights. Constitutional development and the political relationship with the United Kingdom have not advanced much beyond their rudimentary state at the break-up of the West Indies Federation in 1962. Most recently (2006), the Dutch government has extended representation in the Dutch parliament to three of its dependent territories in the Caribbean. Turks and Caicos have advanced their constitution to the point where the jurisdiction has a chief minister and a deputy governor who are Turks and Caicos Islanders. The Cayman Islands, meanwhile, lie mired in a system of voluntary colonialism reminiscent of the nineteenth century.

Caribbean tourism

Tourism as a leisure activity emerged in ancient Egypt between 2040 and 1786 BC, when the building of imposing temples, tombs, and other monuments encouraged regular travel by the nobility for both pleasure and curiosity (Casson 1974, 31–56). Modern tourism had its genesis in the 1850s, when the British tour operator Thomas Cook pioneered tours of Europe. Since that time, travel as a pastime has become a worldwide phenomenon extending across the economic spectrum.

While tourism has been a feature of Caribbean development for many decades, it was not until after the Cuban revolution of 1959 that it spread to destinations other than Jamaica, the Bahamas, Puerto Rico, and, of course, Cuba itself. Before the revolution, Havana was the epicentre of Caribbean tourism, and Cuba was often described as 'the playground of the Americas'. One could drive on board the ferry at Key West, Florida, and 90 minutes later disembark at the port of Havana. It was here that the Mafia, in collaboration with the corrupt regime of Fulgencio Batista, ensured that casinos, rum, music, fine food, fancy hotels, and much more awaited the patrons.

De Kadt portrays the situation vividly:

> Tourism in the Caribbean was initially centered in Cuba and was financed by U.S. capital for the benefit of U.S. visitors. It provided the types of facilities which Americans could not get at home, as well as a climatically attractive winter tourist alternative to Southern Florida. The kind of tourism pursued, especially in Havana, was undoubtedly one reason for the later extreme reaction of Cuba against the U.S. With its termination by Communist Cuba, the increasingly affluent U.S. middle class sought opportunities for taking advantage of the Caribbean's climatic and other natural attractions from one end of the region to the other. ... Such activity provides, of course, an even more significant visual manifestation of Americanism in the Caribbean than other forms of enterprise. It ensures not only the acceptance and ready circulation of the U.S. dollar as a currency supplementary to the local one, but also that increasing numbers of people are brought into immediate contact with the representatives of "the colossus of the north". (De Kadt 1972, 28)

Cuba was the most popular Caribbean tourist destination up to 1959. Tourism fell into decline immediately after the revolution, partly owing to the embargo that the United States imposed on Cuba. Gradually the communist regime drifted back toward tourism. In the 1990s there were reports of a new form of tourism being practised, and it was alleged that Cuba was the destination. In tropical and subtropical areas, tourism always gravitates around sun, sea, and sand. There is, however, another 's', not much talked about in tourism circles in the Cayman Islands. That 's' is sex. In the book *Sun, Sex, and Gold*, Kempadoo (1999) spells out its importance to Caribbean tourism in the subtitle, *Tourism and Sex Work in the Caribbean*.

Currently, little or no evidence exists to suggest that this fourth 's' figures to any noticeable extent in Cayman Islands tourism. In the 1980s, however, there was a thriving 'beach hustling' subculture on Grand Cayman. Young Caymanian males, mainly from the district of West Bay, hung out at the more popular resorts and establishments along Seven Mile Beach and 'hustled' the tourists. The original Holiday Inn was a favourite hangout for beach boys waiting for willing tourist women.

The phenomenon is not new. According to sociologist Dr Rustum Sethna, founder of the Caribbean Tourism Research Centre in Toronto, Canada, 'there are girls who come to the Caribbean on holidays with addresses and references [of beach hustlers] from their friends' (Sethna 1979, 25).

In the same article, Dr Kingsley Ferguson, Chief of Psychology at the Clarke Institute of Psychiatry in Toronto, is quoted as saying: 'There's a legitimate feeling of irresponsibility that goes with a vacation. One of the set of stimuli that you can leave behind are the people who will be critical of your sexual behaviour' (ibid.).

The phenomenon of beach hustlers has now been subsumed under the umbrella term 'sex workers' and is a subject of interest to academics, policymakers, medical researchers, law enforcement authorities, and the International Organization for Migration and other related international agencies.

Although no empirical data exist that describe the behaviour of sex workers in Cayman, it would be premature to conclude that the phenomenon does not exist in Caymanian society. Relations between men and women bear a distinctive Caribbean and Latin American stamp and, married or not, a double standard prevails: girls and women are expected to be chaste, boys adventurous, and men free to roam (Lowenthal 1972, 108).

Indeed, there are those who suggest that a dynamic subculture of sex workers exists in some of the bars and entertainment establishments on Grand Cayman. The suggestion is that these imported sex workers have as patrons men from all sectors of Caymanian society, but predominantly those employed in construction and other transient occupations. It should be cause for concern by the Caymanian authorities, if indeed these practices exist to the extent suggested – particularly given that, after sub-Saharan Africa, the Caribbean has the second-highest incidence of HIV/AIDS infection in the world.

Several factors should alert Caymanian society to its potential role in the web of human trafficking and sex workers. Certainly, the fact that the Cayman Islands are a kind of confluence between South America, Central America, and mainland North America is important. In the second place, the rapid economic development on Grand Cayman is a magnet for large numbers of transient workers in construction and other related vocations. Then, too, Grand Cayman has dozens of bars and entertainment establishments that employ imported female waitresses and barmaids, providing a perfect front for discreet sexual liaisons.

While there is no empirical evidence linking the sex trade in Cayman with the drug trade to any large extent, it is reasonable to speculate that there is some relationship. The Cayman Islands are still a frontier society, and workers' lives are affected by the harsh realities of low wages, a high cost of living, long working hours, and the absence of family as a result of restrictive immigration policies. In a region where fun, frolic, and frivolity are as much a given as industry, prosperity, and success, the balance is not always weighted in favour of the latter.

Regrettably, not enough attention is paid to this issue, since there are allegedly at least two establishments on Grand Cayman engaged in the sex trade. One is reputed to employ 20 female sex workers and to have been in operation for decades. The other employs fewer workers but offers similar services, again operating under a licence to serve liquor. All of the women are foreigners to the island and are in extremely vulnerable positions. They face isolation because of the hours they must work and are often victims of the stigma which surrounds prostitution.

The very nature of Caymanian society should preclude such practices from existing for any considerable period without arousing the interest of officialdom. It is common knowledge in some circles that a research team from the Caribbean Epidemiology Centre (CAREC) visited these types of establishments in early 2004. It would be interesting to learn the results of their research and the government's response to such information. It goes without saying that the existence of such establishments in Caymanian society contravenes the islanders' values.

Attitudes toward sex and sexual mores are intricately interwoven into the fabric of Caribbean societies from settlement, and the Cayman Islands are no exception. The European colonisers in the Caribbean exerted power and control over black women beginning in the sixteenth century. Hilary Beckles wrote that slavery meant 'not only the compulsory extraction of labour from the blacks but also, in theory at least, the slave owners' right to total sexual access to slaves' (Beckles 1989: 141). In modern times, there is a connection between alcoholism and drug use and irresponsible sexual behaviour. In some Caribbean jurisdictions, such behaviour is to a large extent a corollary of the tourist industry, and it is well known that sex tourism is a growing phenomenon.

It seems characteristic of Caribbean – and, by inference, Caymanian – society to separate the images of relaxation, romance, excitement, informality, and risk from those of sober business activities, systematic planning, organisation, and control. For the Caribbean, including the Cayman Islands, that position grew out of the attempt to develop a tourist industry. Tourism is seen as the engine which will drive the Caymanian economy into the twenty-first century and beyond. There could hardly be a more challenging time for the development of tourism in the Cayman Islands.

Tourism in the Cayman Islands

Tourism as an economic possibility in the Cayman Islands had its origin in 1937, as a result of the encouragement of Commissioner Allan Cardinall. In his Address to the Assembly of Justices and Vestry on November 24, 1937, Cardinall said:

> You will have observed not only here but at all times and places how I harp continuously on the possibilities of our tourist trade. And gradually step by step this trade is being created.

> The visit of RMS *Atlantis* in February of this year, followed by that of the *Arandora Star* next year, is a good beginning. The preservation from vandalism and unrestricted exploitation of our magnificent West Bay beach and of the attractive area known as "Hell" was a second step. A third step was taken in September at

the special Session of this Assembly when you passed a short Law facilitating the building of hotels ...

There is too the announcement that in this coming tourist season, for the first time cruising vessels will sail from New Orleans. That promises well for Cayman, because we are definitely on the main route homewards from the Caribbean. (p. 7)

Cardinall took a two-tiered approach to developing the tourist industry. In a unique move, he differentiated between tourists and visitors, and advertising was initially geared toward attracting visitors. While he offered no definition of a visitor, Cardinall, in his Addresss to the Assembly of Justices and Vestry on November 30, 1938, spoke of 'a special type of tourism, almost exclusively devoted to the well-to-do, retired independent. These are the people who would make ideal visitors during the winter months, who would acquire their own properties and who would return annually to escape the severities of northern winters' (p. 50).

It appeared that 'visitors' would be those people who owned their property, much like today's owners of vacation apartments, condominiums, and houses. 'Tourists', then, would refer to the one-time visitors who stayed in hotels or guest houses, or who visited on one of the rare cruise ships making a call in the Cayman Islands.

While reporting to the Assembly that tourist ships had visited in recent years, Cardinall reminded them of 'two disadvantages ... the one is the bad anchorage for large vessels and the second is the weakness in our connection with the rest of the world'. Modern communications have improved Cayman's connections to the rest of the world, including two international airports. The modernisation of the Cayman Islands notwithstanding, the 'bad anchorage' remains a serious limitation, if not a hazard, to the expansion of safe and convenient cruise tourism.

If Allan Cardinall was the initiator of tourism in the Cayman Islands, it was Andrew Morris Gerrard who set it on its modern course. It was providential that John Maloney, writing in the *Saturday Evening Post* (April 8, 1950) described the Cayman Islands as 'The Islands Time Forgot': 'In this Caribbean paradise a furnished house and three servants cost forty dollars a month, and you can make a good living as a beachcomber. Are these the islands you have dreamed about?'

Taking up his administrative responsibilities in the early 1950s, Andrew Gerrard set himself the challenge of building and resuscitating the tourist industry. He wrote numerous letters to the *Saturday Evening*

Post, encouraged Caymanian entrepreneurs to invest in hospitality infrastructure, built modern airports on Grand Cayman and Cayman Brac, and embarked on an exercise to enlighten and inform the Caymanian populace of the benefits of modernisation and hospitality.

An advertisement placed in the *Saturday Evening Post* brought a multitude of enquiries to the commissioner's office. In his usual forthright manner he replied candidly, outlining the rustic state of the colony, but reminding the enquirers of the natural beauty of the beaches and the pristine state of the surrounding waters. Through these and other efforts he worked assiduously to promote the Islands as a tourist destination.

Such efforts must have yielded the desired results, for during the Budget Address to the Assembly of Justices and Vestry on March 16, 1955, Gerrard predicted:

> The growth, on a large scale, of the Dependency as a tourist resort, will make some Caymanians very rich indeed, and it will certainly make all Caymanians a good deal better off, in the material sense, than they are now. But unless we watch our step, I doubt if it will make anyone any happier. The way to watch one's step, if I may put it so inelegantly, is to accept that controlled development is necessary ... But one cannot stop the clock turning round, and development of the islands as a tourist resort is inevitable. (p. 4)

Gerrard, it seems, foresaw what would happen when Caymanians began selling absolute title to their land, for in the same speech, he cautioned:

> I put it to you therefore, Gentlemen, that if you are not to sell your birthright for a mess of pottage, now is the time to do something about it – to go in for planned development, to strengthen the legislation in regard to immigration and aliens, to strengthen the administration of the Dependency which in its personnel each year is growing more overburdened, older, more tired and more discouraged. (pp. 4–5)

Tourism has grown from tentative beginnings in the 1930s through the formative period in the 1950s to being an important, if not the most important, cog in the economic wheel of the Cayman Islands. It is posited here that, as a result of increasing pressure upon the finance industry, tourism will assume an even more pivotal position.

In the foreword to Polly Pattullo's book *Last Resorts: The Cost of Tourism in the Caribbean,* Michael Manley wrote:

> The Caribbean from Cuba to the Cayman Islands, from Haiti to Tobago, needs tourism. Indeed, this industry is now commonly described as "the engine of growth" for the region. Yet if its underlying dynamics are not understood, it can be an engine of short-term cash enhancement and long-term disaster. (Manley 1996)

The charge is not without foundation. In the case of the Cayman Islands, the tourism infrastructure has not been developed with the preservation of the natural environment in mind.

Each political directorate over the past 40 years has tried to make strides in the promotion and growth of tourism. Currently, there are concerns about the tens of thousands of tourists who disembark into George Town on the days when five or more cruise ships are in port. In short, Cayman has entered the mass-tourism era.

Caymanian tourism is characterised by white expatriate management and ownership. Some years ago Caymanian staff was superseded by large numbers of Irish hospitality workers. More recently the trend has been to import workers from the Philippines. Regardless of national origin, it is far from ideal that local establishments must depend on imported labour. However, established Caymanians, unlike the native people in other Caribbean jurisdictions, do not adjust well to the responsibilities of working in the hospitality industry.

The Cayman Islands tourism industry has never attracted young Caymanians in numbers which would allow it to be truly representative of the island's culture, ethnicity, and social make-up. Younger Caymanians even now do not gravitate to the tourism sector the way they do to banking. Many young Caymanians see tourism as an alien industry where non-Caymanian personnel who manage low-level Caribbean staff cater to a non-Caribbean clientele.

The situation is exacerbated by the attitudes of absentee owners and the white expatriate executives who manage their properties, who are often insulting and insensitive to Caymanians of all colours. No genuine efforts are made to establish joint ventures between proprietors, their representatives, and the government or local entrepreneurs, with a view to changing attitudes and developing an understanding of the industry to the economic viability of the Cayman Islands.

The members of the oldest generation of Caymanian hospitality workers have reached, or are rapidly approaching, retirement age, and there are not enough replacements to ensure a Caymanian workforce. Unattractive wages, a hard-to-understand gratuity-disbursement system, long and often irregular hours, and insensitive and prejudiced managers have combined to undermine the satisfaction and enjoyment Caymanians should derive from working in this industry.

Even staff at the condominiums – who, it was originally understood, would be exclusively Caymanians – is now almost completely dominated by white expatriates, sometimes employed by so-called management companies.

Tourism in the Cayman Islands suffers from a legacy of negative social perceptions and unplanned growth. No attempt has been made to assess the strain placed on the ecosystem by the compulsion to increase the number of visitors each year. The fragile mangrove belt has been continually compromised by political directorates which use every kind of rationalisation to justify its destruction. It has escaped the attention of planners and pundits that ecotourism is becoming increasingly important, and even the traditional tourist derives satisfaction from efforts made to preserve the environment.

Tourism development, like much else in the frontier society that is the Cayman Islands, faces a range of difficult challenges. Can the present economic prosperity continue ad infinitum? Is it sound policy to base a developing society's economy on a cornerstone as vulnerable and sensitive as tourism? And – not the least important – if not these cornerstones, what? Given that no natural resources have yet been discovered in the Cayman Islands, there seem to be few, if any, other options. This circumstance should sharpen the awareness of political directorates regarding the importance of extracting maximum social benefit in these development pursuits. Hannerz, in his study *Caymanian Politics: Structure and Style in a Changing Island Society,* asked:

> What happens in the long run to a successful tourist economy? When Caymanians have sold all that land which is attractive to outsiders and when their men have built the houses which the new owners want, what will they do next? What jobs will be open to Caymanians in the new economy in the long run? Will they become a proletariat of beach hustlers, bar tenders and hotel maids, with few entrepreneurs in those crevices of the local economy left unattended by foreign business, and foreign capital? Will their men

start going back to sea, feeling the salt water in their faces again?
(Hannerz 1974, 18)

The Cayman Islands' tourism industry is today dominated and
controlled by foreign capital and investment, and even by foreign labour.
From hotel and condominium ownership, through the establishment
of ancillary services which cater to the tourist trade, to the staff who
look after the tourists' needs, there is no significant Caymanian
representation.

Even in those 'crevices' where it might be expected that Caymanians
would predominate, such participation seems undignified. Witness what
the small and medium-sized taxi drivers and tour operators have to do
on cruise-ship days to ensure that they share in the benefits of tourist
visits on shore. The small and medium-sized operators are
disadvantaged by a system under which a significant percentage of the
tours are prebooked from the cruise liners. Ship personnel make
arrangements with large tour operators whose fleets of 30-seater buses
dwarf the 14-passenger buses that are the largest vehicles of the
individual operators. The Land and Sea Cooperative, which was formed
to bring some semblance of parity to small Caymanian operators, has
failed to level the playing field to any significant extent. There are
constant complaints and expressions of dissatisfaction, and it is only
the laid-back disposition of the operators that has prevented open
confrontation so far.

Compounding these challenges is the recent announcement by the
US Department of Homeland Security that in the near future US citizens
will require a valid passport to re-enter the United States. This western
hemisphere travel initiative (WHTI) means that as many as 200,000
jobs and as much as US$2 billion in income could be lost to the
Caribbean when this requirement is implemented. The magnitude of
this development is exacerbated by the fact that Mexico and Canada,
competitors with the Caribbean for US visitors and their dollars, will
not be affected, at least initially, by this requirement.

Writing in 1977, Chodos estimated that the Caribbean faces a
constant challenge in that 'a large proportion of the tourist dollar
brought into the Caribbean (estimates range up to 90%) goes out again
to pay for the North American food the tourists eat' (Chodos 1977,
55).

I contend that we are using our tourism statistics in a manner which
superficially tells a good story but which does not provide important

information. In the first place, how much do we retain from each dollar earned from the industry? What is the rate of leakage – that is, the amount that goes back to purchase imported goods and services? One has only to visit a few hotels to see the many imported products; even the most basic supplies are imported. Leakage rates for some other Caribbean jurisdictions, described as cents leaked per dollar received, are: Jamaica, 50 cents; Trinidad and Tobago, 22 cents; St Vincent and the Grenadines, 33 cents; US Virgin Islands, 35 cents. In contrast, New Zealand and the Philippines retain 90 cents and 80 cents, respectively, of each tourism dollar.[1]

There have been no studies done regarding the 'multiplier effect' – how much activity is generated from every dollar earned from the tourism product in the Cayman Islands.

Tourism in the Cayman Islands is handicapped by a number of factors which are beyond the control of the service providers. One is the price of petroleum products, especially aircraft fuel. Currently these prices are at a premium, and even when they are not, it is expensive to travel to the Cayman Islands by commercial carrier. This limits the number of visitors.

The Islands' national airline, Cayman Airways, was formed to provide links to the outside world, in addition to offering reasonably priced, convenient connections to the Islands. Along with having to cope with high fuel costs, Cayman Airways has to face competition from large North American carriers with well-developed hubs across the continent and sophisticated international partners. Nonetheless, Cayman Airways has – with a significant government subsidy – managed to continue service. In the aftermath of hurricane Ivan it was the island's sole air link with the outside world.

Through a sometimes controversial and turbulent evolution, the airline has established itself as an integral part of the Cayman Islands tourism product. In this regard, its ultimate responsibility is manifested in its management's willingness to place the airline on call to ferry both tourists and residents off island when a hurricane threatens.

Not surprisingly, Cayman Airways – like so many other aspects of life in ths frontier society – depends on its symbiotic relationship with the government and society as a whole. At the time of writing, the airline has a fleet of five aircraft. Although fuel prices are high, lease costs are low, and there is no shortage of aircraft on the market.

Challenges notwithstanding, both Cayman Airways and the overall tourism product must make improvements to enable them to play even more prominent roles in the economic development of the Cayman Islands. The importance of this obligation has increased given the United Kingdom's position vis-à-vis the Cayman Islands' continuing as a financial centre of international repute.

A 1995 visit to the West Indian and Atlantic section of the Foreign and Commonwealth Office by this writer, in his capacity as a member of the Legislative Assembly, in the company of the second elected member for Cayman Brac, is still a vivid memory. Various matters pertinent to the United Kingdom and the visiting members, interest were discussed. It was the expressed desire of the administering power that the Cayman Islands depart from its established position as an international financial centre of high standing.

When surprise was expressed and the visitors asked the official what the Cayman Islands would be expected to do to make up for such a significant revenue loss, they were advised that the jurisdiction would be prudent to expand its tourism product. It should be no surprise, then, that the demand by international financial regulatory authorities that the Caymanian regulatory agencies impose ever-increasing restrictions on the finance industry was made with the collusion of the United Kingdom. After all, it is the UK Department of Inland Revenue which has brought the most pressure to bear on the Cayman Islands to accede to the European Union Tax Savings Initiative.

Finally, let us briefly examine the development of the Cayman Islands as a model international financial centre and leading offshore jurisdiction. The details of this development are found in another chapter in this book; what will be attempted here is to show how the Cayman Islands crafted its system of catering to the financial confidence of the wealthy, and what factors led so much of the world's money to seek safe haven in the Cayman Islands.

The Cayman Islands as an international financial centre

The evolution of the Cayman Islands, in a matter of a few decades, from a simple seafaring society to the world's fifth-largest financial centre is phenomenal. While not always portrayed as such, the most recent International Monetary Fund report on the Cayman Islands paints a picture of the jurisdiction's being one of the best-regulated markets worldwide.

While there is no question that the Cayman Islands have figured prominently in most major international financial scandals, from BCCI to Parmalat and Enron, such an association bears no direct reflection on the jurisdiction's meticulousness and ability to deliver fast, efficient, and responsible service. Just as the United Kingdom claimed it bore no direct responsibility for the millions of pounds the late Sani Abacha stole from Nigeria and deposited in UK banks, so too the Caymanian authorities, after having exercised due diligence, should not be held responsible for the weaknesses in other jurisdictions where corruption and conflicts of interest led those seeking advantages to bank their money in Cayman.

It is an omnipresent challenge for the financial industry to attract only 'untainted' business, given the proliferation and cleverness of white-collar criminals who devise ever more sophisticated methods to bilk investors and rob governments of revenue. It should be no small credit to the Caymanian financial industry that every time a challenge has arisen, it was defused with the confidence of professional experts.

Financial sophistication and expertise are available in Cayman today; however, the industry had small beginnings. According to Sir Vassel Johnson, the underpinning was the passage of four basic laws: The Companies Law 1961, The Banks and Trust Companies Regulations Law, The Trust Law, and the Exchange Control Regulations Law (Johnson 2001, 148–49).

The fledgling Caymanian financial industry benefited from increased business from overseas and the expertise of expatriates who had exhausted their welcome in the Bahamas after the PLP took power in the 1960s. But the Cayman Islands' rise to prominence as an international financial centre was not a meteoric one.

From its beginnings as a tax haven in the 1960s, the Cayman Islands exploited the almost nonexistent international regulatory system, flexible laws, and discreet but ambitious attorneys and bankers who asked few, if any, questions, to accommodate the suitcases full of cash which streamed into the jurisdiction. Additional factors attracting the money included political stability brought by the Union Jack, good telecommunications facilities, reliable utilities, proximity to the United States, and a socially stable population. With the removal of exchange-control restrictions, the stage was set for the Cayman Islands to progress to the next level.

It was a gradual climb, and it was not until Lynden Pindling and his nationalist agenda came to power in the Bahamas that Cayman achieved anything like international recognition. Pindling's policies culminated in a significant pool of expatriates being uprooted from the Bahamas. Many of these found a welcome in the more sedate and definitely less nationalistic atmosphere in the Cayman Islands. It was this cadre of WASP accountants, attorneys, and bankers who, through their assiduous efforts and almost invisible social presence, allowed the Cayman Islands to mature into a financial jurisdiction of significant international status.

Along the way there were setbacks, many of which have been discussed in this work. What has transpired in the 40 years since is that there is now a small pool of established Caymanians to complement the WASP experts. A certain tension is evident, and there are complaints of discrimination by established Caymanians, who charge that a glass ceiling exists.

A way has to be found to enable the two groups to co-exist constructively. There must be some public acknowledgement of the mutuality of interests, ideally through social dialogue. Continued economic growth in Cayman has always been predicated upon available expertise, political stability, and an absence of social tensions. There are areas of international financial activity where Cayman is on the leading edge, but this will only continue to obtain if the *sturm und drang* is contained.

The presence of a pool of experts enabled the Cayman Islands to stay a step ahead of competing onshore jurisdictions and enact a Mutual Funds Law. In 2000 the jurisdiction saw a 32.7 per cent increase over the previous year in the number of such funds. Registered funds totalled 3,014, with more than US$250 billion in assets. Business comes from all over the world, though about 70 per cent originates in North America (Ibid.)

A stock exchange was established in July 1997, and by June 2001 it had a market capitalisation of $250 billion and more than 400 listings (Ibid).

By 2000 the number of banks and trusts had grown from 10 to 580. Insurance assets had expanded by one-quarter to reach over $14 billion in capital. There were approximately 60,000 registered companies, an increase of 17.6 per cent over the 1999 total. The number of registered companies in 2004, the latest year for which figures are available, stood at about 70,000.[2]

In an interview with the *Financial Times* on July 16, 2001, the then president of the Cayman Islands Law Society explained one of the foundations of Cayman's success:

Confidentiality is important to the banking sector. The Caymanian
confidentiality regulations enshrine the principles practiced in the
U.K. We have made progress in getting critics to understand that
confidentiality is legitimate, but we ensure that confidentiality is
not abused. Because someone seeks confidentiality does not mean
that they are involved in criminal activity.

Cayman's record of success has not been without its negative side.
Periodically there are scandals involving corruption, fraud, and other
white-collar crimes such as money laundering and embezzlement. These
scandals usually bring about mention of the Cayman Islands in the
international press.

In addition to these entanglements, there are the demands of the
international regulatory authorities. In July 2000 the Cayman Islands
were identified by the Financial Action Task Force (FATF), a body
established by the G7 group of industrialised countries to fight money
laundering and other financial crimes, and blacklisted for not having
met its criteria. In spite of this ostracism the jurisdiction consolidated
its position as the world's fifth-largest financial centre. The FATF
removed the Cayman Islands from the blacklist in June 2001 after
legislation was tailored to meet FATF standards. Earlier, the Cayman
Islands government experienced another inconvenience when the
Organization for Economic Cooperation and Development (OECD)
listed the Islands among 30 jurisdictions practicing 'harmful tax
competition'.

Such excommunications seem to have a negligible effect on continuing
business in the financial centre, since the switch had already been made
to institutional funds and high-net-worth individuals with sophisticated
knowledge of the international financial system (*Financial Times*, July
16, 2001).

For whom are we developing?

I will perhaps shock certain members by saying that, in general,
our problems today are not really to get better roads, to eradicate
mosquitoes, and so on. Our real problems are to adjust ourselves
to a difficult and changing outside world and to avoid the danger
of becoming a degenerate community worshipping money. Our
fundamental problem is to create a stable community which desires
to better itself in real terms by bettering its own human material,

by educating its children in proper human values, instead of being hypnotised, as too often happens today, by the belief that happiness consists of the possession of a glossier motor car and a bigger and more sparkling refrigerator than that possessed by one's next door neighbour. (Excerpt from A.M. Gerrard's Budget Speech, March 16, 1955)

It should be obvious that there are many similarities between the current situation in Cayman and that of the Gerrard era. The Cayman Islands' economy is 95 per cent service-based (*Financial Times*, July 16, 2001). While per capita income is listed at US$40,000, studies show that 52 per cent of Caymanians earn less than CI$1,500 per month (ibid.).

The situation is further complicated by the fact that established Caymanians experience competition at both ends of the employment spectrum. At the higher echelons, educated and trained Caymanians have to compete against expatriates who, through their connections, often have the inside edge. This is especially obvious in the legal profession, where experience in the United Kingdom or Canada is valued over the qualifications of young Caymanians.

The same biases occur in banking and accounting. Even among small businesses, which make up 60 per cent of the employment sector, Caymanian applicants face competition from regional and international workers, most recently those from the Philippines and the Indian subcontinent. The imbalance is compounded by some expatriates' pretensions to class and ethnic superiority over all established Caymanians, regardless of colour, and by the presence of a social petulance that derives from contempt for the colonised people by those who see themselves as the colonisers, a privileged elite.

Over the years there has been an absence of meaningful social dialogue which would inform the society and raise the hopes of established Caymanians. In a society where immigrants are more numerous than the established populace (whether permanently or temporarily), it is critical that the society's development philosophy be known and accepted by the local people.

Economic success carries its own set of challenges, and according to the *Caymanian Compass* (June 3, 2005), there is great pressure on the immigration authorities to approve work permit applications: 'Work permit figures from the Immigration Department show that there were 8,945 temporary work permits in effect 31 May compared to some

3,000 a year ago. Annual work permits at the end of May totaled 10,784 bringing the total workers on permits to 18,583.'

In a population of 50,000, where it is widely believed that established Caymanians are almost outnumbered, the presence of so many work permit holders does not bode well for the society's long-term development. Periodically, the question is posed: For whom are we developing Cayman? If there is no unemployment, and if all Caymanians who want to work have jobs, why should there be unbridled growth? Is economic progress being measured solely on the basis of skewed figures representing per capita income and GDP?

Current trends in the society's development should be a source of concern to any informed observer. A recent upsurge in crime that has resulted in the provision of armed bodyguards for cabinet ministers and other high-ranking public officials is costly in more ways than one. It speaks volumes about the sudden transformation of the society from calmness and tranquillity to violence-prone and disturbed. Since the gap between the 'haves' and the 'have nots' is becoming more obvious by the year, it is not far-fetched to predict that within the next decade the society will be significantly more volatile than it is currently. Inadequate affordable housing for the less privileged, failure to integrate the various ethnic groups into the population, and the lack of a coherent development policy all demonstrate the weakness of our current development path.

The Caymanian economy has undergone enormous structural change in the past 50 years. The social aspect is also changed by its relation to the economy. There is a pressing need to address many social challenges if the vulnerable members of society are not to be frustrated and overwhelmed.

With economic prosperity must come affordable housing for the lower middle class and the poor. So too must come programmes to uplift those in dysfunctional family circumstances. Women must be empowered, both by the removal of the glass ceiling and by public acknowledgement of their equal status with their male counterparts. Education and training, with an emphasis on the incorporation of information technology, is the *sine qua non* for the continued success of the jurisdiction. The Cayman Islands have the potential to become the Singapore of the West if certain criteria are met. Not the least among these is that the multinational corporations operating in the jurisdiction must accept a greater share of social responsibility and agree to more meaningful and realistic wages and salaries. This last element will serve to enhance and promote a superior work ethic and a sense of individual loyalty to the organisation. The time has come for Cayman to establish a minimum wage by category as well as more realistic salaries for Caymanians vis-à-vis their expatriate counterparts.

The question of whether, at this stage, there is a direct link between continued economic prosperity and greater self-determination will also have to be answered. Caymanian society seems ready to make that connection. However, civil society, non-governmental organisations, and the political directorate must realise that increasing self-determination should not mean sacrificing long-term objectives and any change must benefit the dispossessed and disenfranchised as much as everyone else.

The privileged are not hesitant to boast of the Cayman Islands' rank among international financial centres. Unfortunately, this statistic is usually offered alone, with no mention of other pertinent facts such as the number of trained young Caymanians succeeding expatriates at the highest corporate levels. Then, too, no attempt is made to measure the contentment of ordinary working-class Caymanians.

There is no denying that the Cayman Islands form a textbook case of economic success. The question is, what happens when the economic success begins to unravel? One way of delaying or even preventing the unravelling of the society is for the corporations operating in the Cayman Islands to exercise a greater sense of corporate social responsibility, defined as 'The distinctive contribution a company makes actively and voluntarily to the advancement of society or alleviation of social concerns, usually through some form of investment in partnership with the community which may include government' (von Tunzelmann 1996, 107).

In *The Post-Capitalist Society,* Drucker wrote that 'Organizations have to take "social responsibility." There is no one else around in the society of organizations to take care of society itself. Yet they must do so responsibly, within the limits of their competence, and without endangering their performance capacity' (Drucker 1993, 97).

Multinational corporations establish themselves in the Cayman Islands without having to pay any infrastructural development fees, impact fees, or corporate tax. Executives employed by these corporations have no direct personal taxes or assessments, and yet their terms and conditions of employment far exceed what is offered to Caymanians.

There has been no need for bodyguards, family security detail, or even drivers, since the hazard-free nature of Caymanian society enables women and children to travel and move around in safety. Since this freedom exists as a result of a lack of the socioeconomic deprivation which triggers resentment and violence in other societies, is there not a case to be made that the beneficiaries should contribute to the maintenance of the 'orderly society'? Experience following hurricane Ivan suggests that not enough corporate entities empathise with the deprivation of the wider society.

Certainly the argument can be made that as a society, the Cayman Islands are changing from one governed by the imperative of community to one governed by the imperative of selfishness. The revolution of rising expectations, it seems, has the possibility of turning the society into a community of philistines whose only objective is to amass personal wealth.

If the society is not to unravel, a profound change in its character will be required, along with a better comprehension of the moral obligation to share the economic success. There must be a greater feeling of connectedness of all elements of society, and corporate entities must develop a culture of philanthropy. Only if individuals and corporate entities alike renounce self-indulgence will Caymanian society attain status as an icon of genuine economic excellence.

In 1978 this writer called for a new sense of community and a new social dialogue – in short, a development strategy based on inclusion and one which genuinely factored in the contributions of both established Caymanians and expatriates. The call was hijacked by an uninformed elite who selfishly and arrogantly saw the effort as a challenge to their entrenched position.

Today the jurisdiction faces a myriad of intractable problems but has made no attempt to arrive at a politics of inclusion and engagement that should enable the many nationalities who make up the society to feel a closer affiliation – to feel 'Caymanian'. As a result, the society is an agglomeration of various ethnic, national, and social groups with little in common except a thriving economy in the background and an increasing drive toward materialism. Crime, including sophisticated criminal conspiracies, is becoming increasingly widespread, yet there is no sustained, coherent attempt to address family and community issues, as if societal breakdown and combating crime have nothing to do with one another.

No solid foundation can be built on such unstable ground. The environment is being stripped, economic shocks are ignored, and there are precious few attempts to come to grips with a sustainable development policy in any sphere. In this writer's opinion, this is a formula for problematic development, if not abject failure. It is a moot question as to where it all went wrong, since 'progress' is still being measured on a faulty report card.

Small wonder, then, that what seems a rhetorical question is becoming ever more relevant: For whom are we developing the Cayman Islands?

Notes

Notes to Introduction

1. In the Cayman Islands today, there is an open rift between Caymanians and some expatriate elements over certain immigration policies. The *Caymanian Compass* newspaper's lead headline on 23 August 2006 was 'Caymanians resent expatriates'. The article quoted a government minister as offering three reasons for such resentment: 1) the 2,850 grants of Caymanian status (citizenship) given by the government in power in 2003; 2) the editorial stance of the competing newspaper, the *Cayman Net News,* which continuously decries 'the divisiveness in the society' resulting from the insularity and shortsightedness – indicated in its adherence to a certain immigration policy – of the current government; and 3) the fact that some expatriates do not identify with the Caymanian way of doing things. The *Cayman Net News,* in its editorial on 25 August 2006 entitled 'Who's to blame?', offers a sobering journalistic perspective: 'The government apparently thinks that, by pandering to and feeding on the xenophobic fringe of our society, which is now even throwing the oxymoron of "Caymanian genetic purity" into the mix, it will generate some electoral goodwill from which it might benefit in three or four years' time.'
2. The term 'frontier society' is used here to connote clannishness, scheming, and a conspiratorial attitude. The term was employed by Hannerz (1974) in his study of the Cayman Islands and finds some substantiation in Kieran (1992). Even today, in the twenty-first century, the Cayman Islands still exhibit traces of frontier-type behaviour.
3. A term used by West Indian historians to denote the colour structure prevalent in West Indian slave societies. The most comprehensive explanation of pigmentocracy is found in the work of Brathwaite (1971).
4. A term used by black people (slave and later freed) to describe a white man or woman. Originating in the eighteenth century

among the Efik and Ibo peoples of West Africa, the term was transported to the Caribbean, where it was used pejoratively by blacks to show their contempt for the white people. In numerous cases in the Cayman Islands it was prefaced by the description 'poor', as in 'poor buckra', to highlight and mock the poverty-stricken conditions in which the white people lived. In Jamaica and some other Caribbean territories, the word is 'backra'.

5. The term 'voluntary colonialism' was suggested to me by Professor Rex Nettleford during the early stages of the development of this work. In the context of this work, it has come to signify the Caymanian decision to sever political ties with Jamaica after the breakup of the Federation and before Jamaica chose independence on August 6, 1962. Voluntary colonialism describes the Cayman Islands' decision to remain a colony of the United Kingdom under a special constitutional arrangement.

6. Monthly Intelligence Report, Cayman Islands, December 1962–January 1963, p. 2 (Public Records Office, London, File CO 1031/4768).

7. Ibid., p. 5.

8. Letter from Allan H. Donald, Commissioner of the Cayman Islands, to Sir Kenneth Blackburne, Governor of Jamaica, September 16, 1958 (Cayman Islands National Archive file 902/111-318).

9. France has the Alliance Française, Germany the Goethe Institut, and Britain the British Council. Recently China has joined the list of countries offering language training and cultural promotion, through its Confucius Institutes. The institutes are partnerships between Chinese universities and local universities in the host country and are designed to meet the growing demand for Chinese-language education. The host country assumes responsibility for housing the institute, while the Chinese partner provides teaching staff and materials.

10. Hedge funds are financial instruments crafted primarily for the rich and the super-rich. Consisting of private capital, these instruments use complex trading and regularly changing methods to generate higher-than-average returns on investment. Ten years ago hedge funds accounted for US$257 billion worldwide. At present there are more than 8,000 hedge funds with a total of 1

trillion US dollars under management (*Economist*, July 1, 2006, p. 68).

11.   The first major political demonstration in the modern Cayman Islands took place in 1963, when Caymanians invaded the Owen Roberts Airport compound and surrounded a Cuban airliner which, it was alleged, had brought passengers from Havana, Cuba, to board British West Indian Airways flights for other Caribbean destinations. The planes were not allowed to leave until the passengers from Cuba reboarded the Cuban airliner for the return trip to Havana. The Caymanian objection was instigated by Americans residing in the Cayman Islands. Of course, the basis of such objections lay in the Castro government's pledge to foment revolution all over the region. The demonstraters, organised by Dr Roy McTaggart and transported to the airport by Craddock Ebanks, a Legislative Assembly member, included children, who were used to block the tarmac and surround the Cubana d'Aviación airplane. The Cayman Islands government conveyed its objection to the British Embassy in Cuba (which had issued the permission and visas for the passengers from Cuba to transit through the Cayman Islands) and requested that the practice be discontinued. After this incident, there were no more such flights and the community returned to its sleepy frontier existence.

12.   Andrew Morris Gerrard, Budget Speech to the Cayman Islands Assembly of Justices and Vestry, March 16, 1955, p. 1.

13.   Edmund Burke, Speech to the Electors of Bristol, November 3, 1774.

14.   Lucian of Samosata (c. AD 120–190), 'How to Write History', trans. K. Kilburn, Loeb Classical Library (Cambridge: Harvard University Press, 1968), 57.

Notes to Chapter 2, Engendering Democracy

1.   United Kingdom, Minutes of the Fifth Ministerial Group on the Dependent Territories, May 1994 (London: Foreign and Commonwealth Office), pp. 5–6.

2.   United Kingdom, The Cayman Islands (Constitution) Order 2003, p. 4.

3.   Hansard Reports April 11, 1979, pp. 11–13.

4.   Hansard Reports 1993 Volume 2, pp. 485–686.

5. Malcolm Rifkind, Secretary of State, to Herbert Hughes, Chief Minster, Anguilla, December 11, 1996.
6. Fifth Ministerial Group on the Dependent Territories, p. 5.
7. Ibid.
8. Ibid., p. 6.

Note to Chapter 3, Settlement, Society, and Population

1. The entire document can be accessed from the Cornell University Library Web site, <http://cdl.library.cornell.edu/moa/moa_search.html>, using the search term 'Grand Cayman Island'.

Notes to Chapter 5, A Nuanced View

1. *(Jamaica) Sunday Gleaner*, February 26, 2006. Amounts in each territory's currency.
2. Cayman Islands Compendium of Statistics 2004, Statistics Office, Elizabethan Square, Grand Cayman, August 2005, p. 43.

References

Augier, F.R., S.C. Gordon, D.G. Hall, and M. Reckford, eds. 1969. *The making of the West Indies*. London: Longmans, Green & Co., Ltd.

Bauer, P.T. 1976. *Dissent on development*. Cambridge, MA: Harvard University Press.

———. 1981. *Equality, the third world, and economic delusion*. London: Weidenfeld & Nicholson.

———. 1984. *Reality and rhetoric: Studies in the economics of development*. Cambridge, MA: Harvard University Press.

———. 1991. *The development frontier: Essays in applied economics*. Cambridge, MA: Harvard University Press.

Beckles, Hilary. 1989. *Natural Rebels: A social history of enslaved black women in Barbados*. London: Zed Books.

Block, Alan A. 1991. *Masters of paradise: Organized crime and the Internal Revenue Service in the Bahamas*. New Brunswick, NJ: Transaction Publishers.

Blum, Richard H. 1984. *Offshore haven banks, trusts, and companies: The business of crime in the Euromarkets*. New York: Praeger Publishers.

Bodden, Roy. 1978. The Cayman Islands: Social, political, and economic development problems from 1950 to the present. Part 2: Some unanswered questions about the future. *Nor'wester*, September and October.

Bolland, O. Nigel. 2002. Creolisation and Creole societies: A cultural nationalist view of Caribbean social theory. In *Questioning Creole: Creolisation discourses in Caribbean culture*, ed. Verene A. Shepherd and Glen L. Richards, 15–46. Kingston, Jamaica: Ian Randle Publishers.

Brathwaite, Edward Kamau. 1971. *The development of Creole society in Jamaica 1770–1820*. Oxford: Clarendon Press.

Byles, Paul. 2005. *Inside offshore: A reality check on the offshore financial world*. Grand Cayman: Focus Communications.

Cayman Islands. 1971. *Proposals for Constitutional Advance: Report of the Constitutional Commissioner, the Rt. Hon. The Earl of Oxford and Asquith, KCMG*. Foreign and Commonwealth Office. London: HMSO.

———. 1999. *Vision 2008: The Cayman Islands National Strategic Plan 1999–2008*. Grand Cayman: Cayman Islands Government.

Chados, Robert. 1977. *The Caribbean connection*. Toronto: James Lovimer and Co. Publishers.

Chambost, Guy. 1980. *Guide mondial des secrets bancaines*. Paris: Editions du Soleil.

Connell, John. 2001. Eternal empire: Britain's Caribbean colonies. In *Islands at the crossroads: Politics in the non-independent Caribbean,* ed. A.G. Ramos and A.J. Rivera, 118–20. Kingston, Jamaica: Ian Randle Publishers.

Corbin, Carlyle. 2003. Political and constitutional implications of self-government in the non-self-governing territories. Paper presented at the Caribbean Regional Seminar to Review the Political, Economic, and Social Conditions in the Non-Self-Governing Territories, The Valley, Anguilla, May.

Craton, Michael. 2003. *Founded upon the seas: A history of the Cayman Islands and their people.* Kingston, Jamaica: Ian Randle Publishers.

Crossley, Sir Julian, and John Blanford. 1975. *The DCO story: A history of banking in many countries 1925–1971.* London: Barclays Bank International Ltd.

Davies, Elizabeth W. 1989. *The legal system of the Cayman Islands.* Oxford: Law Reports International.

De Kadt, Emmanuel. 1972. *Patterns of foreign influence in the Caribbean.* London: Oxford University Press.

Dixon, Liz. 2001. Financial flows via offshore financial centers. *Financial Stability Review* 10: 104–5.

Drucker, Peter F. 1993. *The post-capitalist society.* New York: HarperCollins.

Dumont, René. 1966. *False start in Africa.* Trans. Phyllis Nauts Ott. London: Andre Deutsch.

Duncan, David. 1943. Capturing giant turtles in the Caribbean. *National Geographic Magazine* 84: 177–90.

Dunleavy, M.P. 2005. Does 'hedge fund' mean anything anymore? *New York Times,* October 9.

Ebanks, Benson, Leonard Ebanks, and Arthur Hunter. 2002. *Report of the Constitutional Modernization Review Commissioners 2002.* Constitutional Commission, Cayman Islands.

Elazar, D.J., ed. *Federal systems of the world: A handbook of federal, confederal, and autonomy relationships,* 2nd ed. Harlow, UK: Longman Publishing Co.

Elkins, Stanley M. 1968. *Slavery: A problem in American institutional and intellectual life,* 2nd ed. Chicago: University of Chicago Press.

Elon, Amos. 1996. *Founder: A portrait of the first Rothschild and his time.* New York: Viking Press.

Fergus, Howard A. 2003. Constitutional modernisation in Montserrat and the Cayman Islands: Constitutional advancement or colonial entrenchment? Paper presented at the Caribbean Regional Seminar to Review the Political, Economic, and Social Conditions in the Non-Self-Governing Territories, The Valley, Anguilla, May.

———. 2004. Constitutional reform in some British Overseas Territories (BOTs) in the Caribbean: Modernisation or colonial entrenchment? Presented at the Overseas Territories Conference, Commonwealth Institute, London, June 29.

Fleming-Banks, Phyllis. 2003. Statement of civil society in Anguilla. Paper presented at the Caribbean Regional Seminar to Review the Political, Economic, and Social Conditions in the Non-Self-Governing Territories, The Valley, Anguilla, May.

Foreign and Commonwealth Office. 1997. *Contingent liabilities in the Dependent Territories. A report by the Comptroller and Auditor General.* London: FCO.

———. 1999. *Partnership for progress and prosperity: Britain and the Overseas Territories* (CM 4264). London: FCO.

Freyre, Gilberto. 1976. *The masters and the slaves,* 2nd ed., rev. New York: Vintage Books.

Gaffney, Mason. 1998. *International tax competition: Harmful or beneficial?* Paris: Mason Gaffney.

Greider, William. 1992. *Who will tell the people? The betrayal of American democracy.* New York: Simon and Schuster.

———. 1997. *One world, ready or not.* New York: Simon and Schuster.

Hall, Douglas. 1964. Absentee proprietorship in the British West Indies to about 1850. *Jamaica Historical Review* 4: 15–35.

Hannerz, Ulf. 1974. *Caymanian politics: Structure and style in a changing island society.* Stockholm: University of Stockholm.

Harris, Sophia. 2003. Self-government in the Cayman Islands: The perspective of non-governmental organizations (NGOs). Paper presented at the Caribbean Regional Seminar to Review the Political, Economic, and Social Conditions in the Non-Self-Governing Territories, The Valley, Anguilla, May.

Hart, Keith. 2000. *Money in an unequal world.* New York: Texere.

Higman, B.W. 1984. *Slave Population of the British Caribbean 1807–1834.* Baltimore: Johns Hopkins University Press.

Hintjens, Helen M. 1995. *Alternatives to independence: Explorations in post-colonial relations.* Brookfield, VT: Dartmouth Publishing.

Hirst, George S.S. 1910. *Notes on the history of the Cayman Islands.* Kingston, Jamaica: P.A. Benjamin Manf. Co.

Hobsbawn, Eric. 1997. *On history.* New York: The New Press.

Hoffer, Eric. 1951. *The true believer: Thoughts on the nature of mass movements.* New York: Harper and Row.

Holt, Thomas C. 1992. *The problem of freedom: Race, labour, and politics in Jamaica and Britain, 1832–1938.* Baltimore: Johns Hopkins University Press.

Iton, Andre. 2006. Growth is not necessarily development. *Cayman Net News,* April 24.

Johnson, Vassel. 2001. *As I see it: How Cayman became a leading financial centre.* Temple House, Sussex: The Book Guild.

Kempadoo, Kamala, ed. 1999. *Sun, sex, and gold: Tourism and sex work in the Caribbean.* Oxford: Rowman and Littlefield.

Kieran, Brian L. 1992. *The lawless Caymanas: A story of slavery, freedom, and the West India Regiment.* George Town, Grand Cayman: Brian Kieran.

Knight, Franklin W. 1990. *The Caribbean: The genesis of a fragmented nationalism.* New York: Oxford University Press.

Lamming, George. 1987. *In the castle of my skin.* Port of Spain, Trinidad: Longmans Caribbean.

———. 1996. *The pleasures of exile.* Ann Arbor: Ann Arbor Paperbacks, University of Michigan Press.

Lawrence, Mary. 1975. How government developed in Cayman. *Nor'wester,* October.

———. 1977. Report on the Cayman Islands' delegation's visit to the United Nations. *Nor'wester,* October.

Leckey, Andrew. 2000. *The lack of money is the root of all evil: Mark Twain's timeless wisdom on money and wealth for today's investor.* Paramus, NJ: Prentice Hall.

Lewis, Gordon K. 1968. *The growth of the modern West Indies.* New York: Monthly Review Press.

Lindsay, Louis. 1981. The myth of a civilising mission: British colonialism and the politics of symbolic manipulation. ISER Working Paper no. 31, University of the West Indies, Mona.

Longworth, Richard C. 1999. *Global squeeze: The coming crisis for first world nations.* Chicago: Contemporary Books.

Lowenthal, David. 1972. *West Indian societies.* New York: Oxford University Press.

Manley, Michael. 1996. Foreword to *Last resorts: The cost of tourism in the Caribbean,* by Polly Pattullo. New York: Monthly Review Press.

McLaughlin, Sybil. 1982. Development of parliamentary government in the Cayman Islands, 1832–1982. Unpublished manuscript.

Memmi, Albert. 1965. *The colonizer and the colonized.* New York: Orion Press, Inc.

Mills, C. Wright. 2000. *The power elite.* New York: Oxford University Press.

Naylor, R.T. 1987. *Hot money and the politics of debt.* Toronto: McClelland and Stewart.

———. 2002. *Wages of crime: Black markets, illegal finance, and the underworld economy.* Ithaca, NY: Cornell University Press.

Nazer, Hisham M. 1999. *Power of a third kind: The Western attempt to colonize the global village.* Westport, CT: Praeger Publishers.

Nettleford, Rex. 1995. *Inward stretch, outward reach: A voice from the Caribbean.* New York: Caribbean Diaspora Press.

OECD. 1998. *Harmful tax competition: An emerging global issue.* Paris: Organization for Economic Cooperation and Development.

Ohmae, Kenichi. 1990. *The borderless world: Power and strategy in the interlinked economy.* New York: Harper Business.

———. 1996. *The end of the nation state: The rise of regional economies.* New York: Free Press Paperbacks.

Osterhammel, Jurgen. 1997. *Colonialism: A theoretical overview.* Trans. Shelley L. Frisch. Princeton, NJ: Markus Weiner Publishers .

Palan, Ronen. 2003. *The offshore world: Sovereign markets, virtual places, and nomad millionaires.* New York: Cornell University Press.

Parks, Tim. 2005. *Medici money: Banking, metaphysics, and art in fifteenth-century Florence.* New York: Norton Publishers.

Paton, Diana. 2005. Popular and official justice in post-emancipation Jamaica. In *Contesting freedom: Control and resistance in the post-emancipation Caribbean,* ed. Gad Heuman and David Trotman, 13–17. London: Macmillan Caribbean Ltd.

Porter, Michael. 1980. *Competitive strategy: Techniques for analyzing industries and competitors.* New York: The Free Press.

———. 1985. *Competitive advantage: Creating and sustaining superior performance.* New York: The Free Press.

———. 1990. *The competitive advantage of nations.* New York: The Free Press.

Powis, Robert E. 1992. *The money launderers.* Chicago: Probus Publishers.

Robinson, Jeffrey. 1996. *The laundrymen.* New York: Arcade Publishing.

———. 2003. *The sink.* London: Constable and Robinson Ltd.

Ryan, Selwyn. 1999. *Winner Takes All: The Westminster experience in the Caribbean.* St. Augustine, Trinidad and Tobago: ISER, University of the West Indies.

Sen, Amartya. 1999. *Development as freedom.* New York: Alfred A. Knopf.

Sethna, Rustum. 1979. The phenomenon of beach hustling in the Caribbean. *Maclean's,* March 19.

Smith, Frederick, and Walter Wallace. 1991. *Report of the Constitutional Commissioners* (CM 1547). London: HMSO.

Stone, Carl. 1985. *Democracy and clientelism in Jamaica.* New Brunswick, NJ: Transaction Books.

Strassler, Robert B. 1996. *The landmark Thucydides.* New York: Free Press.

Tannebaum, Frank. 1947. *Slave and citizen.* New York: Vintage Books.

Tocqueville, Alexis de. 2000. *Democracy in America,* vol. 1. Trans. and ed. Harvey C. Mansfield and Delba Winthrop. Chicago: University of Chicago Press. (Orig. pub. 1835.)

Tunzelmann, Adrienne von. 1996. *Social responsibility and the company: A new perspective on governance, strategy, and the community.* Wellington, NZ: Victoria University, Institute of Policy Studies.

Wallace, Elizabeth. 1977. *The British Caribbean: From the decline of colonialism to the end of federation.* Toronto: University of Toronto Press.

Walter, Ingo. 1985. *Secret money: The shadowy world of tax evasion, capital flight, and fraud.* Lexington, MA: Lexington Books.

Watts, Ronald. 2000. Islands in comparative constitutional perspective. In *Lessons from the political economy of small islands: The resourcefulness of jurisdictions,* ed. G. Baldacchino and D. Milne, 17–35. Hampshire, UK: Macmillan Press Ltd.

Archival Materials

Census of the Cayman Islands, June 21, 1802. Cayman Islands National Archive.

CO 137/198, Lawlessness of the Caymanian Population.

CO 137/198 f 318, Papers Relative to the Abolition of Slavery.

CO 137/193 s cc480, Memorandum in Respect of the Cayman Islands.

CO 1031/3392 or /64/19/01, Future Relations between Her Majesty's Government in Jamaica and the Governments of The Cayman Islands and the Turks and Caicos Islands.

CO 1031/324, Cayman Islands Relations with Jamaica after Independence 1962.

CO 1031/3250, Future of the Cayman Islands 1962–1963.

Index

G

Gabby (Barbadian kaiso artist), 199

Gaffney, Mason: *International Tax Competition: Harmful or Beneficial?*, 151–52

George Town, 14, 15, 68
capital moved to, 16, 45
mercantile centre, 187
renaming of Hog Styes to, 15

Gerrard, Andrew Morris (commissioner), xvii, xxx, 18, 56, 224, 242–43
anti-racism of, 58–59
economic prosperity, concerns about, 211, 234
Governor Vesting of Lands Law, 195–96

high calibre of, 42
tourism, contributions to, 233–34
warning against foreigners, 21

Gibbs, Brian (head, Financial Reporting Unit), xix, 38–39, 166, 167–69, 170
as investigator, Royal Cayman Islands Police financial crimes unit, 165
See also Euro Bank debacle

Global Competitiveness Report 2005–2006, 131

globalisation, 119
effect of, on Cayman's financial industry, 129, 132, 144, 173, 179
effect of, on national economies, 140, 183
effect of, on sovereign statehood, 152
power as foundation of, 155

Glover, Nathaniel (first expatriate), 46

Government Savings Bank, 19
closure of, 189

governors
collusion with private sector by, 208
powers of, 210
quality of, 42, 208–10, 225

Great Depression, 18

Greenall, Benson, xxvi, 19, 193, 197, 198
terms of lease of crown lands, 194

Grisham, John: *The Firm*, 143

Guardian Bank and Trust, 143, 144, 162–64

H

Hannerz, Ulf: *Caymanian Politics: Structure and Style in a Changing Island Society*, 181, 183
future of tourist economy, 236
land sales to foreigners, 197, 198
planning regulations, demonstration against, 202–4

Harmful Tax Competition: An Emerging Global Issue (OECD), 73, 150

Harris, Sophia: 'Self-Government in the Cayman Islands: The Perspective of Non-Governmental Organisations', 112–13

hedge funds, 179–80, 249n10

Hirst, George S.S. (commissioner), 17
Notes on the History of the Cayman Islands, 213

Hoffer, Eric: *The True Believer: Thoughts on the Nature of Mass Movements*, 79–80

homosexual acts, legalisation of, xv, 101–2, 115

Hughes, Hubert (chief minister of Anguilla), 105

human rights, 65
democracy, linkage with, 99–100, 228
lack of support for, by National Team, 92

hurricanes, 213
Ivan, xix, 35, 96, 136: early recovery effort, 207–8; effect of, on cost of living, 137; exodus of expatriates after, 206; revelations from, 176, 196, 213–15, 246
Gilbert, 209
Storm of '32, 17

I

immigration (rollover) policy, xxiv–xxv, 64–65, 136
Council of Associations' position on, 97
divisiveness of, 96–99, 125, 226, 248n1
hijacked by politics, 158
nationalism and, 63
protectionism in, 119–20, 137
shortsightedness of, 124–25
in Vision 2008, 98

income inequality, 176–77, 212–13, 215, 243

independence, political
alternatives to, 111–24, 130
undesirability of, 70, 178

outsourcing
competition from, xxiv, xxv, 130–31
confidentiality and control, loss of, 131
Overseas Territories
governors' powers in, 107
distrust of, by United Kingdom, 121, 124
European Union's position on, 130
House of Commons representation for, refusal of, 112
manipulation of, by United Kingdom, 75–76
partnerships with United Kingdom, possible, 121–23
political independence as ideal for, 103

P
Panton, Ernest, 24
Panton, Ormond, xvi, 24, 25, 30, 76
election of 1962, 77, 81–82
Parmalat scandal, 164, 171–72, 239
Partnership for Progress and Prosperity, 72, 74, 108, 113–115, 119
party politics
advantages of, 221
extinguishment of, 28, 82
first appearance of, 27
reappearances of, 39, 81, 93–94, 215–21
suspicion of, 36
team versus party, 33
Pattullo, Polly: *Last Resorts: The Cost of Tourism in the Caribbean*, 234–35
Peloponnesian War, xv, 74
People's Progressive Movement
formation of, 35, 94, 221
position of, on fundamental rights and freedoms, 109–10
victory of, 224
pigmentocracy, 7, 11, 248n3
Cayman Islands as, xiv, xv, 2, 7–8, 46, 53
change from, to class-based hierarchy, 15
See also colour; racial stratification; racism
Pindling, Lynden (Bahamian prime minister), 32, 37, 66, 141, 240
planning, comprehensive
absence of, 177, 228, 236
need for, 234

planning regulations (1970)
demonstration against, 202–5
political parties. *See* party politics; *and specific parties*
poverty study. *See* National Assessment of Living Conditions
power
economic control as, 107
economic well-being as, 103
of expatriate elite, 60–61, 66–67, 68
globalisation based on, 155
imbalance, as foundation of colonial relationship, xv, xix, 72, 73, 105, 106, 112, 113
importance of, in frontier society, 44
of merchant establishment, 79
money as, 145–46
political, after emancipation, 53
private property: differing concepts of, 189, 192–93, 196–97
Private Sector Consultative Committee (PSCC), 150, 153
privilege, white, 56–57, 79

Q
Quincentennial celebrations, xxii, 68, 100

R
racial stratification, 44, 58
after emancipation, 46
ending of, in civil service, 59
in United States, 52
racism, 51–65, 67, 81
legacy of colonialism, 51–52, 208
and mass status grants, 222–23
role of, in development of Cayman as financial centre, 164
Rea, John (banker), 165
real estate business: domination of, by foreigners, 192
revenue, government, 213
revolution of rising expectations, 211–15, 246
government, reliance on, 214–15
origin of term, 212
Rifkind, Malcolm (UK secretary of state), 105
Rifkind letter, 105–7